BLACK BEACH

BLACK BEACH

491 DAYS IN ONE OF AFRICA'S MOST BRUTAL PRISONS

**DANIEL JANSE VAN RENSBURG
AND TRACEY PHAROAH**

PENGUIN BOOKS

Black Beach

Published by Penguin Books
an imprint of Penguin Random House South Africa (Pty) Ltd
Reg. No. 1953/000441/07
The Estuaries No. 4, Oxbow Crescent, Century Avenue, Century City, 7441
PO Box 1144, Cape Town, 8000, South Africa
www.penguinrandomhouse.co.za

First published 2022

1 3 5 7 9 10 8 6 4 2

Publication © Penguin Random House 2022
Text © Daniel Janse van Rensburg and Tracey Pharoah 2022

All rights reserved. No part of this publication may be reproduced,
stored in a retrieval system or transmitted, in any form or by any means,
electronic, mechanical, photocopying, recording or otherwise,
without the prior written permission of the copyright owners.

PUBLISHER: Marlene Fryer
MANAGING EDITOR: Robert Plummer
EDITOR: Alice Inggs
COVER DESIGNER: Ryan Africa
TYPESETTER: Monique van den Berg

Set in 11 pt on 15 pt Minion Pro

Printed by **novus print**, a division of Novus Holdings

ISBN 978 1 77609 693 0 (print)
ISBN 978 1 77609 694 7 (ePub)

I dedicate this book to my mother, Martha, who fought tirelessly
to bring me home, and my wife, Melanie, who humbled herself,
begging for help in raising funds to secure my release
and end my nightmare in Equatorial Guinea.

They never gave up, never lost hope, and the joy of seeing them again
is one of my most treasured moments after enduring nearly 500 days
at Black Beach prison where I was held without trial.

Their unconditional love and support sustains me as
I slowly recover from the hell I endured between December 2013
and my eventual release in September 2015.

Contents

Prologue 1

PART 1 3
1. 'I Do' 5
2. Touchdown 12
3. Blindsided 19
4. *No Entiendo* 26
5. Welcome to Guantanamo 30
6. By the Skin of My Teeth 36
7. Into the Lions' Den 39
8. A Toast to Freedom 44
9. No Way Out 48
10. Déjà Vu 52
11. Courting Disaster 57
12. Judgement Day 62
13. Hide and Seek 66
14. House Arrest 73
15. Permission Denied 78
16. Kidnapped! 81
17. Destination Unknown 88

PART 2 91
18. I Am Not That Strong 93
19. I Will Fear No Evil 96
20. Bangkok 102
21. The Bench 108
22. The Longest Night 114
23. A Place to Call Home 117
24. Breakfast of Champions 123
25. Hell's Kitchen 127

26. Slow-Roasted	132
27. *Feliz Navidad*	137
28. *Mi Familia*	141
29. Ubuntu	144
30. Incommunicado	148
31. Close Shave	152
32. Welcome to News Hour	156
33. Sick	160
34. Until We Meet Again	166
35. Happy Birthday to Me	171
PART 3	**175**
36. Butta My Bread	177
37. Free	182
38. House Arrest at the Bordello	185
39. Malabo Stray	189
40. Boats, Planes and Automobiles	192
41. Land of the Free, Home of the Brave	197
PART 4	**203**
42. Why Is This Happening?	205
43. Enter the Dragon	208
44. Evil Spirits	211
45. *Broda-Broda*	214
46. Tales from the Dark Side	217
47. My Adopted Son	221
48. Ebola	225
49. What's Your Name, Where You From?	228
50. Nothing to Declare	233
51. Fair Game	237
52. Crimes Against Humanity	241
53. Fresh Meat	248
54. *Mucho Gusto*	253
55. Pay the Ransom	257

PART 5	261
56. Western Union	263
57. *Liberdade*	267
58. Final Boarding Call	270
59. Stop the Press	276
60. Until Death Do Us Part	282
Epilogue	285
Author's Note	287

'We must be willing to place all that we have
– not just our possessions
(they may be the easiest things of all to give up),
but also our ambition and pride, stubbornness and vanity
– we must place it all at the altar of God,
kneel there in silent submission,
and willingly walk away.'
– **Elder Jeffrey R. Holland**

FREEDOM
Such a powerful symbol and often taken for granted,
for many it is the most primitive and essential of all human rights,
the cornerstone of morality, but until it is stolen from you,
you will never fully appreciate or understand its essence.

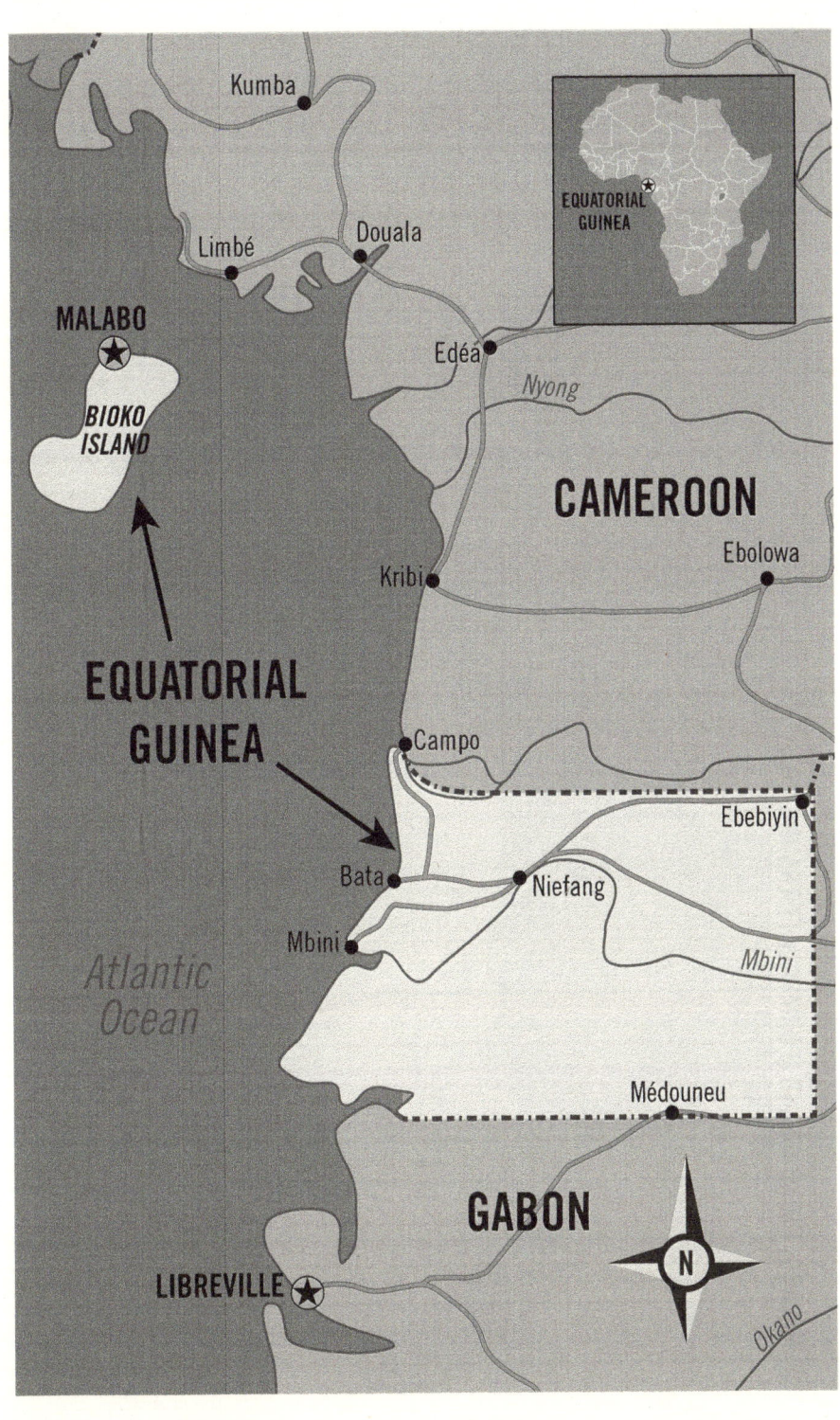

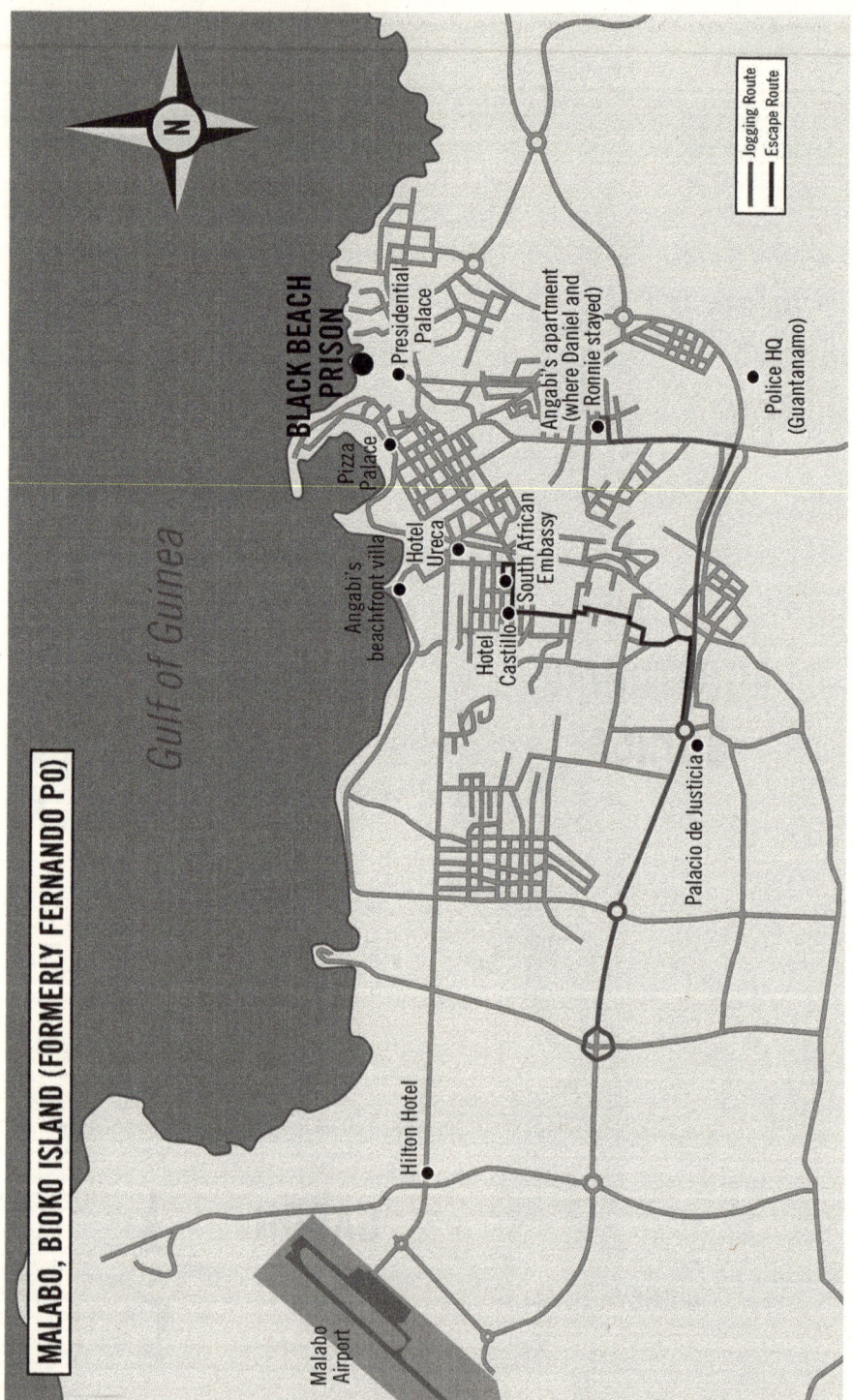

What follows is true to my recollection of the events before and during my detention at Malabo Police Headquarters, my incarceration at Black Beach and my subsequent release. This has been a difficult story to tell, as many events have been painful to revisit, and along the way a few details have blurred in my memory. Dialogue is reproduced as I remember it, and in some cases, I may not have recalled events in the order they occurred. The opinions expressed are my own, and, where necessary, certain information has been changed to protect those involved.

Prologue

The heat is suffocating me, amplifying the claustrophobia that threatens my sanity. Fresh beads of sweat erupt on my forehead, a rash of salty droplets that run into my eyes and trickle down to the tip of my nose. The itch is unbearable, but my hands are cuffed behind my back, the unrelenting grip of steel cutting into my flesh.

I can hear the grunts of exertion from an officer in the next room as he pummels a detainee currently 'under interrogation'. The door is closed, but the sounds create sickening images in my mind.

I am perched on a narrow wooden bench, shackled alongside a panic-stricken man whose terror intensifies my own feeling of dread. Suddenly, the door to the adjacent room bursts open and I catch a glimpse of what is going on in there.

Blood. So much blood. Splattered across the walls, dripping from the end of a baton. Two guards stand over the battered body of a man who lies in an ever-expanding pool of blood on the floor. The man next to me whimpers; his horror mirrors my own.

Another pair of guards emerge from the room and seize the man cowering beside me, unhitching his handcuffs from the rail. His hysterical pleas for mercy fall on deaf ears, and his legs are shaking so uncontrollably that he can barely stand. I see a spreading wet patch at his groin as they pull him roughly towards the room where the other man lies unmoving on the floor. I know that these scenes of suffering will be embedded in a dark corner of my soul forever.

I want to cover my ears to silence his awful cries, but the handcuffs prevent me from shutting them out. Then the door slams, muting the shrieks of the man who moments ago was sitting beside me in this dank, windowless cell at Guantanamo, the unofficial name of the police headquarters and holding cells in Malabo, the Equatorial Guinean capital on Bioko island.

No entiendo – I don't understand. How did I get here? It feels like I have woken into a nightmare. How did this happen? This morning I was on my way home to South Africa, and now I am chained like a rabid dog, staring at the graffiti roughly etched in Spanish on the wall opposite me: *No hay justicia*. There is no justice.

I close my eyes, trying to prepare for the agony that surely lies ahead. The screams in the other room continue unabated. I try to rub my face against the bricks to alleviate the itch of dripping sweat. Nothing helps. I look around the room and find myself staring into the eyes of President Teodoro Obiang Nguema Mbasogo as he watches over the proceedings from a poster loosely tacked to the wall. The poster advocates human rights.

The stark reality of my situation sinks in. Harnessing my faith, I bow my head and begin to pray. 'God protect me,' I murmur as I listen to the unrelenting thump of the baton and the low, tortured moans become quieter and quieter as the prisoner is beaten into oblivion ...

I know that I am next.

PART 1

'There will come a time when you believe everything is finished … That will be the beginning.'

– Louis L'Amour

PART I

1

'I Do'

Hoekwil, South Africa
Thursday, 26 September 2013

Road trip! I've been up since the dark hours before dawn preparing for the long drive from our Hoekwil home in the Garden Route, across the mountains into the hot, dry basin of the Karoo. My wife, Melanie, is pottering around, making sure we haven't forgotten anything, and I'm doing some last-minute admin, typing a few urgent emails before we head out on the road to Loxton for a close friend's wedding.

It's been over twenty years since we travelled from Namibia to visit my parents at their retirement home in Hoekwil for Christmas. Melanie immediately fell in love with this quaint, peaceful village surrounded by mountains, rivers and forests and told me that this was where she wanted to raise our kids. So in 1994, while I was completing a contract in Angola, we bought a beautiful timber home and settled here, enjoying the country life complete with a small village school, church and traditional Afrikaans community where our children could grow up in a wholesome rural atmosphere.

I've been an entrepreneur since my early twenties when I set up my first business offering car-hire services in Windhoek. Later, as consulting work came naturally, I established links with a network of businessmen working in the oil industry in West Africa. Since then, I've assisted multinationals wishing to expand into this burgeoning market, working on a range of projects, from setting up a division of DStv and even sourcing aircraft for politicians and the powerful elite of Equatorial Guinea when owning a private jet became the latest must-have accessory. In a few days, I'll be off to finalise a new airline deal with Gabriel Angabi, the former mayor of the capital, Malabo, on Bioko island.

I met Angabi by 'accident' around 2001 when one of my drivers from the local DStv agency I'd set up had backed into his vehicle. Angabi was not impressed, and as the person in charge, I was summoned to his office to deal with the problem and managed to smooth things over by agreeing to cover the cost of repairs. Our next encounter was under better circumstances and we ended up talking about business opportunities around the town.

The decade that followed cemented our relationship as we worked together while I established a foothold in the aviation business and sourced an aircraft for his airline, Ecuato Guineana de Aviación, which operated under licence with Spanair.

Although I had the utmost respect for Angabi, whom I consider a trusted friend, many others have a different story to tell of this powerful political figure who is a larger-than-life, jovial and shrewd businessman whose reputation for mercurial outbursts is legendary.

It wasn't long before it became obvious that running an airline in a Third World country is fraught with problems, and eventually due to incompetence and a total disregard for safety and compliance, Ecuato Guineana de Aviación lost its licence to fly, but during the ensuing years I continued to supply other aircraft to Angabi.

It was around 2010 that he approached me to discuss setting up a new airline. I initially tried to talk him out of it, as much had changed in the airline industry as a result of the terror attacks of 9/11, but he was adamant, and when Angabi wants something, you don't really have much choice but to comply, so despite my misgivings we forged ahead. Now, at this point, I'm hopeful that the work I've done over the past eighteen months sorting out compliance and regulatory requirements will ensure that the launch of the new airline, Coriscair, will go smoothly.

After my return from Loxton on Sunday, I'll fly to Johannesburg to meet up with our newly appointed airline operations manager, Ronnie, who is perfect for the job. He is an experienced technician, recently retired from South African Airways and not quite ready to sit back and put his feet up. Once Ronnie and I get to Malabo, we'll look for premises where the South African crew I've recruited will establish their base of operations. I plan to stay for about a week, so apart from the mountain of documents, I'll be travelling light, keen to wrap up and move on to new ventures.

I hit send on the last email, and grab a copy of the contract to add to the growing pile of documents I'll be taking with me to Equatorial Guinea on Monday, but for now I'm looking forward to putting all that aside and spending some quality time with my amigos in the Karoo.

Just then, Bubbles, our Maltese poodle, dashes into the study. He loves road trips as much as I do, and it's clear from the vigorous wagging of his tail that he knows there is one on the cards today. From the other room, Melanie announces that she's ready to go, so I shut down the computer and grab our favourite collection of eighties hits on my way out.

I'm looking forward to playing the role of best man to my long-time friend when he ties the knot in true Karoo tradition. Colyn has a sheep farm on the outskirts of Loxton, midway between Victoria West and Carnarvon. He's a typical South African *boer*, a loyal friend and an easy-going, sociable guy. We met back in 2002 while biking in the Karoo, and our friendship has been cultivated over many nights sitting around the campfire with a Jack Daniel's, watching the stars and contemplating life.

I'm really happy that he's found someone special to share his life with him. Being the wife of a farmer in a remote place where sheep outnumber humans is not a choice many women are prepared to make, and he's lucky to have found someone willing to relinquish the attractions and convenience of modern life. There is nothing like the silence of the Karoo – it has an almost hypnotic quality that will either make you crazy or bring you closer to nature and its infinite mysteries. Although I like being among people, the solitude and peace of the desert feeds my soul, and for me, heading off the beaten track is one of life's simple pleasures.

Keys in hand, I call Bubbles and we head out to the car. Melanie is not far behind, looking cheerful as I pop my favourite Queen album into the CD player and the toe-tapping beat of 'I Want to Break Free' fills the car. We sing along as we drive down the Hoekwil hill, laughing when we get the words wrong. A flock of egrets takes flight, painting a ribbon of iridescent white against the purple hues of early dawn over the lakes, setting the tone for what promises to be a great getaway filled with love, laughter and happy times.

We drive along the empty streets of George, catching up with the sun as we cross the Outeniqua Pass into Oudtshoorn and head north through Meiringspoort. The trip is relaxing and uneventful, with Neil Diamond, Meat Loaf and other eighties favourites for company. A little later, we pull in at the Three Sisters roadside stop to fill up and stretch our legs. It's not much more than a pitstop at the junction of two major highways connecting this region to other parts of South Africa. It's not even named for famous sisters, but rather for the three identical hills that are considered the gateway to the Karoo. But this unremarkable spot does have two redeeming features: a patch of grass for Bubbles to run around on and a convenience store where we can get a cup of decent coffee.

While Melanie orders our coffee, Bubbles loses no time dashing around, nose to the ground, making periodic stops to ensure that he leaves his special signature on every scrubby little bush in the vicinity. I stretch and look up at the cloudless sky, feeling the pressures and stresses of the past few months melt away. Life is good; Equatorial Guinea and Angabi's aeroplanes seem as far away as the moon.

Melanie emerges from the store and hands me a coffee and we call Bubbles away from his mission. I put my coffee on the roof of the car, settle Bubbles on the back seat and pull out onto the N1 for the final leg of our journey. After a few minutes, I ask Melanie to pass me my coffee. She looks at me quizzically and it suddenly dawns on us that we left our cups on the roof of the car! Laughing, we continue our journey coffee-less, heading out along the lonely stretch of road that leads to one of the quietest places on earth.

Soon we are surrounded by endless horizons that reach out to touch infinite blue skies. This vast emptiness is dotted with little Victorian-era dorpies where quirky characters live an unhurried existence, and everyone knows one another by name. As in most Karoo towns, the Dutch Reformed church is central to the Loxton community and there is a single coffee shop, bar and convenience store. The primitive corbelled houses, peculiar to this area, are its only notable feature. Water and jobs are scarce, so life is hard for many, but these long-suffering locals are some of the most welcoming folk you'll ever meet.

Bubbles is enjoying the breeze streaming in through the window, his nose twitching at all the exciting smells of new, unexplored territory, his expression of glee unmistakable as we draw closer to our destination, bouncing slowly down a long dirt road, and pull into Osfontein, the farm where we'll be staying for the next few days.

Our friends are waiting to welcome us, and we climb out and hug them as Bubbles scampers off in search of new adventures. The air is filled with the excited chatter of friends reunited, and as soon as we've offloaded our bags and freshened up, we grab a bottle of Jack Daniel's and head over to Colyn's farm, Middelwater, to enjoy a braai with the groom and his family.

The day dawns bright and clear, promising to be a scorcher. The marriage of a local farmer with a long family history in the area is big news, and Loxton is abuzz with excitement. We're up early to help with the preparations. I take a quick, cool shower to dispel the heat, and then get kitted out in my swanky wedding gear that the bride has chosen for us. We're going to look dashing in our dove-grey *Peaky Blinders* scally caps, crisp white shirts with button-down collars, braces and khaki pants. Melanie is looking gorgeous, like a fresh-faced country girl in her summery dress and strappy heels as she applies a touch of lipstick, brushing her long blonde hair while I sit at the timeworn kitchen table polishing my shoes.

With Bubbles back in his favourite spot, we set out along the gravel road, leaving a trail of dust behind us as we drive into town. We park outside the community hall adjacent to the church and make our way into the venue, which has been transformed in true Karoo style.

Tables are arranged around the room, with an area left open for dancing, and in the corner the DJ is setting up and testing his equipment.

The hall is a hive of activity with all the local tannies running the show, bustling about, doing things that are evidently very important and well beyond our realm of expertise. They quickly recruit Melanie to help with the flowers, then commandeer the men to do some heavy lifting, setting us to work lugging crates of beer as they strut around like clucking hens instructing us to make sure there is enough ice and *brandewyn*. Once these most important issues have been addressed, we hover uncertainly, awaiting further instructions, until a beady-eyed old lady spots us loitering and announces that we're getting in the way, and we are unceremoniously shooed out the door.

Laughing, we cross the street and head to Die Rooi Granaat, the local coffee shop where other guests have gathered to escape the rising heat. Midday is approaching and we're all starting to wilt, so I suggest an impromptu pre-wedding 'cocktail' and order pink milkshakes all round. There's nothing better than the cool, sweet taste of a creamy strawberry milkshake on a hot, dry day in the Karoo. In fact, I'd take one of those any time, no matter what the weather or circumstances. Over the years, our friends have teased me mercilessly about this, noting that it does little to boost my 'macho image', but I don't care. The milkshakes arrive festooned with colourful sprinkles and gooey pink syrup, much to the amusement of the older men who have stationed themselves out of harm's way, sipping ice-cold lager and waiting for the highly anticipated festivities to begin. Someone puts some music on and it's as if the wedding reception has already begun.

The ringing church bells signal that the wedding service is about to get under way. Slurping the last drops of pink froth from the bottom of our glasses, we wipe away all traces of our guilty secret from our beards, straighten our caps and head into the gardens outside the church to await the arrival of the bride. A donkey cart slowly clip-clops past the church and I feel like I've stepped back in time. Loxton will do that to you. You can't help but slow down as the stresses of modern life melt away.

Colyn beckons me over, saying that we need to take our places inside. I hand Bubbles to Melanie and we make our way into the church where the harmonious strains of old hymns fill the space. I'm overcome with a feeling of nostalgia, transported back to cherished memories of my childhood in Namibia, the family tradition of gathering for the Sunday morning service and lazy Sunday lunches.

Everyone takes their seats and the first strains of the wedding march announce the arrival of the bride. I glance at Melanie, remembering when, in 1985, during my final year of high school, we first met in Rundu near the Angolan border in northern Namibia. She was in Standard 8 and, luckily for me, the attraction was mutual. I never really shone academically, but we were both sporty and being active was – and still is – a big part of our lives. I enjoyed doing anything that took me outside, away from the bleak, cramped hostel dormitory.

I was always enthusiastic, with an outgoing personality, and my parents never put me under any pressure to do anything other than be happy. Our family was dogged by tragedy, yet despite this my mother was a pillar of strength, coping with the loss of my older brother, who died shortly after I was born, and, years later, in 1989, the death of my sister in a car accident. My father has always been a man of few words, hardworking and practical. His work as a bush pilot took him away a lot, so my mother and I developed a special bond that endures to this day.

Standing in this small church in the middle of nowhere, I remember how I told Melanie on our first date that I was going to marry her, and now here we are, more than twenty years later, happily married and the parents of two wonderful children.

As the bride makes her way to the altar and the ceremony begins, I recall something I once read – that a successful marriage requires falling in love many times over, but always with the same person. How lucky I am to have met and married my soulmate, my heart, my joy and the one person I am sure

I could not live without. As our friends slip on their wedding rings, I silently thank God for bringing Melanie into my life and blessing us with a love that has no end.

Little do I know that these memories will sustain me through the dark days that lie ahead.

2

Touchdown

```
Malabo, Bioko Island
Tuesday, 1 October 2013
```

After a long flight from South Africa with a night stop in Addis Ababa, Ronnie and I arrive in Malabo around midday. As we circle overhead, I remember my first visit to Bioko in 2001, when the 'oil boom' hadn't yet hit and most of the buildings were from colonial times. I arrived at my hotel in downtown Malabo during a torrential downpour at the height of the rainy season and stepped out of the vehicle straight into a river of water flooding the parking area. The lady at the hotel reception didn't speak English and spent a long time shuffling through papers, looking for my reservation, but when she couldn't find anything with my name on it, she eventually handed me a key and I traipsed down the corridor, leaving a wet trail in my wake. The door to my room was stuck tight and the key didn't work, but with a bit of pushing and shoving it finally opened. This was my first welcome to Malabo and Hotel Ureca, the tallest building on the island at the time, and rumoured to be the place where Frederick Forsyth stayed while writing *The Dogs of War*.

As we prepare to disembark, I think about how much has changed since those days and wonder what Forsyth would think of the island now. We gather our things and walk down the stairs onto the blisteringly hot tarmac. Nothing really prepares you for the sweltering heat of Equatorial Guinea, stepping off the aircraft into what feels like a blast from a furnace, and I'm immediately sticky with perspiration. It's early in the dry season, dusty, and the humidity is draining, but fortunately I'm a familiar face at immigration, so we breeze through and head outside, spotting Coco, Angabi's manager, waiting to drive us to the Hilton.

Since 1996, the discovery of vast oil reserves in Equatorial Guinean waters has driven explosive growth, and much has changed in Malabo as the quest for black gold intensified and oil company contractors slowly took over the town, with a long line of local officials and their friends taking a share of the spoils. Now, the Hotel Ureca is a distant memory, having been replaced by the five-star Hilton, where beautifully manicured, landscaped gardens and a sparkling pool have taken the place of the flooded parking lot of my memories.

Malabo is an old colonial town, dating back to the days of slavery, its roots evident in the language and architecture emulating the style of eighteenth-century Spain, in stark contrast to the surrounding derelict buildings and shacks constructed from wood or corrugated iron. The town is a microcosm of extremes, where poverty and wealth intersect along the edges of a recently constructed highway connecting the airport to the town centre. The south and central regions of the island are beautiful natural areas of tropical rainforest, nestled at the foot of a dormant volcano in a region that is relatively untouched, with some agricultural activity. Frequent torrential rain causes mudslides as it flows down its slopes, flooding the narrow roads around the town.

The urban district where we're headed is where businessmen lured by the promise of oil and profits enjoy five-star living at luxury hotels. I've clocked many miles jogging around the town, but first-time visitors often find it difficult to comprehend the extreme contrasts of everyday life here. The island is slowly being overtaken by greedy First World corporations hoping to strike it rich. Life is laid back and the culture is heavily influenced by its Spanish colonial past. Wealthy locals reside in palatial beachfront mansions, while just out of sight of the promenade the majority of the island's population live a hand-to-mouth existence in squalor on muddy streets with limited access to water, electricity and sanitation.

The Río Cónsul river runs along the edge of the residential area, meandering north until it flushes into the ocean alongside Black Beach, the notorious prison infamous for its human rights atrocities. With each visit, as Western influence grows, I can see the changes being wrought on this tiny, remote island. The gap between rich and poor is becoming more apparent, and as with all things when you have something valuable, inevitably someone else wants it.

In 2004, Nick du Toit, a South African soldier of fortune, and Simon Mann, a former British SAS army officer, were imprisoned here following the failed Wonga plot, an attempted coup by a team of mercenaries led by Du Toit and Mann and linked to Mark Thatcher, the son of former British prime minister Margaret Thatcher. (Thatcher has always denied any involvement in the plot.)

I was working in Malabo at the time, and was briefly detained with these men as I happened to be in the same bar when they were arrested. But I was quickly released and allowed to continue working when they discovered that I had no ties to the group. The plot drew international media attention and soured relations between the Equatorial Guinean political elite and foreign businessmen, particularly on the part of President Obiang, who has been suspicious of foreigners ever since, and it wasn't long before the police and military began to roam the streets.

We arrive at the newly built Hilton, which happens to be constructed on land co-owned by the president's son and Angabi, who are both majority shareholders in the hotel. Even though I've stayed here on previous trips, as access to a stable internet connection in the well-equipped business centre makes it the perfect base from which to operate, extravagant living is not the norm for me. The architecture is regal, with a grand columned entrance that ushers you across a majestic foyer to the expansive reception desk where we are greeted with a warm African welcome. The check-in process is quick and painless as I am a familiar face here too, and we hand over our passports to Coco to arrange work visas before heading off to our comfortable suites overlooking the pool.

Later, Ronnie and I meet up at the poolside bar to discuss our plans for the coming days while enjoying steak sandwiches, salad and fries washed down with #33 beer, a popular local brew. Angabi usually provides a Land Cruiser for me to get around in, or he'll send a driver, but as everything happens on 'African time' they are generally unreliable and frequently late.

As the temperature rises throughout the day, most inhabitants of the island follow the Spanish tradition of taking a siesta, so Ronnie and I head for the comfort of our air-conditioned rooms until Coco arrives to take us to visit the new offices and apartments arranged for management and the incoming crew. I'm feeling relaxed and confident: everything is going according to plan, and all that remains is to secure the final payment, so after a light supper I turn in early.

As I drift off to sleep, I remember the first time I sourced an aircraft for Angabi, way back in 2001 when I'd been working on setting up the DStv agency. The shrill ringing of the phone in my hotel room had jarred me awake at 2 a.m.

'Daniel,' a now familiar voice boomed down the line. 'Come now ...'

Still groggy with sleep, I thought I was being summoned to tune Angabi's decoder, but when I arrived twenty minutes later, I discovered he had much greater needs requiring my urgent attention: he wanted an aeroplane and he wanted me to source it *now*!

The island of Bioko is not directly opposite mainland Equatorial Guinea but further to the north: it's about 35 kilometres from Cameroon and 235 kilometres from the rest of Equatorial Guinea. To commute to the mainland you need an aircraft or boat, and as many of the country's wealthy elite own homes here on the island, there is a huge demand for goods from the mainland and neighbouring countries. The outrageous extravagance of the country's leaders knows no bounds in a place where, despite its vast wealth and relatively small population, almost a quarter of children will die before their fifth birthday and most citizens will not live beyond fifty years.

The international press frequently documents unlawful killings, torture, arbitrary arrest, and restrictions on the freedom of speech. Anyone who dares to demand justice for the people of Equatorial Guinea is sent to rot in the notorious Black Beach prison, which is located in a stinking swamp in a dark and forgotten cove behind the presidential palace. Angabi is closely connected to the Obiang family, who have been in power since 1968, facing numerous charges for human rights violations and fraud investigations into the embezzlement of state funds, acquiring aeroplanes, luxury vehicles and homes around the world with overflowing bank accounts that fund their excesses.

I managed to pull off the impossible and within a week had arranged for the delivery of an MD82 for the new national airline, Ecuato Guineana de Aviación, as its aircraft were being serviced and would be out of action for a few months. Needless to say, Angabi and the presidential family who had green-lighted the deal were thrilled with their new toy, and a golden era of short-haul flights between Bioko, the Equatorial Guinean mainland and neighbouring Cameroon and Gabon ensured that the plane was always crammed to capacity.

Angabi is not the only powerful politician in Malabo to enjoy the prestige of having his own planes, and since those early days I have become known as one of the go-to guys for aircraft, sourcing everything from a Fokker F28, a G1 and a Learjet to cargo planes. For the commercial market, nothing beats the Hawker Siddeley 748, known around here as the 'banana plane' because of its bright yellow paint job depicting Angabi's company logo. It had some quirks – like a Land Rover of the skies – but its saving grace was its lightning-fast turnaround time, and as long as we had a mechanic, it was as reliable as an old-school Nokia phone, like the one I always carry around as a backup.

The success of these early ventures paved the way for a mutually beneficial business relationship as I assisted Angabi in setting up his fledgling airline, acquiring a total of six aircraft over the next few years and forging a friendship that saw me spend many happy hours with him and his family. But it hasn't all been champagne and caviar: although the airline flourished, Angabi's team regularly came under fire for lack of compliance, and planes were often grounded because the airline hadn't paid its fuel bill or because safety and maintenance requirements were not met. In some cases, the leased planes were deemed unserviceable and returned to their owners, and new planes were acquired to replace them.

Over the years, I learnt a lot about the pitfalls of setting up a high-yield cash enterprise. One of our biggest problems was cash ticket sales, as invariably the cash didn't end up in the bank and when the fuel bill had to be paid there was no money to pay it. Scheduling was another challenge because a typical African minute can sometimes equate to an hour or more. This laid-back approach to check-in times hampered scheduling and the filing of flight plans for trips on and off the island. But somehow we made it work, the robust and reliable Hawker Siddeley 748 often coming to the rescue. Ultimately, though, the serious issues of compliance and maintenance resulted in the aircraft being grounded and I'd have to find another to replace it.

In November 2010, Angabi broached the subject of starting a new airline, but after all I'd experienced over the past decade, I was dubious and noncommittal, returning home to Hoekwil for Christmas to think it through. While I was shopping at the local mall, Angabi called to say that he'd deposited almost US$200 000 into my bank account to secure the lease of an aircraft for his new airline, Coriscair. Vaguely alarmed, I flew back to Malabo in early January to try to persuade him that it was a bad idea due to the tough regulatory changes in international aviation regarding safety compliance and other issues post-9/11, not to mention that Equatorial Guinea had been put on an aviation blacklist by the EU as a result of safety concerns, meaning that all local planes were banned from flying internationally. Considering his track record when it came to airline ventures, I also made it clear that things would need to be handled differently this time to avoid being shut down. At that point, I was aware that the government had purchased several new Boeing 777s and were impatient to get the ban lifted so that they could be put into service, meaning that some headway was being made in terms of conforming to international safety standards, opening up new opportunities for everyone.

Angabi understood that this time we had to follow protocol, so armed with a five-year plan I'd drawn up, I immediately arranged a plane for domestic use only, but while sourcing a crew I was confronted with yet another complication. Angabi's airline operating licence had been revoked and we had to cancel the order and lost that plane, but I am confident that the new contract will cover all these bases and I have used the funds he's provided to sort out compliance with the new International Air Transport Association (IATA) rules and regulations governing airline operation and navigate the complexities of setting up the airline to run on an Aircraft, Crew, Maintenance and Insurance basis while travelling around the world in search of a crew and robust aircraft with a carrying capacity of around eighty passengers that is suitable for frequent short-haul flights.

Now, after months of negotiation, my go-to guy for aircraft Ray Richardson and I have finally brokered a deal with Cemair in South Africa. All that remains is to secure a final payment from Angabi and we can deliver the Bombardier CRJ100 I've secured. The months leading up to this point have been exhausting, with trips locally and across Africa. I've even ventured as far as Dubai in search of a suitable aircraft and crew, not to mention the numerous flights to Equatorial Guinea to meet with Angabi and his team in an attempt to resolve their licensing issues and have the IATA embargo lifted.

It took until July to help him get his licences to operate approved, and in the three months since then, I've managed to source an aircraft and a team to get the Coriscair project under way. After all these false starts, the endless months of negotiation and paperwork seem to have paid off and now I am here in Malabo to collect the final payment so Coriscair can at last take to the skies.

I switch off the light and settle in for the night, waking up to head out for an early morning run to start the day. Later I meet Ronnie for a quick breakfast and we settle in at the poolside to relax as the temperature rises. You find a lot of people hanging around at the Hilton waiting to be summoned to meet with a local VIP, as typically one waits a day or two for meetings to be scheduled – the decision-makers of this tiny but enormously wealthy country have an annoying habit of feeding their sense of self-importance by granting foreigners an audience only once a few days have passed. Having worked in the region for more than a decade, I'm familiar with this protocol, so I factored it into my schedule and my return flight is only booked for the end of the week.

The following morning, Coco takes me to the bank, of which Angabi is a director, and I'm shown the amount allocated for transfer. The bank manager advises that it will be processed into a local account in my name, which I find surprising as I haven't signed any documents for this purpose. A few days pass and I still haven't met with Angabi. Coco tells me that his boss has left for medical treatment in Brazil, so I extend my stay on the island indefinitely as he is vague regarding dates for Angabi's return.

Later in the week, I pop into the bank to follow up on the transaction as the funds have not yet materialised. I'm left waiting for some time but eventually I'm ushered into the bank manager's office. Our meeting is awkward as he seems evasive and can't give me a straight answer regarding the delay. Clearly there's a problem, but I'm not overly concerned; I'm used to the way things work here and am sure that everything will be resolved, so I go back to the Hilton to wait.

Days pass and I visit the bank a few more times but make no headway. I can't understand why there's a problem, and alarm bells are starting to ring, but I set aside my concerns, feeling vaguely reassured by the fact that the bank has issued guarantees for the funds, and, besides, we have an ironclad contract with all the official stamps, notarised by the courts and drawn up by a top South African legal firm with a transcript in Spanish by an internationally accredited translator.

Although I am baffled by the delay, I've worked with Angabi for many years so I know that this is not so uncommon – it's something to be expected when doing deals in a Third World country. I trust him and feel pretty confident that all will be resolved when he gets back from South America.

3

Blindsided

```
Angabi's Residence, Malabo
Thursday, 24 October 2013
```

It's been more than three weeks since we arrived in Malabo and Ronnie and I have now settled into one of Angabi's apartments while we wait for him to return from South America. Although he's getting on in years, Angabi enjoys the thrill of new ventures, which is why he's the principal shareholder and financier of Coriscair. He never misses an opportunity to put in an appearance and proclaim his supremacy with a hearty handshake and magnanimous gestures, but he's seldom involved in putting any plans into action. He has people like me for that, and I don't think he realises how much work has been done to get to this point.

We received our temporary air operator's licence in July, as well as the South African Civil Aviation Authority's acknowledgement of intent to operate in Malabo. We've also prepared the aircraft I sourced from Cemair on an Aircraft, Crew, Maintenance and Insurance basis, and one of Angabi's representatives has inspected it, so once the final payment is made, we're good to go.

Angabi has strong ties to the Obiang family that has ruled Equatorial Guinea for over forty years. The upper echelon of Malabo society is loyal to this powerful family, particularly those with close personal ties to them like Angabi, who is the brother-in-law of Constancia Mangue Nsue Okomo, the president's number-one wife, and uncle of Teodorin Obiang, the president's son. They're partnered in many lucrative ventures, including business, property and resource investments such as the Hilton hotel.

Having concluded many deals with Angabi, I'm struck that he is not the most well-educated businessman I've ever come across, but he seems adept at hiding this. He is a pioneering force behind the modernisation of Malabo, has enjoyed a long political career as a senator and is counted among a handful of powerful elite controlling Equatorial Guinea, largely for their own benefit.

I've always been impressed that a semi-literate man has achieved as much as he has. It's a testament to his intelligence and resourcefulness, even though he might be considered 'ignorant' by Western standards. In fact, the more time

I spend here, the more I'm reminded that Africa does not need redemption, education or handouts from the West. Vast resources, innovation, diversity and a sense of community drive a culture of entrepreneurship on the continent. Corruption is rife, but this is true of governments around the world, and in Africa it's a little more complex, with unwritten laws honouring ancient alliances dating back centuries, even though some might call it nepotism. I've seen first-hand how not all great things are achieved because they are for the good of the people. Wealth and power are obvious motivators, no matter where in the world you are. Africa marches to the beat of a different drum, and Western powers would be wise to adopt a less patronising attitude towards their African counterparts.

Although the unnecessary delays are frustrating, it's all part of the game. I've always thought that Angabi had an immense capacity for self-worship, which fuels a desire to string people along. We're on his playground, so we must play by his rules, and if we have to wait then that's what we do. I've been under the impression that everything was in place on this side and that we could launch Coriscair on delivery of the aircraft, but in reality not much has been done, so there's plenty to keep me busy until Angabi returns.

Early one evening, Coco calls to say that Angabi is back and a driver will collect me for a breakfast meeting at his beachfront mansion in the morning. Relieved, I put down the phone and tell Ronnie the good news. I've been here for almost a month, but at last we can finalise the payment and I can return to South Africa to collect the aircraft.

The morning dawns hot and humid. When the driver arrives, I grab the contract and some other documents on my way out, calling to Ronnie that I'll see him later. As we make our way to Angabi's villa, I think about how our working relationship has brought me a level of respectability around Malabo. I enjoy working with him, despite having heard about his mercurial temper (a friend once compared him to the two sides of a coin – one day heads, the other day tails). But although he's pompous and self-absorbed, I respect him and feel privileged to have been welcomed into his home and treated like family, an honour not bestowed lightly in African culture. I am humbled by the trust he has in me, and even though he's unpredictable and not everyone is impressed by him, often whispering subtle warnings that he's not to be trusted, I've never experienced any animosity in all the time I've known him.

As an ordinary, middle-class South African, experiencing the lifestyle of the super-elite is surreal. Angabi's world is one of obscene wealth that exists for a select few, the level of opulence astonishing and almost pornographic in its excess. It's incredible how the discovery of oil has brought such tremendous wealth to this obscure corner of Africa that few people have even heard about, except in relation to slavery, black magic, cannibalism and attempted coups. And yet here I am, sitting in an air-conditioned, chauffeur-driven vehicle, on my way to a meeting with a powerful, politically connected African businessman in his beachfront villa.

Aurora, Angabi's secretary, is waiting and gives me a quick hug. She's gained a few kilos since I last saw her, a sure sign that she's become accustomed to the high life. She leads me upstairs to the dining area on the balcony overlooking the ocean. The patio is cool and a slight breeze wafts in from the ocean, helping to diffuse some of the cloying humidity. Angabi is pacing about, waving his cigar while talking loudly into his phone. He acknowledges me with a nod and I wave a greeting in return. Coco is seated at the breakfast table and introduces another guest, one of Angabi's lawyers. Aurora pours me a coffee and the aroma of freshly baked pastries tantalises my tastebuds as I grab a crisp, golden-brown croissant from the buffet platter laid out for breakfast, adding a few pieces of fruit for good measure.

Angabi is still going full throttle, so I drizzle a little honey over my croissant and attempt to make small talk with Coco and Aurora, but they seem edgy, more formal than usual. I give up and watch the fishermen down on the beach prepare to launch their boats as the early morning fog clears. Finally, Angabi sets his phone aside, lumbers over and collapses heavily into a chair. Aurora fetches him a coffee as he reaches for a fresh cigar and looks over at me. His expression is inscrutable.

'I want my money back,' he says without preamble.

I stop chewing and look at him blankly. 'I don't understand,' I say slowly, in utter confusion. 'What do you mean you want your money back?'

Angabi glances at the others, who remain poker-faced, busying themselves with their breakfasts.

'Daniel, don't be difficult,' says Angabi, turning back to me and taking a long drag on his cigar. He exhales. 'I want my money back.' He leans forward, his voice flat and menacing, jabbing his finger on the table to emphasise the point. 'We are not going ahead with this project.'

'What do you mean?' I ask in confusion, looking up at him. '*No entiendo.*

I don't understand. You can't just cancel the contract, that's not how things work, there must be a reason,' I tell him.

To mask my bewilderment, I pick up the contract and flip through it, frowning as the pungent aroma of his cigar smoke wafts over me, but determined not to let him intimidate me. I tap the spot where he's signed and it's been notarised by the courts.

'Here,' I say, pointing to his signature. 'You see, this document is legal and binding. Here is where you signed … You can't just say the deal is off!'

As the words leave my mouth, I realise that I've made a colossal mistake. Questioning Angabi's authority in front of an audience is a really bad idea. Worse, these people are his employees, his subordinates. But it's too late, the words are out and there's no taking them back.

Like a shadow passing across the sun, Angabi's face darkens, and for the first time since I met him all those years ago, I'm finally confronted by the man that everyone has warned me about. I feel a shiver run down my spine and struggle to keep my expression neutral as I try to figure out what I've missed. Why does he want to cancel the deal? Where has this all fallen apart?

'Daniel, don't tell me what I can and can't do!' he bellows. 'You will not leave this country until I have my money!'

He slams his fist on the table. Dishes rattle, my coffee spills into the saucer and a butter knife bounces off the table and clatters to the floor. Coco and Aurora quickly grab hold of their cups, and the croissant I've been enjoying lies abandoned amid a sea of scattered crumbs. For a moment, it feels like we're at the epicentre of an earthquake. As the rattling subsides, I consider my options: Should I act or retreat? I know that it's unwise to argue with Angabi in this state of mind, but a part of me is completely baffled. I want an explanation, so even though it's reckless, I look him straight in the eye.

'That's impossible,' I tell him. 'We have a deal; we have a contract. You can't just cancel without explanation.'

'Who are you to question me?' he roars. 'You are a thief and a liar! There are no aeroplanes! There never were!'

I look at him in absolute amazement. *There are no aeroplanes?* I'm totally bemused. The immaculate Bombardier CRJ100, which his employee inspected in July, is waiting to be collected from Johannesburg. How can he accuse me of ripping him off? It makes no sense. As for repaying him, that makes even less sense considering the expenses I've incurred getting us to this point. I take a moment; I need to stay calm and level-headed before I respond to his irrational outburst. After we've spent two years working on this, he's clearly lost the plot, but arguing will just add fuel to the fire. Even though I am confused and feeling betrayed, I realise that he needs to calm down before we can discuss this rationally. I try a different approach.

'Mr Angabi,' I say in a conciliatory tone, 'I'm sorry, but I am very confused. Can you please explain the problem? I've never given you any reason to mistrust me. If you want to cancel the contract, then we need to follow the proper procedures.'

I lean across the table and place the contract in front of him, pointing to the section that covers cancellation. He grabs it, glances at it briefly pretending to read, then rips it up, flinging the pieces into the air.

'I told you, if you want to leave this country and see your family again, you need to repay my money,' he says, his tone ominous. 'That's the end of it.'

My mind is racing; nothing makes sense. No one else at the table has said a word, and I'm pretty sure that right now they wish they were elsewhere. I try again.

'But I've been working on this for almost two years, Mr Angabi,' I say. 'Costs have been incurred. Please just tell me what is going on. I cannot be held liable to repay the deposit. All that money has been used up on licences and costs to get us to this point. I can't get it back now. If you want to cancel the contract, there are procedures to follow.'

I am confident that as long as I don't challenge him, we can sort this out. But I need to stand my ground. I'm well within my rights and our contract is legally binding. In fact, if he chooses to cancel the contract at this point, he would probably owe me *more money*, but I decide that perhaps now isn't the best time to mention this.

No one moves and the silence weighs heavily, surrounding us in a suffocating blanket. Angabi's mask has slipped. He glares with such venom that I quickly decide that silence is the better course and watch impassively as he heaves himself out of the chair, its metal legs scraping along the floor and setting my teeth on edge. He reaches for one of his phones, punches in a number, and barks down the line in Fang.

Whatever he has to say, he doesn't want me to understand it, but he's clearly enraged as he disappears inside. The others follow, leaving me alone on the veranda wondering what the hell has just happened. Minutes pass and no one returns, so I dig out another copy of the contract, flipping through it, toying with the idea of leaving and arranging another meeting once he's calmed down, but leaving may add fuel to an already volatile situation. Perhaps the most powerful weapon is silence, so I wait, wishing I could rewind the clock just a few minutes.

We have a contract; he's signed it and I've fulfilled my legal obligations. I've done nothing wrong. All of a sudden, there's a commotion outside. Sirens blare and tyres squeal as two Rapid Intervention Force (RIF) vehicles screech into the driveway. I lean over the balcony, curious to see what's going on as they grind to a stop and a team of operatives leap out, armed to the teeth, and race towards the house. Some surround the building, while the others head over to where Angabi has come out to meet them.

The RIF is an elite tactical unit within the Equatorial Guinean police force, similar to SWAT in the USA. They're a familiar sight on the streets of Malabo, but they can only be summoned by someone with serious power. Even Angabi isn't high enough on the ladder to have that level of influence over the police. Despite my own troubles, I realise that someone's day is about to take a turn for the worse. I'm lucky that these guys aren't here for me.

I sit down and pick up my coffee. It's cold, but I drink it anyway. Boots thunder on the stairs and the team of RIF operatives bursts onto the balcony, assault weapons at the ready. They pause, apparently momentarily surprised to find a solitary, seated businessman calmly drinking coffee and reading through some papers.

It takes me a moment to realise that they're here for me. I lower my cup and start to get up. They immediately raise their weapons and surround me. I can't believe this is happening, but I quickly raise my arms in surrender as I hear the synchronised clicking of safety catches being pulled back on a dozen weapons pointed in my direction.

Angabi strides out onto the balcony and, ignoring me, has a heated exchange in Fang with the lead officer. They seem to reach an agreement and the officer turns to two of his men, ordering them in Spanish to restrain me. They step forward, grabbing me firmly by each arm, and bundle me back inside the house and down the stairs. Angabi does not follow. Aurora, Coco and the lawyer are nowhere to be seen.

Outside, a few curious bystanders are peering into the yard to see what's going on. I'm hustled towards the RIF vehicles, but once there, the men appear to be in disagreement as to what is to be done with me. It's probably the first and only time they've been deployed to arrest a mild-mannered entrepreneur attending a breakfast meeting at a beachfront mansion, and it almost seems as if they're disappointed that they're not going to be able to fire their weapons.

The officer in charge has realised that I'm not a threat, so he instructs the two men to release their hold on me. They hand me my phone and shove me into the back seat of one of the vehicles, standing on either side to be sure that I don't try to escape. Equatorial Guinea is always conscious of its appearance to the outside world, wanting to portray a positive environment to encourage foreign investment. The very public arrest of a South African businessman by their elite RIF unit in an upscale neighbourhood of Malabo is bound to draw the wrong kind of attention.

While sitting in the back of the vehicle, I quickly realise that an invisible hand is at work behind the scenes, probably the person Angabi called before the RIF arrived. In Equatorial Guinea, everything works in a pyramid system, and if you do anything that might reflect badly on the country or a superior, you risk drawing the wrath of those who are merciless when it comes to saving face. So, to my knowledge, even if you just need a signature, it has to go all the way to the top. My instinct tells me that the president's son, Teodorin – Angabi's nephew – may have authorised this little show, which does little to silence the voice in my head whispering that there's a good chance that things are about to go horribly wrong for me ...

4

No Entiendo

Guantanamo — Police Headquarters, Malabo
Thursday, 24 October 2013

The Rapid Intervention Force vehicle hurtles through the streets of Malabo at breakneck speed, sirens wailing. Seated in the back, I have no idea where they are taking me until we pull up outside Guantanamo, the police headquarters. Recently completed, it's a brutalist block of a building, conceived as the crowning glory of Malabo's law enforcement division. But when we pull up at the gate, I see the boom is unmanned and out of order. An officer climbs out of the vehicle, raising it manually.

I'm frogmarched to the building entrance, where one of the glass doors is broken. After a bit of grappling, my guards manage to force it open just wide enough for us to squeeze through. So much for the brand-new flagship architectural marvel; it's so run down it looks like it's been operational for at least fifty years.

The locals named it Guantanamo while it was still under construction because of its windowless facade. The atrocities that are said to take place behind these walls have ensured that the name has stuck, although no one talks too much about what goes on here.

Inside, the air is stale, reeking of sour sweat and other smells that I'd rather not identify. A few officers are milling about in the corridor. Others, wearing black berets and combat boots, are busy in the interior courtyard, investigating the contents of a few hessian sacks. Their distinctive reflective yellow jackets are labelled with the words 'Unidad de Investigación', providing a clue to their official function. About twenty shirtless prisoners are lined up against the back wall, hands cuffed behind their backs. They watch warily, anticipating the unwanted and possibly unwarranted attention of the officers examining the sacks.

We approach the front desk where the duty sergeant is lounging on a dilapidated chair, feet up, watching soccer on a small television. He lumbers to his feet, less than thrilled to abandon the game, and after a brief discussion it's clear that no one knows what crime I'm supposed to have committed. The officers leave and he scratches around on the desk for a pen, presumably to take my statement, his irritation evident as he keeps glancing at the TV. He finally locates the document he needs and scribbles something at the top of the page.

'With whom do you have a problem?' he asks in Spanish.

'Angabi,' I reply.

His attention finally diverted from the television, he looks at me, his eyes widening. And then he sniggers.

'Angabi?' he says, shaking his head, throwing down the pen and shuffling around from behind the desk, muttering to himself in Fang. He seems to be thinking: *You poor bastard, you have just made an enemy of the wrong person.*

'Okay,' he tells me. 'You will see, this is Angabi's way, but first we must wait for him to come ...'

He tells me to raise my hands and conducts a cursory body search. I don't resist and he doesn't bother to take my name or write anything on the booking sheet. Satisfied that I don't have any hidden weapons or contraband, he tells me to remove my shoes and belt, places them with my cellphone behind the desk, and then escorts me down the passage. He hasn't noticed my other phone, the old Nokia, which can only make voice calls and send SMSs but has a battery that never dies. It's pretty small and easy to overlook, so I don't mention it. He stops in front of a dingy office, pushes open the door and ushers me in.

'Wait here,' he says, shutting the door and walking back down the passage to catch up with his soccer match.

The room is dark and gloomy with a few recessed downlights, most of which don't work. One flickers incessantly. Still somewhat bewildered, I find a broken chair to sit on, pull out my little Nokia and quickly type a short text to my mother in Afrikaans: *'Bid! Bid! Bid!'* (Pray! Pray! Pray!)

The SMSs are limited to a few characters, so I can't provide more detail. I slip the phone back into my pocket and prepare to wait it out. I'm not too worried, but I want to make sure that someone back home is aware of my situation, just in case. It's not every day that you get taken into custody at gunpoint by a team of elite RIF operatives. I'm pretty sure Angabi will have a change of heart; he probably wants to scare me and put me in my place by showing me how powerful he is. I'm confident he'll tell them to release me. The whole situation is so ludicrous that I'm hoping I'll see the funny side later when I'm back at the apartment, telling Ronnie what has happened. The fact that the desk sergeant didn't write anything down, not even my name, makes me think the entire incident will be off the record, so I'm not particularly concerned. These are scare tactics. I regret confronting Angabi; challenging him in front of his staff was a stupid mistake. Hopefully it'll just cost me a few hours of wasted time in this soul-sucking concrete box. I still don't understand why he wants to cancel the contract.

It's clear that no expense has been spared on the construction of the building, and yet this room is in a pitiful state. I'm appalled by its shabby condition. Broken furniture is scattered around and stacked in corners, and the steel filing cabinets have been forced open, most likely because the keys have been lost. Some of the custom cabinetry is broken too, the doors dangling at odd angles. The window facing the passage has dusty blinds that are bent and twisted but do a good job of making my sense of isolation complete.

Being closed in makes me anxious. I shift in the chair, trying to find a comfortable way to sit without it keeling over or ripping a hole in my jeans. The more I look around, the more I realise that everything is defective or mutilated. I shudder, realising that the state of this place is remarkably similar to the state of some of the once-pristine aircraft I've sourced over the years. I hope it's not an omen for the new airline we're trying to set up. So far, it's been an uphill battle, and now this. Clearly, none of the people working here take pride in their fancy new offices, and I doubt that any maintenance crew will be put to work fixing things. It's a stark reminder of what I've got myself into, again.

Time slows. I sigh, wondering how long I've been sitting here. A few hours at least. Outside, there is a whole world going on – kids playing in the streets, mothers shopping for tonight's meal or preparing lunch, elders having a siesta, taxis racing by, lovers taking a stroll ... Claustrophobia is setting in. I feel like I've entered a parallel universe, stuck in a room where the hands of the clock have come to rest at 10.10, and whenever I look at it, they haven't moved. I'm starting to feel disconnected. Cut off. Stuck in a time warp.

Seconds, minutes, hours pass.

No one comes.

I wait.

My phone buzzes in my pocket. I take it out and have a quick look before switching it off and putting it back. *'Welman, ons bid vir jou.'* (Welman, we're praying for you.)

The message is comforting, but I hope my mother doesn't mention my situation to my wife. Thinking of my family is a distraction, and I wonder what Melanie and Bubbles are doing. It's the height of summer there, so they're probably in the garden. It's best not to worry her, but at least my mother is aware that something is up; if things get out of hand, she can start asking questions. I have a short conversation with God, telling him that I don't know why I'm here and what lessons I am about to learn, but I am grateful that He is beside me and protecting me. My faith is strong. Knowing that God is in control and watching over me is reassuring and gives me a fresh boost of confidence.

I am not alone.

5

Welcome to Guantanamo

```
Police Headquarters, Malabo
Thursday, 24 October 2013
```

It's been hours and the claustrophobia demons lurk, ready to take me hostage in this airless, stuffy room. My temples are throbbing, my mouth dry, anxiety manifesting as a blinding headache. I reach up, massaging the base of my neck, and take a few deep breaths to ease the tension. I have no idea how long I've been stuck in this miserable room. The musty smell heightens my sense of confinement, and without my smartphone there's nothing to distract me. I know I can't take much more of this, and besides, I need to pee. I lean back, closing my eyes, but the chair threatens to keel over every time I move, so I get up and pace the length of the room instead, going nowhere.

I stop in front of the window and pull the blinds open a crack, peering down the passage, but it's as if I'm alone in the building, maybe even on the planet. Perhaps I can sneak out and find a bathroom – the dull ache in my groin is compounding my misery. Sighing, I pull the blinds a bit further aside. A few people have come in and are talking to the sergeant, who gestures in my direction. The RIF are back. They head my way and tell me to come with them.

It's a relief to escape the stifling office as we gather at the front desk. I'm about to ask where the bathroom is when the high-pitched metallic screech of the door scraping along the tiled floor announces some new arrivals. We all turn to see a massive figure appear, filling the space with his unmistakable presence. Angabi. He's accompanied by his minions, including Aurora and Coco, who attempt to manhandle the door back into place as he barrels towards us.

Imperious. Arrogant. Larger than life. He's holding a cigar in one hand and three mobile phones in the other, his commanding and authoritarian manner proclaiming that he knows we all know who he is. He's not wrong.

Angabi is used to people jumping to attention, and right now he's in his element, revelling in his power as a grovelling army of sycophants clusters around him. This is his superpower, the politician in action. He's a formidable man, both physically and on another less tangible level. He ignores everyone else and turns to me, his eyes brushing over me with undisguised contempt as he demands to know why I am not in handcuffs.

'This man is a liar and a thief,' he announces in Spanish, pointing at me. 'He may be white on the outside, but he says he is an African like us!' He sneers. 'I am telling you that he is just like those Europeans that have come here to rob us and steal the wealth of the Equatorial Guinean people. He thinks we're fooled because he says he is an African. He's worse than the Europeans. Look at him standing there like he is an innocent man. But I know the truth. He stole my money. He is a trickster. We must punish him!'

I listen to his preposterous accusations, flabbergasted. The irony is not lost on the officers as they look at me dressed simply in Levi's and a T-shirt, barefoot, while Angabi is decked out in expensive clothing and designer shoes, flaunting an extravagant watch that's worth more than their combined annual income. Careful not to let him see their reaction, they glance at one another with raised eyebrows and wry expressions, while he rages on about my sins. They probably haven't been paid in months.

Angabi has worked himself up into a froth, yelling furiously, switching between Spanish and Fang as he waves his cigar around, spilling ash all over the floor.

'I have welcomed this supposed "African" man into my home, treated him like family,' he bellows. 'We have eaten together, he knows my wife, my children, and yet he insults me. He thinks I am stupid. He thinks he can make a fool of me.' He pauses and then glares at me and hisses, 'If he is an African then he must be punished like an African!'

I look at him in stunned silence as the barrage of accusations rain down, not least the worst sin of all: betraying a fellow African. He insists that I must be punished right here and now. The officers must show no mercy. He threatens them with terrifying consequences if they fail to carry out his demands immediately.

Finally, he runs out of steam. No one moves until the RIF officer speaks up, quietly reminding him that I am a foreign businessman and it would look bad for the country if word got out that I'd been imprisoned or tortured, so perhaps a more subtle approach is advisable. I watch Angabi turn purple with rage. He grabs one of his phones off the desk and makes a call, barking into the phone in Fang and then thrusting it towards the officer. The man takes it and instantly jumps to attention, listening intently. After a while, he hands the phone back to Angabi.

A deathly silence hangs over the room. It feels like we're standing in a mausoleum. No one says a word. Fear is a universal language. You can see it, feel it, smell it, taste it ... And at this moment, I can tell that the officers' fear far outweighs their contempt for him and everything he represents. Apparently satisfied that his supremacy has been reinstated, Angabi lights a fresh cigar.

'Now,' he says with finality, 'you will take this man down to La Oficina and beat him like an African. He looks like a European, but he is not a European! He is an African! Like you. Like me. He says he is our brother; let's show him what we do with lying, cheating, stealing African brothers!'

Snarling at me in contempt, he stomps away, trailed by Aurora and Coco, and disappears around a corner as we watch in silence. Until this moment, I've always believed that I am an African through and through. Yes, I am a white person, but I'm a third-generation African, born on this great continent; it's in my heart and soul, my bones, my blood. But as I stand in this newly built yet decaying monument to corruption overseen by sociopaths masquerading as respectable leaders, I realise that I am utterly alone. I wish I'd never been born an African, never been to Equatorial Guinea, never encountered Angabi. At this moment, I would like nothing more than to be a pampered First World businessman, sipping gluhwein in front of a cosy fire with my beautiful wife in a Swiss chalet after a hard day's skiing somewhere in the Alps.

Once Angabi leaves, there is some discussion in Fang between the officers. They seem to reach a consensus and grab me roughly by my arms, marching me to the courtyard where I am searched again. This time they find my Nokia and take it, and they tell me to place my hands behind my back. A set of handcuffs is slipped on and fastened with a click, the metal cold and tight on my wrists. I prepare to face a bleak reality.

Angabi's interpretation of justice becomes clearer with each passing minute, and it has nothing to do with due process or upholding the law. It seems I will now face the same reality that ordinary folk with no money or influence find themselves in if they fall foul of someone with the right connections and an axe to grind. Judging by my experience so far, it seems that law enforcement officers carry out instructions without question if they're issued from high up in the chain of command.

I know it would be political suicide for Angabi to act without support from above, so I suspect that someone else has authorised my detention. I think he must have the blessing of at least one of the 'holy trinity' – the president, his wife, or his son. My money would be on the president's son, Teodorin. He and Angabi are tight, and for some reason I'm yet to understand, Angabi has concocted this story of theft, perhaps to justify his actions should news of my arrest and incarceration be leaked.

Over the years working in Equatorial Guinea, I've been aware that much has been done by those in power to clean up the country's image so that international corporations see it as a friendly place to invest. Of course, that doesn't mean that human rights abuses don't still happen, just that they are less likely to come to light. For Angabi to have pulled this stunt despite our ironclad contract, I suspect he must have the full support of someone with immense power.

The two officers seem satisfied that I can now be escorted elsewhere and take me back inside. We head down a long, dimly lit passage. At some point there are stairs, but with no windows facing outside, I become disorientated, not knowing if we're going up or down, feeling like I've been granted a free pass to hell. I've heard enough stories to know that whatever lies ahead is going to involve a fair degree of pain and suffering.

The guard's footsteps echo on the hard concrete floor, their rhythmic beat bouncing off the walls and hanging in the air around us. I'm not wearing shoes, so my movements are soundless, apart from the clinking of the handcuffs at my back. It's as if I am already a ghost.

Perhaps this is Angabi's intention. If I am not here on paper, then I don't officially exist. A sense of foreboding takes hold. It's clear that I'm not leaving this place unscathed. Ahead, through the gloom, I can just make out the silhouette of a gate, its steel bars blocking the end of the passage. As we draw closer, the sign above it leaves me with no doubt as to where I have arrived: Celda de Detención – the infamous holding cells of Guantanamo.

My legs turn to lead as the officers drag me through the gates. The thought of what lies ahead chills me to my bones, and I pray for God's protection. A guard slips a key into the lock, slides it open and pushes me through. The gate clangs shut behind us, the sound echoing into the darkness, cutting me off from the outside world. I hear the faint but indistinct echo of voices in the dark. I know that I'm standing in one of the most feared places on the island, second only to Black Beach, and that I'm about to have a meeting at La Oficina – The Office – a place with a notorious reputation for suffering, torture, isolation and missing people. A place where no one and no sound escapes.

They take me to a room where I am searched again, and, irrelevantly, I realise I no longer need to pee. Rough hands poke and prod, probing every inch of my body. They are thorough, malicious and degrading. I don't know what they're looking for, everything I have has already been taken, but with my hands cuffed behind my back, I have no choice but to surrender to the humiliation. If their goal is to intimidate me, it's working.

I feel violated and helpless. I've heard stories about the horrors that take place here, but it all seemed so far removed from the world outside where the sun shines and people are free. Until this moment, in this dark place, none of it seemed real. For the guards, this is just another day at the office. I wonder when it is that your compassion for another's suffering is suspended because you are 'just following orders'.

They drag me to the adjacent room and suddenly the muted voices I heard earlier are amplified. A man is chained to the wall, sobbing in despair, his fear tangible. It's easy to understand why. From behind the closed door of the next room come the desperate cries of a soul in terror, sounds that come from a place so deep and dark that I know they will haunt me forever.

The room we're in is bare, apart from a bench where the man is chained. I'm dragged across the room, forced down beside him, and my handcuffs are attached to the metal railing mounted on the wall behind us. A visceral, primal fear takes hold of me, carrying the warning that I'm about to encounter something beyond my darkest nightmares.

I'm Daniel in the lions' den, and the beasts are circling, drawing nearer until I can almost feel their breath on me, hot and fetid. Beads of sweat erupt on my brow as I take a deep breath to bring my emotions under control. Suddenly, the fate of the man who is next in line for interrogation matters more to me than anything in the world. I'm not interested in the crimes he did or didn't commit. I don't care if he is guilty, only that he is about to suffer unimaginable horror. I pray for him. I ask God to give him strength. I pray for his salvation. I pray that his suffering will not be unbearable and that God will grant him refuge. I pray because the alternative is to think about myself, to think about my enemy, to think about how alone I am, and to think about my fate, about the power and control these men have over us. A black man from

Mali and a white man from South Africa chained together side by side; we are worlds apart, two men who have never met and yet are now inextricably united in this moment, facing unknown demons together. Once they take him, I know that I will be next.

There has been a long silence from the adjacent room, and then the door bursts open and the guards seize the Malian, dragging him in. The door slams shut again, muting his screams. I wonder if I will ever see him again. What was his crime? Will he live or die? I wonder if his family will ever know his fate. I close my eyes and bow my head, trying to find a place to hide while I find the strength to endure what is sure to come, reciting Psalm 23 out loud:

Yea, though I walk through the valley of the shadow of death,
I will fear no evil;
for thou art with me;
Thy rod and thy staff,
they comfort me ...

Talking to God is a daily ritual and a sense of calm washes over me, slowing the frantic beating of my heart as I take a deep breath. My faith is strong; I need it to provide the determination to face what lies ahead. The tension leaves my body and I feel safer, believing that God will protect me, providing a refuge to endure whatever is to come. I open my eyes and look up, confronting the image of the president advising me to take note of my rights. It's almost laughable, considering the circumstances.

Slowly, I become aware that I am no longer alone in the room. A man dressed in a white safari suit stands at the doorway watching me enigmatically. I don't know how long he has been there.

'Don't worry,' he says in Spanish. 'We are waiting for Angabi to leave the building, then you can go. We are not going to harm you.'

Praise God! I think, not knowing that this man, known as the Devil's right hand, the man in charge of La Oficina, is one of the most feared in Malabo.

6

By the Skin of My Teeth

Guantanamo – Police Headquarters, Malabo
Thursday, 24 October 2013

A short while later a policeman enters, detaches my handcuffs from the railing and leads me out of the room. Is it over? I'm too scared to hope that I'm being released. As he escorts me through the dark and confusing labyrinth, we pass a few poorly lit cells and it becomes clear that leaving is not on the itinerary. A row of small windows set high in the wall allows some light in. It's still daylight outside. Have I really only been here for a few hours? It feels like the longest day of my life.

We pass a cell filled with a bunch of rowdy women, most sporting garish make-up and outfits that leave little to the imagination. It's immediately obvious how they make their living and probably explains why they're here. They rush to the front of the cell, shouting '*Blanco, blanco!*' – an obvious reference to me, the only white man in the vicinity – and press their bodies against the bars, laughing raucously, making erotic gestures and yelling 'jiggy, jiggy' as the guard tows me past them.

Next door are a few men who are more subdued, lost in their own turmoil. They show little interest in me. I can usually tell who's local, and these men appear to be foreigners, from Mali, Cameroon, Senegal or Nigeria, men who have come to Malabo to seek their fortunes. No matter where they're from, it does little to change their current situation, and considering the reputation of this place, they're probably wondering if this is where they'll be spending their last days on earth, miles from home. Will their families ever know the truth about what happened to them? Are they wondering if it was worth it in the end, as I am?

The soupy atmosphere thickens with the rancid odour of unwashed bodies and stagnant air. It's hard to breathe, humid and damp, and the sweat stings as it pools in the cuts where the handcuffs are digging into my wrists. The guard stops in front of another, larger cell. It's bedlam in here and the commotion reaches fever pitch as we approach.

'*Blanco, blanco, blanco …*' they chant, crowding the bars at the entrance to the cell. Clearly, not many white men make it into this chamber of suffering. The cell is overcrowded, everyone jammed up tightly against one another, and I'm sure that these inmates are all locals. I can't imagine how they can possibly fit another soul in here, but apparently there is space for one more ...

The guard pushes me inside, quickly slamming the gate shut. In an instant they swarm over me, grabbing with fingers like talons, scratching my flesh, ripping my shirt in their frenzied search to find anything of value.

'*Basta*! Enough!' I bellow, trying to drive them off by kicking and twisting my body. My ability to defend myself is severely limited as my hands are still cuffed behind my back, so I lock my fingers into the steel bars of the cell to secure myself and avoid falling under the crush of bodies scrambling to get a piece of me. Slowly, I inch along the perimeter until I reach a corner where I can wedge myself in. Fighting them off is nearly impossible, but they're abruptly distracted by the arrival of a prison official who peers in, announcing that he is the 'Jefe de Castel', the chief of the jail, and if I want anything I will have to pay him. Since I have no money on me, and because I am still dealing with the unwanted attention of a few persistent prisoners, I ignore him and he leaves, the novelty of a white man here quickly losing its allure when he sees that I have nothing to trade.

Before long, everyone ignores me. I lean my head against the wall, my body bruised, my arms aching from being stuck in such an awkward position behind my back. The smell is so rank and fetid it's like inhaling a toxic substance. It's hard to believe that I have only been here for a day; it feels like weeks. And after the Jefe de Castel mentioned payment if I want anything, I am starting to doubt that I'll be getting out of here any time soon.

Despite being spared the agony of the torture chamber, it's not enough to lift me above the uncertainty of what lies ahead. It's like I am stuck in a virtual reality game without a reset button, but I know I can't give up; they win if I start thinking like this. Even though I'm exhausted and overwhelmed, I dare not close my eyes. My shoulders ache deep into my bones. It's impossible to get comfortable with my arms wedged in behind me, so I focus inwards, praying, praying, praying. Prayer has always calmed me, bringing clarity. Placing my life in God's hands fortifies me. I block out everything and just breathe.

I sense someone squeezing in beside me. He starts tapping me on the shoulder. Irritated, I sigh out loud. I'm close to breaking point. When I turn to face him, I find myself staring into the eyes of a young boy. I know that sometimes these kids are the most dangerous, but he looks harmless, so I don't want to believe that he is deceitful or devious. What on earth could he have done to end up here? His wide-eyed innocence makes me fear what will happen to him if he spends too much time in here with these vultures.

He holds up a bottle and shakes it. I realise that he's offering me water and I accept gratefully. He presses it against my lips, pouring it slowly into my mouth, washing away the dryness in my throat. I am humbled by his kindness and strengthened by the knowledge that not everyone in this hellhole is pure evil. I nod to him. *Gracias.* Thank you.

7

Into the Lions' Den

```
Guantanamo — Police Headquarters, Malabo
     Thursday and Friday, 24—25 October 2013
```

I watch the sky turn pink through narrow windows as the sun sets and dusk approaches, and start to feel empty and helpless again. Despite the crush of humanity pushing against me, I have never felt more alone. Previous inmates venting their anger at the system have destroyed the lights, and as darkness descends, any hope that I will be leaving here tonight is lost.

It's been a rough afternoon – hot, sticky and never-ending. My fellow prisoners have offered me everything from food and water to a cellphone and drugs, but with nothing to trade, everything is out of my price range. As night falls, the incessant buzzing of roving mosquitoes out for blood becomes my latest torture; they home in on the exposed parts of my body, and with my hands cuffed behind me I can't swat them away.

A steady stream of detainees flows into the cell; for every three in, one leaves. Shutting out the noise is impossible. In the early hours of the morning, a few lucky ones are released after their families pay the necessary fees. A sense of detachment builds inside me. The guards turn up with annoying regularity, banging on the bars to summon their next victim for a rendezvous at La Oficina. Some do not return; others are thrown back in the cell, battered and bloodied.

Not much can be done for them; they require emergency medical treatment that we can't provide in this filthy rat hole. The floor is slippery with their blood, vomit and shit, by-products of the butchery inflicted on them. There is no mercy or compassion from the savages who revel in the control they have over us, and they forbid us to help the injured without permission. I spend the night sitting upright, jammed into a corner against the wall with hot, sweaty bodies pressed up against me.

I don't want to move around too much and draw attention to myself; the inky blackness provides cover for predators on the hunt for fresh meat. Despite my exhaustion, it's impossible to sleep. Even though I've had nothing to eat and very little to drink, my bladder feels like it's going to burst. It's all

I can think about, and I try to figure out how to deal with this increasingly urgent need. The toilet in the cell has long since been dismembered. I've noticed others using empty bottles to answer the call of nature, but with my hands cuffed behind my back, I can't undo my pants, let alone hold a bottle.

Being helpless is its own form of cruelty, and it throws me off balance knowing I am unable to perform even the most basic human function with dignity. Here, I am nothing; I have nothing. Not even my self-respect. My only option is to ask one of the thugs to recognise my predicament and help me get the job done.

When I can't take it any more, I turn to an old man wedged in beside me. His pockmarked, scarred face tells of someone ravaged by a hard life on the streets. He's been quiet, not getting involved, staying invisible and out of sight of the rabble-rousers. I weigh up the odds, and then, mortified, explain what I need. He agrees to help, struggling in the poor light to undo the buttons on my jeans, but finally managing to get everything in the right place. As the bottle fills, my sense of relief is immeasurable. I'm grateful that the cell is dark, so there aren't too many witnesses to my discomfort and humiliation. I'm torn between gratitude and shame, but the man seems to think nothing of it, returning to his spot and hunkering back down for the night.

I lean back against the wall. What is all this suffering for? A contract? Money? Again and again, I ask myself, *Why?* What went wrong when Angabi and I were so close to finalising the deal? Sleep is impossible. I try not to think as an invisible clock ticks on, moment by moment, endlessly counting down the hours towards daylight as I try to block out the moans of the men who lie mangled at my feet. Slowly, through the narrow slits of the windows at the top of the wall, the subtle hues of dawn herald the arrival of another day in hell.

As the dim light brightens, I face the grim evidence of our captors' handiwork – it's not pretty and does little to alleviate my fear and dread. A few guards appear, shouting for roll call. We're told to line up against the wall, which is impossible in the overcrowded cell. Some pull the injured to their feet, holding their limp bodies upright as the guards call out our names. Two names are called repeatedly with no response. Have they been released during the night or succumbed to the brutal beatings they sustained? We'll never know.

The guards leave and the morning drags on, monotonous. Towards midday it starts to rain, bringing some relief from the stifling heat. In contrast to the chaos of the previous night, a relative calm descends – even the agony of my arms still twisted behind my back has faded into numbness. A few prisoners tell me why they're here and are in turn eager to discover how a white man has ended up in this place.

When I mention Angabi, they're even more astonished to hear that I managed to leave La Oficina unscathed. They tell me that the commander of the prison is a 'disciple of the Devil', with no fear or pity, and answers only to the president. They believe it's a miracle, that I must be under God's protection, because no one ever leaves that room unharmed. We pray together, united in the misery and uncertainty of our situation, seeking solace through our faith.

A prisoner squats beside me, sharing his water while others tell me that they've been here for weeks, beaten and interrogated without charges being laid or without appearing before a judge. I find their stoicism and sense of hope baffling, although I also get the idea that it's a case of 'this is just the way things are'.

As the day wears on, I realise that because Guantanamo is close to town, it's easy for prisoners' family and friends to visit, bringing food, water and cigarettes. Most inmates bribe their way out or spend two or three days here before appearing before a judge and being released or ordered to pay a fine. For those accused of serious offences, the outcome is bleak – they are sent to Black Beach.

No one wants to end up in Black Beach. It's considered one of the world's worst prisons, infamous for extreme brutality and a laundry list of human rights abuses. The government takes few steps to prosecute or punish officials who perpetrate these abuses, and according to my fellow inmates, if you're part of the politically connected elite, you're completely above the law. The members of this exclusive club run businesses, often threatening competitors or simply taking over their companies after arranging their arrest. If you criticise a member of this elite or are even involved in a fender bender with one of them, you can find yourself facing detention.

The prisoners tell me that it doesn't happen often, but if by some crazy chance one of the elite or their children are arrested and end up here, it's only a matter of hours before an unmarked vehicle arrives, whisking them to the airport where they're put on a flight to Spain – a popular way to resolve problems with wayward family members. Listening to these stories, I understand that there are two sets of laws here: one for petty criminals and those without money or influence, and a second for politicians, the wealthy and the connected.

There is a steady stream of visitors, and many of my companions have cellphones and stay in contact with their families or friends on the outside. Obviously, I'm not afforded that luxury, and with nothing to trade I am unable to make any calls. Besides, I don't know who could help me.

Throughout the day, guards turn up calling for prisoners. I don't know if I want to hear my name being called. Will it mean I'll be released or that I'm about to be dragged to face my oppressors in La Oficina? The uncertainty takes its toll, my imagination working overtime, making me desperate and willing to agree to anything to get out of here. I hunker down in my corner, escaping inwards, my thoughts drifting away from the bleak reality of my situation, dulling the noise and chaos around me.

It takes a while to realise that my name is being called. I struggle to my feet and push through the throng towards the gate, where the guard is waiting for me. Feeling disorientated and decidedly wobbly from sitting in the same position for hours, I stumble along beside him. I'm filthy, my clothes are ripped, and now that we're on the move there is a nagging pain in my arms that throbs with each step. We round a corner and the guard directs me towards a door; he knocks and we enter a grand space filled with elegant dark wood furniture. An imposing man is seated behind a large mahogany desk. So far, this is the only room I've seen that isn't falling apart; it's obvious that the man behind the desk is a high-ranking official. Sitting opposite him is Coco, who avoids making eye contact, barely acknowledging my arrival.

The officer nods brusquely at the guard and tells him to remove my handcuffs. As the lock clicks open, my arms drop heavily against my sides. The pain is intense and immediate, shooting like an electric current down to my fingertips and back up to my shoulders. It's agony as I wriggle my fingers to stimulate the blood flow. Slowly, I raise my hands in front of me. They're covered with streaks of dried blood and there are deep gashes in my wrists where the cuffs have dug in, but my arms are free at last and the sense of relief almost brings tears to my eyes.

Coco and I go back a long way – I know him well as Angabi's manager and have worked with him for years – yet now he is cold and indifferent as he points to a document on the desk, telling me that I have a choice: sign a declaration admitting to stealing Angabi's money and that I will pay it all back, and I'll be released immediately – or else ... His expression makes it very clear what 'or else' means.

I don't hesitate. I don't even care what it says. I know that anything signed under duress won't be admissible in court, and I am not denying that I have received money from Angabi. I have. Stealing it is something else altogether, but if saying that's what I've done is my ticket out of here, that's fine by me. Coco hands me a pen. Shakily, I reach for it and sign.

I am free to go.

8

A Toast to Freedom
Central Malabo
Friday, 25 October 2013

I follow Coco out into the sun, dizzy with relief, my eyes stinging as they adjust to the intense glare. It's a typical afternoon in Malabo, the sky bright with a bank of clouds rolling in over the horizon. Savouring this moment of freedom, I remember my wife saying that I run on solar power, and I stop to 'recharge', looking up at the endless blue sky, feeling the sun's warmth on my face and enjoying the taste of fresh air. The moment doesn't last. Coco is impatient, yelling at me to hurry up.

I'm not keen to hang around here too long anyway and hobble across the courtyard after him, still stiff from being crammed into the overcrowded jail cell, my body aching with each step. The car waiting for us is idling, and I climb in. As we pull away, the ominous walls of Guantanamo loom over us, casting a long shadow, but in the bright light of day it's almost impossible to believe what goes on behind them, hidden in plain sight in the middle of a city bustling with people going about their daily business.

As we head into town, I watch the anonymous, foreboding structure receding in the side mirror, my mind grappling to understand what I've just been through. I don't know where Coco is taking me, but no matter where it is, it can't possibly be worse than where I've just been. I'm furious with Angabi and can't understand why he has turned against me, but I have no interest in discussing it with Coco. The atmosphere in the car is strained, and as much as I'm glad to be out of Guantanamo, I'm still on edge, acutely aware that I have no control over anything. I'm mildly concerned about where we're going, but Angabi can't take matters much further than he already has if he wants me to pay back his money, so I gaze out the window, savouring the simple pleasure of being free and able to watch the world go by.

It seems we're heading for Angabi's apartment where I've been staying with Ronnie. I puzzle over how just minutes from here there's a torture chamber where people are beaten, murdered and treated like vermin, sometimes at the whim of a politician. I'm acutely aware of the armed policemen at the intersections, patrolling the streets outside the market area. I look at them differently now as we head down a familiar jogging route. I know that they avoid entering the market; maybe they don't like to get their boots dirty, preferring to leave the policing of petty crime to the locals who make a living there.

The radio is on and I feel rather than hear the lyrics filtering into my thoughts. I recognise the simple acoustic track by Bob Marley – 'Redemption Song'. It almost feels as if it's been selected by an unseen hand, sending a message to me: to emancipate myself from mental slavery and to free my mind.

Minutes later, we round the corner and pull in outside the apartment block. Coco finds a parking spot, grabs a set of keys from the dashboard, and together we walk up the stairs. He opens the apartment door and ushers me inside, remaining on the threshold as he hands me the keys. He tells me that Ronnie has been sent back to South Africa and I need to arrange to get Angabi's money if I want to leave the country too. As he walks away, I watch until he disappears out of sight and then shut the door and lock it, leaning heavily against it.

The apartment feels abandoned, almost sinister in its emptiness. Even though Coco said that Ronnie is gone and there is no sign of him, I check his room, knocking on the door and waiting a moment before opening it. The bed is neatly made and nothing is out of place, as if no one ever stayed here. I open the cupboards. Nothing. This is not a good sign for the future of Coriscair. But I have other things on my mind right now as I become increasingly aware of just how alone I am and how limited my options are.

Sighing, I walk through the apartment, worrying about what lies ahead, even as part of me takes solace in my seclusion, savouring my first moments of freedom, of having my own space after being locked up in that crowded, filthy cell. I go to the kitchen and, too exhausted to make any calls, send a quick text message to my mother, thanking her for her prayers, explaining that I've been released and will update her when I have more information. Then I open the fridge to get something to drink. A pink milkshake would be great right about now, but as that's not an option, I settle for refreshing cold water, straight out of the bottle. At this stage, there is no guarantee that my problem is going away. I need to work on an exit strategy before I involve my family. The phone rings and, thinking it's them wanting to make sure I'm okay, I pick it up. Glancing at the caller ID on the screen before answering, I see that it's a local number. Angabi.

He wastes no time getting to the point. 'Daniel, I am out of patience. Let me warn you, if you don't give my money back, you will never leave Malabo again. I guarantee it.'

He's deadly serious and I believe that my life is on the line. I don't want to spend another minute in this apartment. I've now seen what he's capable of and don't want to risk staying here and regretting it later, or, worse, not living to regret it at all.

There is only one person who can help me: Mike Polokwane. I've worked with Mike since early 2001. He's well connected and one of my closest friends in Malabo, my 'local brother' who is familiar with the inner workings of conducting business in this region. It was great to have found someone who speaks English, as most townsfolk speak Spanish, and I've spent many happy evenings with him and his wife. Mike is larger than life, with a perpetual smile lurking at the corners of his mouth. Nothing fazes him, and he has connections in local government. His advice in dealing with the politicians in Malabo has previously proved invaluable. Unlike Angabi, I believe I can trust him.

I scroll through my contacts and dial his number. Hearing his booming, friendly voice has an instant calming effect on me. I tell him what I've just been through, and although he's dismayed, he doesn't seem too surprised. He tells me to come to his house, *pronto*.

Fortunately, his home is nearby, so I throw my things into a bag, grateful that I've been travelling light. I peer out the windows to see if anyone is watching the apartment. It looks clear. Even though I am desperate for a shower, I lock up quickly and go downstairs. Outside, I scan the dark streets for anyone loitering as I try to blend into the background, walking briskly and sticking to the shadows where possible, feeling jumpy and paranoid, checking for occupants seated in the cars parked along the road.

I breathe a sigh of relief when I reach Mike's home. His wife has prepared a simple meal for me, while Mike hauls out a bottle of Jack Daniel's and pours me a stiff one, saying that his driver is on standby, waiting to take me to a friend's apartment. For the first time since being released, I feel like I can breathe again, knowing that Mike will do what he can to help. After saying goodnight, I head off with his driver to my new temporary accommodation. The whole situation feels unreal, like I've landed a starring role in a spy thriller, except that no one bothered to give me a copy of the script. I hope it ends well…

I feel marginally safer at the apartment as I doubt Angabi will find me here, but I know this is only a temporary solution. Malabo is a small town and Angabi could have eyes anywhere, so I need to stay out of sight until I can get legal advice. For now, I just want to wash away the grime and memory of the past two days.

I get into the shower, leaving my clothes in a heap on the floor. Steam rises against the glass, enveloping my body in a comforting mist as the soothing water cascades over me. I scrub myself vigorously, trying to erase all evidence of the past thirty-six hours. But even as I relish the sensation of the hot, stinging water, I realise that the horrific things I witnessed have left an indelible stain that no amount of soap or time will erase.

I turn off the shower and towel myself dry, examining the damage to my body. The only noticeable signs are a few bruises and scratches. By far the worst are the deep cuts to my wrists where the handcuffs dug in. I scratch around in the bathroom and find some ointment to rub into the wounds, hoping that they don't become infected. To think that I was almost tortured for a crime I didn't commit seems surreal.

Later, after a coffee, I go to bed, but as exhausted as I am, sleep eludes me. Uppermost in my mind is the fact that Angabi has my passport. How am I going to find my way back to South Africa? The night drags on and I am plagued by nightmares. I wake up often, sweating and disorientated. But I am free, and safe for now.

9

No Way Out

South African Embassy, Malabo
Monday, 28 October 2013

I'm hot and feverish, my head pounds and I feel like I've battled five rounds with Connor McGregor, but I'm fuelled by a sense of purpose. The injuries I picked up in custody are superficial and will soon fade, unlike my issues with Angabi.

From now on, no more surprises, I tell myself. I'll focus on climbing into the ring and emerging victorious. Mike will probably know a lawyer I can talk to before I tell my family what's going on. Coco said that Angabi is in Cameroon for a week; I'm not sure what can be done in his absence, but hiding out, waiting for his henchmen to come, isn't an option, so I'm going to see if the South African embassy can help.

I head to the kitchen to make some coffee. The Coriscair contract is on the counter, open on the page outlining the cancellation process. I've read it so many times that I could probably recite it backwards, and although I've experienced the dark side of Equatorial Guinea, I have faith that the courts are impartial and will honour the law.

The fact that Coco took my passport when I arrived is more of a concern, as without it I can't leave the island. I'll ask the embassy what can be done if Angabi refuses to return it and put them in the picture in case I disappear again. The more people I have in my corner, the more confident I'll feel. It's hardly a plan, but it's better than sitting around waiting for Angabi to make his next move.

I take a taxi to the embassy feeling pretty upbeat – getting out of prison will do that to you. Things don't always go as expected when working in Africa, but I've certainly never been jailed or threatened with torture. Angabi clearly doesn't play by the rules, but I've done everything by the book, so I'm hoping that going back to the signed contract should get things back on track.

The embassy is located in what was formerly a Spanish-style residential home. It has a distinctive mustard-yellow exterior and is enclosed by high walls and a razor-wire fence. When I arrive, the South African flag is fluttering lazily in the breeze. I settle with the taxi driver and head inside. Even though I'm still in Malabo, it feels like I'm setting foot on South African soil, walking into the home of an old friend, familiar and safe. I hope I'm not being naive or delusional putting my trust in the system.

While I wait, I admire a life-size poster of a happy couple enjoying a meal at the V&A Waterfront in Cape Town, the iconic Table Mountain in the background. Home! I feel better already. Maybe when I get back, Melanie and I will take a road trip to Cape Town and have lunch at that exact spot.

Eventually, a young woman calls me to her office, barely glancing up as I walk in. She seems to be a typical government employee, used to shuffling papers and completing forms, and not inclined to deal with anything requiring too much effort. She listens impassively, making notes as I recount the events of the past few days. When I'm finished, she puts down her pen, shaking her head.

'Unfortunately, this is outside our jurisdiction,' she tells me flatly, explaining that the embassy can't help as this is a civil matter rather than a criminal, military or religious affair. Judges in civil and criminal courts have different roles and powers. Criminal court judges can punish you for breaking the law by sending you to jail, while civil court judges handle disputes, usually financial in nature, listen to both sides, reach a verdict and order you to pay a fine if found guilty. The bottom line is that the embassy cannot intervene until the issue has been cleared in civil court.

I leave a little later feeling like I've been punched in the gut. Angabi has just won round two. Storm clouds are gathering over the horizon, dark and ominous, devouring small patches of blue sky as they roll in towards the shore. A perfect manifestation of my current state of mind. I'm frustrated and angry that there is nothing I can do until a judge rules on the issue. Standing outside the only place that represents home and everything I love heightens my sense of abandonment. Angabi won't be back for at least a week, I think, and suddenly my headache is back with a vengeance. I feel hot and prickly all over.

I'd planned to walk back to the apartment, stopping at the market for supplies and to top up my airtime, but I'm feeling thoroughly disheartened and don't fancy a long walk in the heat. I wave down a taxi and head back to the apartment to lie low, having accomplished nothing. When I pay the driver, I glance around to see if anyone is watching me. There aren't many places for me to hide in this town, and I'm sure Angabi's men are keeping tabs on me, but right now there's no sign of them.

Inside, I switch on the television for company and check the bathroom cabinet for headache tablets. It's well stocked and I throw back two pills with a swig of water, hoping to stop the pounding in my head. I know I can't put off calling my family any longer and mentally prepare a watered-down account of recent events so that they will believe everything is under control. As I search my contacts and select my mother's number, I remember that I am low on airtime. I make a mental note to walk to the market once the coming rain has passed and it's a little cooler.

My mother's relief is tangible when she answers the call and I reassure her that I am safe. I tell her I visited the embassy, but I don't elaborate. I'm running out of call time, so I ask her to send my love to everyone, promising to make contact again once I've appointed a lawyer and the judge has heard my case.

Afterwards, I stare blankly at the TV, feeling utterly alone and miserable. I can't summon the energy even to make something to eat, so I focus on TVGE, the Spanish-language Equatorial Guinean state television channel, which usually broadcasts pro-government propaganda. Today is no exception – the broadcast is a rerun of the recent forty-fifth anniversary of independence, celebrating Obiang's rise to power. I remember that there was a parade along the promenade a few weeks back. Judging by the footage, it was a showy attempt at portraying the unity and might of Equatorial Guinea: marching bands, and police, military and naval displays, followed by women dressed in colourful flamenco-style dresses and children cavorting happily under the watchful eyes of their minders. The monotony of the broadcast makes me feel drowsy. Or maybe it's the effects of the medication. I drift off while the marching band drones on in the background.

I wake from the twilight of my dreams and don't know how much time has passed. I'm sweating profusely, and when I try to sit up, my body doesn't want to cooperate. Lightheaded and disorientated, I roll into a sitting position. My skull feels like it's about to split open as I stumble to the bathroom and throw up into the toilet, hanging onto the edge of the porcelain, retching until there is nothing left inside me.

Malaria. It doesn't take much to recognise the symptoms. All I can do is wait for the hell to follow. I'm allergic to malaria prevention medication, and as I was only going to be in the country for a few days I hadn't worried about it. Getting treatment is imperative, but I don't even have the energy to drag myself to bed. I lie on the bathroom floor, drifting in and out of consciousness. I've run out of airtime so I can't call anyone.

Malaria is utterly debilitating, healing is slow and symptoms often resurface even several years later. It's so common here that health workers don't need to perform blood tests to confirm a diagnosis. The sooner you begin treatment, the better your chances of survival. Depending on the strain, it can be a death sentence, especially for those reliant on state facilities, even though the supply of antimalarial drugs is funded by the government. Once again, the greedy hand of those with access to lucrative contracts means that pharmaceuticals destined for hospitals are sold through local pharmacies. No prescription is necessary; families must scrape together significant amounts of cash to buy the medication and then return to the hospital for it to be administered to the patient. As a result, most poor communities rely on the informal market in the town, where wily salesmen prey on the desperate, selling counterfeit drugs that are inconsistently effective or expired medication repackaged with new expiration dates. Families with limited resources have little choice and take what's on offer with a roll of the dice.

Every time I wake up, I down a few more tablets for the headache and fever. It's important to stay hydrated, but I lose all sense of time as I drift in and out of consciousness. Finally, I pull myself up off the floor. Weak and unsteady, I take a shower, pull on some fresh clothes and make my way out of the apartment to get help. As I step onto the street, I spot a pickup with two guys who seem to perk up when I appear and watch me intently, but I'm past caring. I've reached such a low point that I can't imagine things getting any worse. I climb into a taxi and direct the driver to take me to Mike's home.

Mike is alarmed to see the state I'm in and takes me to a local clinic where they put me on a drip and administer a course of antimalarial drugs. He then insists that I stay with him to recover. Coriscair and what had promised to be a business venture of a lifetime have led me into a nightmare. Physically, I'm in bad shape. Emotionally, I'm drained. All I want is to go home.

10

Déjà Vu

```
Angabi's Residence, Malabo
Wednesday and Thursday, 6–7 November 2013
```

Mike and I discuss my options and he urges me to keep a low profile until I've seen a lawyer, but fate deals me a different set of cards. Angabi has returned from Cameroon and summons me to meet him. Mike is adamant that I shouldn't go, horrified that I'm even considering it and insisting that Angabi can't be trusted. But I am stubborn and don't want to throw in the towel just yet. I refuse to believe that the situation is beyond salvation. I want answers. I still can't fathom why Angabi wants to cancel the deal. And besides, he has my passport.

Despite Mike's misgivings, I head off to Angabi's mansion, where I'm told to wait outside. Before long, my shirt is sticky with perspiration. Baking in the hot tropical sun is not fun when you're recovering from malaria, and I'm struck by the stark contrast between my last visit and today. No freshly baked bread, no cooling breeze, no sign of Coco or Aurora, just a hot gravel driveway and a posse of unfriendly security guards watching me as if I'm about to make off with the crown jewels. I ignore them, but after more than an hour of kicking stones in the heat, I'm starting to think that maybe Mike has a point and meeting Angabi is a bad decision on my part. But now the front door opens and a servant beckons me inside, leading me to Angabi's office.

It's a relief to be out of the heat, but Angabi is in a foul mood and our meeting is short, accomplishing nothing as he demands that I return the money and I tell him that it's all been spent on acquiring the plane and sorting out the licences and other fees. My words fall on deaf ears. Angabi is adamant, refusing to listen to logic. Finally, I tell him that if he cancels the deal we must follow the guidelines in the contract. Just then, I hear police sirens. I look at him in horror. Surely they're not coming for me again?

If this wasn't so serious, it would be almost laughable. Angabi doesn't get up when two policemen burst into his office. He takes a deep drag of his cigar, watching dispassionately as they pull me roughly to my feet. Once again, I'm handcuffed, this time with my hands in front of me, and bundled out and thrown into the back of a stinking police van waiting outside.

Within moments we're hurtling through the streets, sirens blaring. I'm flung around the metal cage manufactured specifically for transporting supposedly dangerous criminals. I try to hook my fingers into the steel mesh as we tear around a corner, but lose my balance, bashing my head against the metal framework. A razor-sharp wedge of steel hooks into my shirt, ripping the sleeve and slicing into my forearm. It suddenly dawns on me that Angabi wasn't planning to negotiate with me at all; the meeting was orchestrated for the sole purpose of having me rearrested as he resented the fact that I'd been released in his absence. So, with total disregard for the law, I am once again in handcuffs, cut off from the outside world, en route to an unknown destination. I have a horrible suspicion that I may have been there before.

Thinking about how things have just played out, I realise that Angabi probably arranged for the police to be there, but that I arrived before they did, so he was forced to stall. Mike was right: I was naive to trust Angabi. Until now, I've been reluctant to believe that the deal is off, especially after so much work has gone into it. I've finally received the message, loud and clear.

It's Thursday and I know that the courts are closed between Friday and Tuesday, so I'm in for a long and harrowing wait. Could Angabi be so diabolical that he'd force me to endure four days behind bars just to make a point? I'm starting to believe that he is.

The sights and sounds of mid-morning life in Malabo whizz by until the van comes to an abrupt stop outside Guantanamo, my body slamming against the side of the vehicle. They pull me out and drag me into the central courtyard, by now a familiar space. I know how this will play out. Knowing doesn't make it any easier, but I summon my strength. Angabi cannot win.

Visions from my previous visit flash through my mind. Am I headed for La Oficina, or will I be shoved into a cell to face a frenzied mob? Either option is terrifying, but there's nothing I can do to change it, so I submit to a body search without protest. My hands are still cuffed in front of me, so I'm marginally better off than I was last time. At least I can pee without asking someone else to help me. Thank God for small mercies.

The guards complete their search. My valuables are removed and I'm hustled down a long tangle of dark, dank passages to an overcrowded cell brimming with thugs. As before, my appearance is a novelty and I'm subjected to an initial groping to see what treasures I will yield. I know that some of these people may be violent criminals, but they're not the real threat; it's the ones sporting badges and in uniform that do the most harm. But as a protective measure, I shove my way into a corner with my back to the wall and spend the afternoon slow-baking with the other prisoners pushed up against me. Space is at a premium. It's hot. Sticky. Sweat streams off my face and my armpits are soaked.

I disconnect, emptying my mind, ignoring attempts by the others to communicate with me, shutting off, as if I'm watching a movie of myself with the sound turned down. The heat is unrelenting and we're all lethargic. Even the guards seem sluggish and don't turn up as frequently to take prisoners away.

The longer I huddle in the corner battling claustrophobia, the harder it becomes not to open the doorway in my mind that leads to a labyrinth of horror. It's as if I am pacing in front of it. I know I shouldn't go in there, but the pull is overpowering, even though stepping across the threshold will lead me to a dark place.

I can't resist, and then it's impossible not to flick the switch illuminating the images now flashing through my mind. A film reel on fast-forward. Bloody snapshots. Prisoners battered and beaten. Crowded cells. Groping hands in the dark. Handcuffs chafing my wrists. A man begging to be spared as he is dragged to La Oficina. An infinite loop. Real, and at the same time not real.

'God, help me!' I scream silently. I am once again Daniel in the lions' den. My focus shifts with this thought; God is always there when I need him. I can do this. I breathe deeply, reminding myself that dwelling on what was and what might come will destroy me as effectively as a trip to La Oficina. I cannot allow the fear of the unknown to take hold of me. Squeezing my eyes shut, I whisper a solemn prayer, asking for guidance and strength.

Shutting down the horror in my mind takes everything I have, but I feel the panic subside and slowly open my eyes, gazing around the dimly lit cell. The other prisoners are quiet. It's all in my head. Still, the uncertainty of what lies ahead weighs heavily as the day drags on. It takes all my willpower to keep the demons at bay when the light fades and darkness creeps through the cell, bringing an end to my first day back behind bars.

All the horrors I've witnessed inside this building seem amplified at night, and the likelihood that I'll encounter the torture chamber is becoming impossible to ignore, especially since the guards are now turning up more frequently. So many of us are crammed together in this filthy, unhygienic space. Young. Old. Strong. Bold. Some silent, hunched over, gazing into the abyss, just as I did earlier. Do they share my nightmares? What have they seen? What have they done? Who have they crossed? How is this justice?

Angabi seems to be above the law and has robbed me of my faith in humanity by snatching away my freedom on a whim. I think I will be able to handle the physical side of the torture chamber, but having the mental strength to stay positive for my family, Melanie especially, is what I'm praying for. If word of my imprisonment gets out, I pray that Melanie will find the strength to cope, to believe that I can get through it.

With thoughts of my family giving rise to panic, I beg one of my cellmates to let me use his phone. He hands it over reluctantly, and even though I have nothing to offer him in return, I type a short text message telling my mother that I'm behind bars again, asking her to break the news to Melanie gently in case she hears it from other sources. My mind flits between dread and despair, my anxiety levels spiking every time I hear footsteps approaching along the corridors. Are they coming for me?

Finally, dawn arrives, not that it makes much difference, apart from more unrelenting humidity and discomfort. Around mid-morning a few guards turn up and conduct a cursory roll call. The others have accepted my presence here and chatting to them is a distraction, but as the day wears on, time hangs heavy in the sweltering heat, sapping our energy and stripping us of any motivation, even to talk. Fatigue overwhelms me and I surrender to it, dozing fitfully in my corner, a hot press of bodies jammed against me. The monotony is broken when I am jolted awake by the sound of heavy footfalls and the rattle of keys in the gate.

My name is called.

I break out in a cold sweat, instantly on the alert. A surge of adrenaline makes me feel lightheaded and nauseous. Am I being summoned to La Oficina? Dare I hope that I am being released? I'm reluctant to weigh the odds for fear that the scales are tipped against me.

They call for me again, impatient now.

I'm led along a warren of passages. Lights flicker intermittently above us, doing little to illuminate where we're going. I'm sleep-deprived and suspicious of everything. A man could disappear in here, I think.

How quickly it becomes easy to imagine the worst rather than hope for the best. The guard is irritated by my hesitance. Ironically, after wishing to get out of here, I'm now reluctant to leave a place where there are potential witnesses. Since the guard pulled me from the cell, we haven't encountered anyone. He shoves me through a door and I blink rapidly as my eyes adjust to the unexpected brightness. It's raining. We're in a deserted parking area with just one solitary vehicle. I freeze. A well-dressed man in civilian clothes gets out of the vehicle and comes towards us, running through the rain, and leads me back towards it. What's going on? Who is this? Where is he taking me? The guard has disappeared inside.

Alarm bells ring in my mind as I take stock of the facts. There are no official markings on the car and the man at my side isn't wearing any kind of uniform. Why would he arrive out of nowhere, late on a Friday afternoon, to pick me up? It doesn't make sense. I stop, refusing to take another step. Handcuffs or not, I'm not about to disappear without putting up a fight. The man seems to realise what I'm thinking.

'No worries,' he says, reaching into his pocket, pulling out his ID card and explaining in Pichi that I'm going to see the judge.

I am astonished. *Really?* Although I want to believe him, part of me thinks it's yet another ploy by Angabi, but what choice do I have? There's only one way to find out, so I climb into the car and we're soon speeding down the highway towards the Palacio de Justicia.

From the outside, the Palacio is an imposing building. No expense has been spared on the state-of-the-art surveillance equipment, yet I have my doubts whether the impressive-looking technology is functional or maintained. Earlier this year, there was an official inauguration ceremony for this new building dedicated to the pursuit of morality and justice, but based on my recent experiences I have the feeling that it's unlikely that justice will prevail, no matter how honourable and righteous the judiciary. But despite my lack of faith in the system, my spirits lift. The driver wasn't lying.

We pull up through a side entrance sporting a drive-through vehicle security inspection system capable of detecting explosives and weapons. Again, I doubt that it's operational. The driver pulls up, flashing his ID card, and the guard listlessly drags the automated gate open. Yet another piece of equipment that doesn't work. We follow the road down through a black metal sliding door into an underground basement where prisoners are transported in and out of the courthouse.

It seems that I will have my day in court at last.

11

Courting Disaster
Palacio de Justicia, Malabo
Friday, 8 November 2013

We pass through an unmanned 'secure' checkpoint and head into the building. To the left is a row of holding cells, a waiting area just beyond them. Through a barrier to the right are a few offices, the doors shut. It's dark and gloomy, but I'm not sure if the lights are switched off or if they ever worked. My escort finds a guard and they ignore me, methodically going through the motions that could potentially lead to my freedom with a distinct lack of interest that borders on apathy. Their indifference is unsurprising; from what I've heard, most public servants don't get paid for months on end.

The barrier screeches in protest as the guard drags it open – yet another fine piece of equipment that doesn't work. Seeing the remotes and body scanners scattered on the desk, I imagine they don't either. He waves me through, conducting a cursory search that is little more than a superficial pat-down. I'm relieved that for once my dignity has been spared. The driver has disappeared.

The space beyond the barrier is empty and quiet. I'm escorted past the cells to the waiting area and sit down, reading the plaque on the closed door which tells me I'm outside the judge's chambers. A sliver of light shows through the gap at the bottom of the door – a sign of life inside. I lean back and stretch my legs out in front of me, savouring the silence and the feeling of space around me. It feels good not to have stinky, hot, sweaty bodies pushing against me from all sides.

Until now, I wasn't certain I could believe the guy who drove me here, but perhaps even those in power are required to allow their victims to appear before a judge. Finally, after all the horror and wasted time, I'll get to tell someone in authority my side of the story. In most countries, it's illegal to detain a suspect for an extended period without officially laying a charge against them. I'm sure the same applies here, but as Angabi makes his own rules and seems to be above the law, I can only pray that justice will prevail and I'm more than happy to wait here to find out.

Gazing around the shabby room, it's clear to me that, like Guantanamo, not much maintenance has been done. Even though it was completed less than a year ago, it looks decades old. It's also clear that this space wasn't designed as a waiting area; it's poorly ventilated and stiflingly hot. I don't see any restrooms and although there is a desk for a secretary outside the judge's chambers, no one is sitting there now. Still, I feel the tension leaving my body, appreciating the simple pleasure of sitting on a chair. This is the most comfortable I've been in the last forty hours.

Compared to the chaos of Guantanamo, everything here seems more orderly. Some cells in the detention area have glass walls, while others are fitted with full-length steel doors and a small ventilation hatch at the top, probably reserved for dangerous felons, but they all appear to be empty; apart from the guards and whoever is in the judge's chambers, I seem to be alone here. I hope Angabi doesn't turn up, but I brush all thoughts of him aside for now. Even though I can't leave the building, I'm grateful to be sitting here rather than locked up in the cells, which look dark and claustrophobic.

With freedom potentially within reach, I sit and wait, once again on African time. Finally, there seems to be movement in the adjacent room and someone summons the guard. He disappears into the office, returning with a man in handcuffs, and tells me to go in; the judge will see me now. I get up and stand uncertainly near the doorway. The judge is sitting at his desk and motions for me to enter the room. I take a seat opposite him and greet him respectfully, introducing myself. He asks who I have a problem with.

'Angabi,' I say.

He shakes his head, muttering under his breath, shuffling through the papers on his desk. He finds what he is looking for and skims through it. He peers over his glasses at me.

'Mr Angabi has laid a charge of theft against you.'

I tell him that I have not stolen anything from Angabi, explaining that we have a contract for which I have received a deposit to procure an aircraft and to pay the necessary licences and permits, but now Angabi wants to cancel the contract and is demanding the money back. The judge listens impassively and then asks me if I have a lawyer. I tell him I don't and he grimaces, scribbling a note on the document. He tells me that I can leave but must return on Tuesday with a lawyer and a copy of the contract, and to arrange for Angabi and his lawyer to be there too. And just like that, it's over. I am free to go.

I walk outside, where it's been raining. The streets are slick, shining in the twinkling lights of a Friday evening. I realise that I don't have my keys, phone or wallet and it's about five kilometres back into town, but after being cooped up in a crowded cell, I relish the thought of being out in the open and decide that the walk will do me good.

Ironically, the closest place to where I am happens to be Angabi's apartment where I stayed with Ronnie before things fell apart. I realise that returning to it borders on insanity, but I am stubborn. Besides, God and the law are on my side, so even if it seems that I'm poking an angry cobra with a short stick, I don't think Angabi can do anything to me now that the courts are involved.

The freedom of being outside lifts my spirits and I feel a thrill of pleasure at the thought of telling Angabi that I've been released. Mike is not going to be impressed with my reckless decision, but I've done nothing wrong, and I'm fed up with Angabi's bullying tactics.

It's quiet and peaceful outside. Thunderstorms are unusual at this time of year, but now the skies are clear and the waxing crescent moon casts a faint glow over the street. I'm walking on air, untouchable and determined not to let the fear of what might happen control me as I head down the wide avenue leading to the traffic circle connecting the eastern and western parts of the island.

There's not much traffic at this time of night and the road is well lit, even though in some places the lights flicker intermittently. There are security cameras everywhere, but I know that they're not maintained and don't work, and if they did, there would be no one watching the feed – the Israeli company that installed them was summarily dismissed and no one bothered to train the locals to use the system. Instead, the government relies on the RIF to employ extreme measures to maintain law and order. I keep an eye out for any of them patrolling, but this is still a little too far from the main attractions at the centre of town where foreigners, mostly employed in the oil industry, cruise the rutted side streets, hanging out at bars and restaurants, drinking the night away with their pick from the flock of ladies looking for a good time and a fast buck.

A gentle breeze comes off the ocean, keeping the temperature at around twenty-seven degrees, which is bearable, despite the humidity. I take a shortcut diagonally across the road and walk along the left side of the double-lane motorway, keeping an eye out for anyone who might be following me, but there's no one about and only the occasional car passes, paying me no attention.

I reach a small, wooded area which I recognise from one of my regular jogging routes. There is a maze of small alleyways here, but I stick to the tarred road so I don't get lost in the dark. I pass the time imagining being back home with my family, picturing Bubbles running around, tail wagging, yapping happily, until I reach another intersection that brings me closer to civilisation.

I pass tracts of open land interspersed with factories and warehouses, and then the Santa Maria central market. Angabi's apartment is not too far now. Mike's home and the South African embassy are in the same general vicinity, but still quite a distance further. Walking there would take some time, and by now I am exhausted, so I stick with my decision to go to Angabi's apartment. I pick up the pace as the thought of a cool drink and something to eat spurs me on.

It's a little busier as I enter the downtown district where street vendors are setting up stalls for the evening trade, couples are out walking, musicians are tuning their instruments in the open-air pubs and people are heading home from the market. The casino is always a popular destination, and I imagine that's where most of the Friday-night crowd will be gathering; karaoke hour has yet to kick off in the popular bars and taverns in the area. Turning a corner, I see the apartment block up ahead and hesitate. Should I really risk everything just to make a point? After a moment's hesitation, I decide there is only one answer: absolutely.

Still, I hang back a little, watching the apartment for a few minutes from the shadows. The lights are off; no one is home. There's nothing unusual on the streets, no men in black suits waiting in cars, no indication that it's anything but a typical Friday night. As far as Angabi is concerned, I am where I should be, locked up in a rancid cell at Guantanamo. I doubt that news of my release has reached him yet.

Getting into the apartment is going to be tricky. I need the keys and decide to call Coco. I approach a Malian trader and convince him to let me use his phone to make a quick call. Luckily, I still remember Coco's number, and after a few rings he answers, caught completely off guard when he hears my voice. He's even more surprised when he hears what I want. He tells me to wait at the apartment and I hand the phone back to the trader and lean against a crumbling wall in the shadows outside an abandoned building, wondering if Coco will tell Angabi.

An hour passes and I'm starting to think that maybe I am being a bit reckless; I could have been at Mike's by now. Maybe Angabi is gathering his hounds for the chase and I've taken an unnecessary risk by putting myself back in his sights just to make a point. I should have carried on to Mike's house.

Just as I begin to doubt the wisdom of my decision, I recognise Angabi's navy-blue SUV turning into the street and pulling up outside the apartment. The engine stops and Coco emerges, looking around. I hang back, waiting to see if there are any other vehicles or suspicious characters with him. He's alone. I cross the road and jog over to meet him. As he sees me approaching, I can tell by his expression that he is unimpressed, but he hands over the keys. He then pulls his phone from his pocket and dials a number. After a brief conversation, he passes the phone to me. A deluge of venomous hatred spews down the line. Angabi is livid and launches into a tirade of abuse, bellowing and threatening until he runs out of steam and abruptly ends the call. Nonchalantly, I hand the phone back to Coco, toss the keys into the air, catch them again, and walk towards the apartment entrance with a wave.

'See you in court,' I call over my shoulder as I head into the building.

12

Judgement Day
Central Malabo
Monday and Tuesday, 11–12 November 2013

The weekend passes quickly. On Monday, I head off to deliver a copy of the contract to the judge. At the Palacio de Justicia, an officer directs me to the basement. There's a notice at the entrance advising me that this is where appointments are scheduled and cases filed, and a woman is busily tapping away at a computer. She tells me to wait until I'm called, so I take a seat and page through my papers.

Mike told me that this woman is a legal secretary, responsible for recording statements and scheduling appointments with the judge. It's a position of tremendous power and she has a reputation for being fierce. Rumour has it that she's not averse to accepting 'payment' to expedite your hearing.

She eventually calls me over and I introduce myself, making sure to be respectful – I'm not willing to pay any bribes, but don't want to jeopardise the process. I explain that I've already seen the judge and will be appointing a lawyer this afternoon, adding that I've been told to return in the morning with Angabi and his lawyer. She makes a few notes, attaches them to the contract, and says that the judge will review the documents today and she'll see me tomorrow. It's all very quick and efficient, and in no time I'm outside again, hailing a taxi to go to my next appointment, where I hope to appoint my legal counsel.

Arriving at the law offices, I'm ushered into a room where a young woman sits at a conference table with a laptop and notepad beside her. She's young but looks businesslike and efficient, and I incorrectly assume that she's the lawyer's secretary, only just managing to cover my surprise when she introduces herself as my potential new lawyer. My future is in this young woman's hands, and I try to recover from my blunder with an embarrassed smile. She laughs, explaining that it happens a lot. And so we get down to business.

I like her brisk manner as she reads through the notes I've made summarising the events of the past few weeks and including details about my dealings with Angabi and an overview of the contract. She arranges some coffee and listens quietly as I fill in the details, and then takes a thorough look at the contract, making notes in a journal. She tells me that I have a strong case and nothing to worry about, everything is in order, and she is willing to represent me. We end by agreeing to meet in the morning outside the Palacio de Justicia.

All in all, it's been a productive day with encouraging results. On my way back to the apartment, I stop in at a travel agency to see what flights to South Africa are available for later in the week and then spend a quiet afternoon relaxing and reading. Later, as the evening brings some relief from the stifling humidity, I go for a jog along the central highway, and at around 9 p.m. I go to bed, sleeping well until the alarm wakes me.

I get up feeling refreshed and invigorated, excited to end this chapter involving Angabi and his airline. It's annoying that I've wasted so much time on it, but ultimately what is most important is family. Doing a job that you enjoy if you're working with people that you don't respect doesn't quite measure up. All I want is to get back to my family; they are everything to me and I can't wait to go home.

I leave the apartment feeling a little anxious but believing I'll be exonerated, and hail a taxi, jumping in as it pulls to a stop beside me. As we slip back into the traffic, I lean forward to tell the driver where we're going and a sticker on the dashboard catches my eye. My spirits lift and I take a quick snap of it on my phone as a reminder of how faith can restore hope: *El Poder de Dios esta aqui presente.* The Power of God is present here.

Feeling upbeat, I arrive to find my newly appointed legal counsel waiting on the steps at the entrance. She smiles and waves, exuding confidence and charm. Together we sign in and head downstairs to the judge's chambers. Even though I have a lawyer at my side and the judge has confirmed that Angabi doesn't have a case against me, an agitated swarm of butterflies has taken up residence in my gut. It's not easy to shrug off the events of the past few weeks. The memories are still too fresh, too raw.

We're early, but as we round the corner, Angabi is already there, dominating the space and holding court loudly in the waiting area. I recoil at the look of utter contempt that passes over his face as he sees me and realise that this man's stubborn determination to win must not be underestimated. He has a score to settle. But I am not going down without a fight.

I've never given it much thought before, but it suddenly dawns on me why

Angabi has always had a team of lawyers at his disposal. Today, he has brought the big guns with him: his 'number one' lawyer, Camila Núñez, and her wingman, Mariano, whom I've dealt with before and who is one of my least favourite people in Malabo. He's a typical yes-man, officially employed by the African Union but acting as Camila's deputy. Having butted heads with Mariano several times, I suspect that he's relishing the thought of having power over me today. His arrogance gets under my skin. The lawyer herself is a powerful adversary; I've seen her in action before when she defended Angabi against an oil company when he didn't pay his aviation fuel bill. Together, the three of them are a formidable pack.

Angabi stops mid-sentence, glaring at my lawyer in stony silence. I know she hasn't met him before and I want to hold her back as he summons her over, turning his back to me so that I can't hear what he's saying. Initially, she argues with him, but as Angabi's voice gets louder, the conversation becomes more one-sided. Even though I can't hear the words, there is a menacing undertone that is disconcerting.

Finally, my lawyer makes her way back to me and busies herself collecting her files and hoisting her bag over her shoulder before announcing that she will no longer be representing me, adding that I must pay Angabi the money immediately. She doesn't look back as she walks away briskly, leaving me dumbstruck. Just yesterday she was full of fire and righteous indignation, but after minutes with Angabi she is walking away. She knew all along that we were up against him, so I am shocked by how quickly she has backed down, especially considering that she's read the contract and knows the law is on my side. The only possible explanation is that Angabi has threatened her, possibly telling her that he has the support of the untouchable elite. In a small town like Malabo, the fear is real, and even though I understand her predicament, I'm frustrated that it's apparently so easy for her to walk away, leaving me with no choice but to represent myself.

I fall heavily into a chair, as far away from them as possible. Before long, Angabi grows tired of waiting; ironic, given that he always makes people wait hours or even days before granting them an audience. He makes a great show of leaving, announcing loudly that his lawyer and Mariano will sort out this matter. The room fills up with others waiting to see the judge, and after some time Angabi's lawyer leaves too. Only Mariano remains, and we spend the next few hours avoiding one another, waiting for my case to be heard.

Eventually, my name is called, and the judge gets straight to the point, asking where my lawyer is. I explain that she is no longer interested in pursuing the case and I will be representing myself. He frowns, clearly annoyed, then shakes his head, seeming to understand. I don't envy him his job; it must be frustrating dealing with all these cases that are largely centred on the political aristocracy trying to eliminate their competition or intimidate their opponents. He tells me that he's read the contract and is satisfied with the details and won't need any more information from me, then he turns to Mariano and asks if he has read the contract. Mariano shakes his head. No, he has not. The judge glares at him and then launches into a tirade, ripping shreds off him for wasting the court's time, telling him to get out and adding that once he's read the contract, he must explain to Angabi that he has no case against me and that I'm free to leave the country. I'm not usually a spiteful person, but I feel a moment of absolute glee imagining this insipid parasite having to deliver the news to Angabi. Oh, to be a fly on the wall. I chuckle to myself; today is turning out to be just great!

The judge gets up with an air of finality, saying that the contract is binding and Angabi should stop wasting his time. If there is any further dispute it should be taken to the civil court, not to him at the criminal court. I quickly ask him if I can get my passport back and leave the country, to which he says: absolutely, yes, I am perfectly within my rights to leave the country. It's official, my problems are over and I'm going home.

Minutes later, I head out of the building with a big smile, strolling down the steps a free man.

13

Hide and Seek

```
South African Embassy, Central Malabo
      Tuesday, 12 November 2013
```

I'm still smiling as I walk along the street outside the courthouse, the thrill of victory adding a bounce to my step. I've been vindicated. The world seems to mirror my optimism with clear, bright blue skies and a fresh breeze, and I can barely contain the sense of euphoria that fills my heart. Life is good. I'm going home.

My cellphone rings. I take it out of my pocket and answer the call. Instantly, Angabi begins hurling abuse at me, warning me that this is not over and that he does not accept the court's decision.

'Daniel, I am warning you,' he bellows. 'You will pay.'

I roll my eyes and let him rant as I keep walking, gazing up at the sunny sky, feeling confident and untouchable. He finally runs out of steam and I tell him that there's nothing further to discuss, I'm leaving and he'll be hearing from my lawyers. I end the call, enjoying the satisfaction of cutting him short. I've finally been pushed to my limit and can't wait to get as far away from him as possible. I've nothing more to say to him. Angabi has put Coriscair into an unrecoverable death spiral and I am bailing out; I'm not going down with him.

The judge told me Angabi should return my passport immediately, but after this phone call, I'm pretty sure he won't comply. Perhaps I can arrange a temporary passport through the embassy. I look out for a taxi, but the streets are quiet, so I walk down the main boulevard towards town. Even though it's hot, I'm enjoying being out in the open with nothing to fear. Maybe later I'll spoil myself and go out for a beer to celebrate.

I feel like I've had a system reboot and my anxiety melts away in the heat. I stop at a street vendor and buy a bottle of water. While I'm paying, my phone rings again. It's Mike. I can't wait to tell him the good news, but I immediately sense the urgency in his voice as he asks me where I am. I start giving him a rundown of the morning's events, but he interrupts, saying I must get out of sight quickly. If Angabi refuses to accept the judge's ruling, then he may order vehicles to look for me. I must stay out of sight and get to the embassy as soon as I can, then contact him once I'm there. He rings off abruptly.

I stop in the shade of a tree, scanning the area. Even though there is very little traffic, every vehicle that passes suddenly looks suspicious. I quickly duck into a side street and take cover in the doorway of a dilapidated shack to consider my options. The embassy is still quite a distance away, and with no taxis about it's going to be tricky to get there quickly. Luckily, I'm familiar with this part of town, having jogged these routes for years. I probably know the back streets of Malabo better than Angabi, who has most likely never even set foot in this part of town.

The roads in the slum are little more than narrow dirt tracks and my chances are better if I stick to the side streets where it's almost impossible for a vehicle to pass. They wouldn't think to look for me in this maze of small alleyways, likely assuming I'll be in a taxi, so I leave the relative security of the shadows and pick up the pace, heading deeper into the shantytown. As I hurry along the dirty streets, I'm distinctly aware of the danger I'm facing. Mike is generally calm and unflappable, but he sounded genuinely concerned on the phone, the urgency in his tone undeniable. I need to get to the embassy quickly.

Fortunately, there's a fair amount of foot traffic that provides some cover, although a well-dressed European drenched in sweat, running through the slums of Malabo, does draw a few curious glances. But they know better than to get involved, and ignore me. As I get closer to the embassy, I slow down, trying to blend in and not draw any attention to myself.

On the outskirts of suburbia, there are more vehicles about and less foot traffic. I keep my head down and stay close to the buildings, approaching cautiously until I'm about a block away from the embassy. I stop outside a small corner store where a few locals are gathered and mingle with them, picking up a newspaper and peering over it, watching for any sign of surveillance. I immediately spot two cars parked outside the embassy and I freeze, knowing without doubt that these are 'official' vehicles. They have arrived ahead of me and are lying in wait.

I can't stay here much longer without drawing attention to myself, so I retrace my steps up the side street, moving into the shadows of a nearby derelict building where I have a better view of the embassy. The glare of the afternoon sun makes it difficult to see who or even how many are inside the vehicles, but I doubt that they can see me. Other than them, the street in front of the embassy is deserted. It's far too risky to approach, even though they'll probably expect me to arrive by taxi and won't be watching the pedestrians passing by, but if I walk past now, I'll have no chance – they'll spot me in an instant. I'll just have to wait.

My unease grows by the minute. Safety is a stone's throw away, but there is no way to approach unseen. Even as I try to figure out what to do, part of me is suspended in disbelief. Am I really being hunted down on the city streets of a remote island off the coast of Africa? My life is starting to feel like something out of a Hollywood movie; it's almost too bizarre to be real. But there is no way I'm going back to Guantanamo. And judging by the phone call and Angabi's reaction to seeing me this morning, there's a good chance that he has other plans for me. It's not hard to imagine that I might just disappear altogether. My only option is to get inside the embassy; now that I've been exonerated, they will protect me.

It seems as if time stands still as I watch and wait, fresh out of ideas. The vehicles don't move, but soon one of the occupants gets out and approaches the other vehicle, leaning in through the window to speak to the driver. I'm quick to spot the firearm clipped to his belt. These guys mean business. I'm glad I waited. The last thing I want is to die as a fugitive evading arrest outside the gates of the embassy in a pool of blood. I can already see the headlines: 'South African businessman shot while resisting arrest in Malabo.'

I wonder if I should sneak away and call Mike. He could send someone to pick me up somewhere nearby and I could go to the embassy when Angabi calls off his hounds. But I am so close, just a few hundred metres away. I don't want to give up so easily. The embassy is the only place where I'll be fully protected from this madman and his ridiculous vendetta against me.

Clearly, the men are not planning to leave without me. I'm running out of options. But then a group of teenage students approaches from the school a little way up the road behind me, their carefree laughter and happy chatter carried towards me by the wind. As I watch them approach, so engrossed in their world of teenage intrigue and drama that they don't even notice me, an idea begins to form in my mind.

They're going to pass right by me, heading towards the embassy. This might be my only opportunity to approach undetected. As they draw nearer, I decide that, despite the risks, hiding in plain sight is the only way. I almost laugh at the audacity of my 'plan' and begin walking, matching their pace, trying to blend in, keeping them between me and the street, hopefully obscuring any view the occupants of the vehicle might have of me as we approach. The students hardly notice me, absorbed in the mundane chatter of school life. Too late, I remember the weapon I saw holstered and realise that I could be endangering them if I'm spotted and the men start shooting.

Each step closer heightens my anxiety; I'm worried for these kids too, cursing myself for making such an impulsive decision and not thinking it through, but I'm committed now and keep walking alongside them, hoping I look casual and nonchalant despite the frantic pounding in my ears. Sweat pours off me, my heart feels like it's going to blast right out of my chest the closer we get. The vehicles feel like magnets pulling me towards them. I feel compelled to look in their direction, and it takes everything in my power to resist. I'll know soon enough if they spot me, and I focus on keeping pace with the kids, who have no idea of the potential drama playing out right here in the midst of their happy group.

I have to trust that God is protecting me and them. Finally, I'm close enough; if the men see me now, I can make a run for it and be inside the embassy before they can give chase. The kids take no notice as I manoeuvre myself between them so that I can slip into the entrance as we pass by.

The vehicles loom large in my peripheral vision, and, from what I can make out, at least three men are seated inside the first one, but I'm too close to the other one and can't risk taking a look. The engines are running, either to keep the air conditioning on or maybe so they can make a quick getaway.

The men are looking the other way and hope surges as I realise that they might not even notice my arrival at all. My heart soars, I can't believe that I'm going to pull this off, the gate is just steps away! I get ready to dodge into the entrance, praying that it's unlocked and that the guard isn't on a break. Not far now. Safety is within reach. Keeping my head down, I slip away from the group. The embassy guard recognises me and lets me in, closing the gate behind me. I've made it!

I risk looking back and almost laugh when I see that the men are still watching the street and haven't noticed their prey slipping through their fingers. I feel like James Bond as I turn to head inside. Behind me, a car door opens. I don't turn to look but hurry into the embassy, slamming the door shut. Through the window I see that all hell is breaking loose outside as three of the men rush to the gate, banging on it and yelling to the guard to open up.

It's pandemonium. A woman rushes out of her office and dashes over to the window; just then a man appears from one of the other offices, demanding to know what's going on. I tell them that the men outside are here to kidnap me and may even try to kill me. They eye me with suspicion and I realise how dubious my story sounds, but my anxiety is clear, and after a moment, the woman crosses to the intercom and tells the guard not to let the men in. I breathe a sigh of relief and collapse onto the couch, safe for now as they gather around, wanting to know more while we all keep a wary eye on the gate outside.

The woman quickly realises that I'm in shock and does her best to reassure me. Giving me a pat on the shoulder, she gets up and disappears into another room. I hear her talking to someone before returning to sit beside me. She tells me that her name is Thandi and she is the South African consul in Malabo, and then introduces me to her colleague, Sengani, who is the first political secretary. She explains that they are currently the only diplomatic employees manning the embassy, as the ambassador has been recalled and his replacement has yet to arrive. I can tell by the way she takes control that I'm in good hands. A tray of coffee and biscuits quickly materialises, and before long we're sipping from sturdy mugs while I tell them everything that has led to this point. It's a surreal moment, as if we are under siege, which I suppose we are, and yet here we sit, chatting and dunking our rusks like there aren't a bunch of gun-toting goons skulking outside.

They are outraged by my story and visibly concerned, which makes me feel guilty for dragging them into this mess, but Sengani quickly assures me that I've done the right thing by coming to them. They make a call the Department of International Relations and Cooperation (DIRCO) in Pretoria to establish protocol and to make sure that whatever we do is by the book. It's clear that they take their role as diplomats very seriously. Having them on my team renews my spirit and gives me confidence, as I no longer have to handle this on my own.

Thandi is in her forties, vivacious and kind, with a broad smile that immediately makes me think of home. She distracts me from worrying about the men outside by telling me a bit about herself: she's married to a Belgian man who lives here in Malabo with her, but she's nearing the end of her contract and is excited to be moving to Milan to take up a position at the embassy there soon.

Sengani embodies all the characteristics of a diplomat; he is stocky, well dressed, with close-cropped hair and glasses. He seems to be a devoted family man, explaining that he has brought his two daughters to live here with him in Malabo. I can see that he's a serious and dependable person who will always follow the rules to the letter, reinforcing my feeling that these two are professional diplomats who I can trust to do whatever they can to help me. But the problem is that I have barged in unannounced, an uncomfortable inconvenience, and I know they're going to need to harness everything in their diplomatic armoury to help me out of this mess.

Every time we check through the windows, we see that the men are still lurking and show no signs of leaving. Yet, despite the threat, I'm amazed to see that the guard hasn't left his post. I'm grateful that I don't have to face them alone, but we've reached a stalemate – the men outside can't enter, but it's not safe for me to leave either, and obviously calling for police backup is not an option.

Nervously, we watch them pacing outside the gate, wondering if they're planning to storm the building. Although dressed in civilian clothing, they seem like well-trained and armed Special Forces guys who get a kick out of flaunting their power and intimidating people. The lone embassy guard is not only outnumbered, but he's not authorised to carry a weapon, so he won't be able to offer much resistance if they decide to force their way in.

Technically, the embassy is sovereign South African territory, so any unauthorised entry by a team of armed men could be considered an act of war. Alarming as things are, I'm fairly confident that not even Angabi will take our bitter feud that far. Having the embassy in my corner gives me hope.

I doubt many diplomatic staff have ever had to deal with a situation like this, unless perhaps they work for the Russian embassy, and I am surprised that there is even a protocol in place for such events. I can hardly believe that my dispute with Angabi is at the centre of what could end up as a major international diplomatic incident.

The men still show no signs of leaving and Thandi and Sengani set to work organising the paperwork and making calls to the judge's office. After a few hours pass, I get the feeling that it's a long road ahead, as being bound by diplomacy means the wheels turn slowly. I have no idea where it will be safe to stay while I wait, distinctly aware of just how small my world has become – there is nowhere to hide, and although the embassy is considered South

African territory, there is no real security here and no guarantee that I'll be protected. And setting up camp on the couch in reception is not an option, so it's clear that I can't stay here.

Finally, as the evening approaches, Thandi calls her husband, Herwig, and the two of them decide that I must stay with them as she is an official appointed by our government. They feel that it is her duty to protect me and she cannot in good conscience put me out on the streets to fend for myself. A little while later, Herwig arrives to collect us, and as their vehicles and home are protected by diplomatic law, I am able to leave with them and remain safe from Angabi's men. As I settle into the comfortable room they have offered me, I am deeply grateful that this woman and her husband, who has never met me before, have opened their hearts and home to a fellow South African in need, with nowhere else to turn.

14

House Arrest

Central Malabo
12 November – 18 December 2013

The days that follow are incredibly frustrating. I'm essentially under house arrest at Thandi and Herwig's home. It's not safe for me to go out, as we know that armed thugs are constantly watching out for me. We're still waiting for an official letter from the minister of security confirming that I am free to leave. It's the only document standing between me and my plane ticket home.

It's been nearly two months since I last lay beside my beautiful wife. We are soulmates, and having spent the past twenty-five years together, I miss her and the simplicity of our life back home. Some days are worse than others, like a physical ache tearing at my heart. Being housebound means that there is little to distract me from my thoughts of going home. What should have been a five-day trip in October has turned into weeks; it seems a lifetime ago that Ronnie and I arrived at the Hilton hotel, excited about our new venture and looking forward to giving Coriscair her wings.

Thandi and Herwig go out of their way to lift my spirits, keeping me safe and well fed. I'm grateful to this amazing couple and I know the bond of friendship that we've formed will last beyond these dark days. Herwig is a Belgian expat, and we enjoy many lively discussions over a beer or two. He's a crazy character and I'm thankful for the distraction his companionship provides while we wait for the embassy to navigate a way out of this mess. His unique worldview makes me look at life differently, and our discussions leave me with much food for thought. I take stock of where I've been and what I've been doing over the years, and spend time reflecting on my life and the choices I've made.

Coriscair is beyond resuscitation, and although it's cost me dearly in time and effort, I don't want to work with a madman who, my recent experiences have shown me, is manipulative and without a moral compass. I've always tried to put family and God first; honesty and integrity are cornerstones of my faith, and while I am in 'exile', separated from home and everything I love, I realise just how important that is to me. Much as I enjoy the thrill of a new business venture and travelling abroad meeting people and exchanging ideas, it all pales in comparison to the joy I feel thinking of home.

One evening in early December, we're enjoying a nightcap when Thandi receives an urgent phone call. Our beloved Madiba, former president of South Africa, is dead. Even though he has been ill for some time and was ninety-five years old, we're deeply saddened by the news. As an anti-apartheid icon who spent twenty-seven years in prison before being released in 1990, he is seen as the father of the new, unified South Africa; his life is a symbol of the struggle against racial oppression and, ultimately, of freedom. His message of reconciliation, not vengeance, has inspired the world. Having spent just a few days in prison without committing any crime, I am in a reflective mood as I turn in for the night, realising the magnitude of his sacrifice for justice and equality and how we can all learn from his legacy of hope and forgiveness.

Just a few days later, Thandi arrives home triumphantly waving a document. The last piece of the puzzle has just been put in place: the official letter from the minister of security has arrived. I rush off to call Melanie with the good news. The children are home from university for the Christmas holidays and my parents are there too, and I laugh as I hear the whole family erupt into a cheer in the background; even Bubbles joins in, barking with excitement. Going home will be the best Christmas present ever. I almost can't believe it. I'll be home for Christmas! I've missed them all so much, it feels as though a decade has passed since we were at my friend's wedding in the Karoo.

After that, things move quickly. My emergency passport arrives and I am finally free to leave the country. I'm filled with joy as I rush to pack my bag. I can't wait to leave! I take a quick shower and choose a smart but comfortable cream jacket, a white shirt and jeans for the trip home, looking every inch the businessman rather than a fugitive on the run. I do a quick check of the room, making sure I've left it neat and tidy, before closing the door for the last time.

Outside, one of the embassy's diplomatic vehicles is waiting to take me to the airport. I throw my bag onto the seat and climb in, sitting back comfortably as we set off, relieved that this day has arrived at last. I say a quick prayer of thanks to God as we arrive at the airport, where the embassy staff accompany me into the terminal building to hand in all the necessary papers issued by Equatorial Guinean officialdom. Even though everything is in order, I can't help feeling apprehensive. Angabi has caused chaos in my life, and I'm concerned that he won't give up. I pray that it's all behind me. Maybe once I'm home I can try to figure out what went wrong, but for now all I'm interested in is getting out of Malabo and as far away from him as possible.

I check in and pass through security. The airport is not particularly busy today and I join a short queue at customs, happy but on edge, hypervigilant as I glance around, taking note of the people in the vicinity as I approach the counter and hand my passport to the official. The process is simple, I've done it a hundred times before, but I feel as though I'm in a state of suspended animation, watching as he takes my papers and casts a cursory glance over them, stamping my passport and handing it back to me. I sigh with relief; I have been officially cleared to leave Equatorial Guinea. It's almost anti-climactic. Where is the fanfare? Where are the marching bands, dancers and musicians, the banners and balloons? Even if they're not there in reality, it's as if they are in my heart as my spirits soar.

The embassy team haven't left my side and my sense of euphoria is contagious. Everyone is smiling, and even the security officer who waves me through treats me like a visiting celebrity. With my boarding pass in hand, we head to the waiting area where I can see the plane on the tarmac, bags being loaded into it.

It's then that I spot Aurora, Angabi's secretary. She is the last person I want to see here. I turn away quickly, hoping she hasn't seen me, and whisper to Sengani. He glances around and says that she's definitely watching us. Does this mean Angabi knows that I am leaving today? Has he sent Aurora to monitor the flights? I decide that I won't allow Aurora, Angabi and his team to ruin this moment, and put them out of my mind. After all, I've been 'cleared for take-off' by Equatorial Guinea's top officials.

I make my way to the boarding gate, taking a seat to wait for my flight to be announced, and Sengani bids me farewell. Everything is under control. Not long after, I hear the boarding call and head off, stopping briefly to show my passport and boarding pass to the airline staff, and then join the other passengers heading towards the plane. Suddenly, there's a commotion behind me. Glancing back, I spot Angabi barrelling towards me at full throttle, like an angry bull chasing a red flag. It's like a sketch from a Zapiro cartoon in the Sunday papers. I shake my head in amusement. I'm in the clear and have nothing to be afraid of; his tenacity, while remarkable, is totally absurd. I turn around, following the other passengers to the plane, where the cabin attendant waits, smiling and welcoming us aboard.

As the queue moves forward, I watch Angabi approach. He's bellowing with rage, actually shaking his fist, and I am *almost* concerned that he might have a heart attack. Behind him, a policeman rushes out and tries to force him back, but Angabi, imperious as always although wheezing with exertion, jabs a finger in my direction and instructs him to arrest me. Airport security vehicles race up, lights flashing, and boarding is instantly halted. Surrounded by a furious Angabi and the team of officers, I weigh up my options: make a run for it onto the aircraft, or try to explain to these men that Angabi is the problem, not me.

I realise that boarding won't change anything. If Angabi is hell-bent on detaining me, he'll send security onto the aircraft and pull me off the plane, so I turn to the nearest official and show him my boarding pass, telling him that everything is in order. At the same time, Angabi is yelling in Spanish, commanding them to arrest me. The officers are completely confused, not sure what to do. I tell them that Angabi is mistaken, here is my passport, here is my ticket, it's all been stamped and I'm free to leave. If they detain me, they will be committing a crime.

They don't know how to handle the situation. Angabi is a threatening figure, but they try to reason with him, explaining that everything is in order. I have cleared customs; there is no legal reason to deny boarding. Angabi glares at them. I've seen that look before. He pushes me aside, talking to them in Fang, his tone low and menacing. I quickly tuck my passport and boarding pass into my jacket pocket and pull out my phone to call the embassy.

As soon as they answer, I tell them what's going on, but before I can end the call, Angabi spins around with surprising agility for a man his size, grabs my phone, stuffs it into his pocket and stomps away. An officer takes my arm, guiding me back towards the building, apologising profusely, saying that unfortunately he cannot allow me to board the plane and we have to go to the commissioner's office to sort this out.

As we walk, I pull out my little backup Nokia and call the embassy again, telling them to get here quickly. They're horrified and promise to come right away. I'm hoping that this can be sorted out in time for me to be booked on the next flight out. Surely Angabi can't wield this much power? I get the uneasy feeling again that there is someone else behind all of this.

Minutes later, I'm in an office with guards posted outside the door. The commissioner walks in and quickly makes a call. I can hear the urgency and respectfulness in his tone and suspect he's talking to someone of high authority, but as the conversation is in Fang, I haven't a clue what he's saying or who is on the other end of the line. He ends the call and leaves the office. While I'm alone, I pull out my Nokia again and make another call to the embassy. They tell me that someone is on their way and not to worry, the situation will be sorted out. Thank God.

Sengani arrives, as does Angabi, and soon the office is bursting at its seams. Angabi dominates the room with his bulk and the sheer force of his rage while Sengani tries to reason with him, but Angabi just growls, telling him not to interfere, adding that he is going to make sure that I never leave Equatorial Guinea alive. The airport police are frozen in shock and about as useful as shop-display mannequins. Sengani again tries to reason with Angabi, who lunges at him, grabbing him and shoving him out the door. No one can lay their hands on a foreign diplomat and get away with it, but Angabi clearly believes he is untouchable. The door slams and they continue to argue in the passage, blocking my only escape route.

I'm surrounded by policemen, my fate being decided by a madman on the other side of the door. On the runway, the engines of the aircraft that represents my ticket to freedom start up. The plane begins its departure, turning onto the apron and speeding down the runway and into the air. A feeling of dread overwhelms me. I feel numb. Is this where it all ends for me, like the cowboy in a Western who disappears with the sunset, nobody knowing if he will live to see another sunrise?

15

Permission Denied

Malabo International Airport
18 December 2013

Angabi does not make idle threats. After all I've been through, and with a ticket in my hands, I don't want my life to take yet another dark turn. I don't want to believe that there is no way out. I don't want to believe that I may never see my family again. At this point, whatever Angabi may have planned would surely be much worse than Guantanamo. It's made no difference that I've been cleared by the courts and granted permission to leave the country. It seems he'll see to it that I 'pay' – if not by returning the money, then with my life.

Outside the room, Angabi rains a torrent of abuse on the embassy staff, who now seem powerless to protect me. He repeatedly vows that I won't leave the island alive. I know that someone very senior must have authorised his actions, so whatever lies ahead is sanctioned by them and is the stuff of nightmares from which I am sure that without God's help there will be no escape.

I pull out the small Nokia and look at it despondently. The small, backlit, monochrome screen glows green – the only link between me and my family. I run my fingers over the well-worn keys, thinking about all the messages I've sent and the calls I've made on this humble device that connects me to the world. It was the latest and greatest in high-tech gadgetry almost a decade ago but smartphones have evolved; the only reason I still carry it is that its battery never dies. I'm struck by the irony that there's a good chance that this outdated device might outlast me. It will quite possibly also be delivering the last message I will ever send.

How do I start? What do I say? How do I explain what's going on in just 160 characters? How do I say I'm not coming home? Do I say goodbye? Despair sets in. Do I want my last words to my soulmate, the love of my life, my reason for living, to be via a text message that offers no real explanation of what has happened here today? What if, by some miracle, things work out and I put her through hell unnecessarily? The one thing I can be sure of is that I won't be returning home today, but what do I say?

I know that whatever lies ahead is going to be dark, very dark. I don't know if it's the kind of darkness that just ends in nothing, but even if that is the case, I can't send a text message just saying 'goodbye'. How do you tell someone just how much they mean to you in a few short words? How do you tell your high-school sweetheart, life companion, mother of your children and one true love that you might never be coming back, that you may never see one another again, never hold one another again?

And why, I think angrily. Because a business deal went south on an island thousands of miles away? There is nothing I can say to her. Nothing that will give her any peace if I never come home again. I make a solemn oath to do whatever is necessary to get back home and hold her in my arms and tell her how much I love her, how much she means to me.

I unlock the keypad and start typing a message to my mother instead:
Angabi has taken me again.
I am in serious danger.
Dit gaan donker raak. (It's going to get dark.)
Be strong.
Take care of Melanie.
Pray. Pray. Pray.
God is in control.
I press send.

My mind empties, shutting down. I don't want to think about what happens next. I am numb. I can't think about home and the possibility that I may never see Melanie again. I don't want to think about cycling in the mountains or spending time with my kids or hanging out with Bubbles on the beach. I'm not ready for it to be over; there is so much living still left to do.

My thoughts are like quicksand, dragging me into the depths of despair. I focus on my breathing, closing my eyes, trying to control my emotions as I become aware that Angabi and the others have moved further down the passage, the sound of their voices muted. I feel utterly alone and disconnected, as if everything I'm experiencing is happening to someone else and I'm watching from a distance.

The door suddenly crashes open and four RIF officers brandishing assault rifles and dressed in full official regalia burst into the room, followed closely by Sengani, who looks absolutely panic-stricken. I want to tell him that I'll be okay, that I know that these men are here to take me into custody, but the words don't come. I get to my feet quietly.

I know the drill and lay out my wallet, phone and belt on the table. I look down at my hands, at the only piece of jewellery I've ever worn. Slowly, I remove my wedding band and press it into Sengani's hand, asking him to take care of it for me. My heart is breaking; this is the first time I've removed my ring in twenty-five years. Looking at Sengani, I can see that he is also distressed, and I know that my pain is tangible.

'Please keep this safe and see that my wife gets it back,' I say, my voice choked with emotion. At least now that Sengani has my ring, I know that if anything happens to me, this small and almost insignificant symbol of my love will make its way back to Melanie. Cold comfort. Nothing now stands between me and what lies ahead. To resist is pointless. The officers cuff me and manhandle me out of the office.

I am escorted through the building past gaping passengers and airport staff and dragged towards a vehicle parked halfway up the curb at the entrance, its lights still flashing. I'm forced into the vehicle, and as the door slams I see that Sengani has followed us out. He looks on in despair as the car pulls away. I doubt I'll ever see him again.

16

Kidnapped!

Malabo
18 December 2013

The vehicle careens out of the airport, heading away from the city towards the less inhabited mountainous central highlands of the island, a wild no man's land of deep rainforests, mystery and tales of black magic. A man could get lost out there …

Until now, I've clung to hope, not wanting to believe that I will die today, but the stark reality of how dire my situation is has set in. We've reached the point of no return. Flashbacks from Angabi's rants and threats fuel my fear that these men are taking me into the forest to kill me.

The atmosphere is tense, the officers solemn, even though they seem confused about where to go and make numerous phone calls interspersed between long silences. No one speaks to me. Once their assignment is concluded, I'm fairly certain that there'll be one less occupant in the vehicle. Even though I am not ready for it all to be over, I have accepted that there is nothing I can do to change it.

I pray fervently, realising that I've been too trusting, expecting others to behave honourably. Honesty and integrity are sacred in my book. How could I have not seen what Angabi is capable of? Why am I surprised at this outcome? Have I been too proud, too defiant? Maybe I should have been less stubborn and uncompromising, but would it really have made a difference?

Before God, I know that I am innocent. He is the only judge I must face, and I know I can arrive at His door secure in the knowledge that I've tried to live a good and honourable life. But as we travel deeper into the forest, this brings me little comfort. It's hard to breathe as panic threatens to overwhelm me, so I bow my head, close my eyes, and keep praying. God is my only hope.

A phone rings, shattering the silence. Is it Angabi calling to check if the job is done? I hear snatches of conversation in Spanish, but not enough to make sense of it. We change course abruptly, heading back towards town. What has changed? Dare I hope for a reprieve?

We pull up outside Guantanamo and the officers make another call.

Memories of what I saw in the torture chamber come rushing back. I'm not ready for it all to end here either. Why are we here; how has the plan changed? Has God heard my call? Does He have a plan? I know I stand a small but fighting chance away from the isolation and anonymity of the forest; there are other people here, witnesses. Maybe I can get a message to Mike or the embassy; maybe I can bribe my way out. Even though my options are limited, I'll take any crumbs that I can get.

Despite the threat of La Oficina, Guantanamo offers a small kernel of hope. If it means I can live, then I will endure the torture chamber, I will cope with the dark nights in an overcrowded cell. Anything is better than becoming a rotting, bullet-riddled corpse deep in the forest where I will be lost forever, with no one to tell my story, no one to bear witness to Angabi's ultimate betrayal. But there are no guarantees, and the possibility that I will just 'disappear' once I am behind these walls is still likely. I could end up with the same fate, the same forest, the same bullet-riddled body, the only difference being that I would have had to face the torture chamber first and endure whatever cruel and brutal punishment is dreamt up by Guantanamo's sadistic officials. I hear Angabi's voice in my head: 'He must be punished like an African, like one of us …'

The phone rings and moments later we're on the move again. Maybe Guantanamo and the horrors there are best left behind, but the fear of the unknown is just as terrifying. Our aimless meandering feels like another form of torture, as there seems to be no logic to it. All I know is that no matter what happens or where they take me, I don't want to end up dead in a ditch in the forest, left to rot, eaten by animals or, worse, chopped up for muti.

Panic rises again and I force myself to focus on one moment at a time. It's not over yet. As long as I am still breathing, there is hope. I look up as the vehicle slows and we pull up outside the Palacio de Justicia. It's deserted, not a soul in sight, as they haul me to the judge's chambers.

Minute after agonising minute ticks by. I ask the officers to let me make a call, just one. They tell me to shut up. I persist, but they ignore me. It's as if I already don't exist. After a while I give up. I hear footsteps approaching and glance up to see a man coming towards us, dressed casually in shorts and sandals and looking extremely unimpressed. He is an official court judge. My fate has been passed like a rugby ball and is now in his hands. I wait. What else can I do?

Not long after, I hear the murmur of voices and look up to see Thandi and her translator hurrying towards me, the first friendly face I've seen since the airport. She hugs me.

'I'm so sorry, Daniel,' she says, looking at me, tears glistening in her eyes. 'We have tried everything, but there is nothing more we can do to help you right now.'

She says she's going to take my fingerprints. I don't understand. It's not as if I've robbed a bank.

We go over to a table where she unpacks a box she's brought with her containing all the necessary paraphernalia. She lays it out and then, as my hands are still cuffed, awkwardly presses my fingers into the ink, rolling them one by one on the spot on a form with my name and the date written neatly at the top. I'm confused and ask why this is necessary. She busies herself with the task and I can tell that she's struggling to answer my question, but she finally says quite simply, too simply, that it's 'for later', in case they need to identify my body at the morgue.

I shake my head in disbelief. No trial? No chance to defend myself? How does one respond to that? I watch in silence as she places the form into an envelope and seals it. She gives me a pat on the shoulder, saying she must go now but that I must be strong and have faith; they'll do what they can to sort this out. Then she gathers her things and hurries away.

I flop back down into the seat, deflated, out of options and out of hope. The judge hasn't bothered to acknowledge me at all, focused on completing some forms and stamping them. Is he signing my death sentence? Finally, he closes the file and hands it to the officer, then leaves. That's it, job done. My fate, whatever it may be, is sealed. No one has said a word to me, and as far as I'm concerned these papers serve one purpose only: to cover Angabi's ass and somehow provide justification for whatever happens next.

Apart from Thandi, not a word has been spoken to me by anyone. Nobody has asked for my opinion. Nobody has told me what I'm accused of having done. Nobody has asked for my side of the story. Nobody seems to believe that I have any rights whatsoever. I've been completely ignored. It's as if I've faced the firing squad already and this is just a last little bit of paperwork before they bury me forever.

One officer remains, and he leads me past security, steering me towards the holding cells. I remember seeing them the first time I was brought here, on the day I was allowed to walk free, and yet here I am, back again.

The officer leads me down the passage between the rows of anonymous doors, solid metal with a small ventilation gap covered with steel bars at the top, the only identifying feature being the number painted on each one. It's impossible to tell if there is anyone behind them.

We stop outside cell number nine. It reminds me of a TV game show where contestants are randomly selected from the audience and asked if they would like to find out what's behind the door. *Ladies and gentlemen, a game of chance! What's behind door number nine? Daniel, you're up next! Let's see what's in store for you…*

I am pretty sure that I don't want to find out what's behind door number nine, but I don't have a choice. The guard unlocks the cell and pushes me inside. The door clangs shut, leaving me in the dark. It's cramped and stiflingly hot in here. The walls are chipped and glow with the sheen of thick coats of cheap, glossy paint in that nondescript colour one finds in public toilets around the world. Holes and cryptic messages have been gouged into the paint by frustrated prisoners, and without warning, the sense of the oppression, of being closed in, threatens to overwhelm me. I'm sure everyone locked up in here, guilty or innocent, feels a pervading sense of hopelessness, desolation and doom. It's going to take everything in my power to keep the dread at bay.

My mind is in a dark place where light only occasionally breaks through, confusing me and throwing me off balance. Waves of anguish and loss intersperse as fear surges like a storm over the ocean. The feeling of being out of control and not knowing what happens next, when or how they will strike, makes the passage of time irrelevant and impossible to track. A myriad of thoughts assault me. I'm trapped in a void between time and space where nothing has meaning. The outside world ceases to exist; it's as if I've been plucked from reality and catapulted into oblivion where nothing changes, it just is. Has it been minutes? Hours? Days?

I try to escape to thoughts of home, but it's too painful and I feel like I can't breathe, suffocating beneath the weight of futility pushing down on me. I'm trembling and dizzy, my body tingling, and suddenly I'm running out of air, losing control, my mouth dry, looking for a way out. But there isn't one.

At some point, I curl up in a foetal position, my hands still cuffed in front of me, and fall into a fitful sleep. I dream of riding my bike, being carefree, the air filled with laughter and love, the rich smell of the earth comforting, the forest floor crunching beneath my wheels as I whizz along a winding track. Up ahead, there's a bend in the path, and as I draw nearer the atmosphere changes, and I stop pedalling. The air feels different. Cold. Dank. Suffocating. Shivers run down my spine as the malignant smell of decay cloaks the forest, silencing the birdsong. The trees move, looming larger, surrounding me, choking the light from above, and the path behind me closes, cutting off all means of escape. The only way is forward ...

I wake up in a cold sweat and it takes me a moment to realise where I am. I remind myself that what I'm feeling is just a sign of panic. Claustrophobia. I cannot allow the irrational fear of a confined space to overwhelm me. They're just thoughts. I pull myself up off the floor. How long have I been here? I think I hear something outside. Is someone coming down the passage? Or is my mind playing tricks on me?

I lean closer, putting my ear to the door. I'm pretty sure someone is there. I step back as a key rattles in the lock. The person on the other side seems to be having some difficulty, then suddenly I hear a grunt of surprise as the door swings open, revealing a man in civilian clothing. He grins happily at me and lurches against the doorway. He's drunk. Smiling idiotically, he motions for me to follow him through the deserted building. On the way, he stops at the desk and finds the key to unlock my handcuffs. This is a good sign. I am beyond grateful, rubbing my aching wrists as head into the restricted basement parking area beneath the courts that's reserved for bringing prisoners in and out of the building.

A rusty, dilapidated Toyota sedan is parked haphazardly, pulsing with the persistent beat of African music. It's pretty dark in here and I have no idea whether it's day or night or how long I've been here, so I ask my companion what day it is. He seems surprised that I don't know, then laughs, shaking his head. I ask him where we're going, but he just gives me a quizzical look and doesn't answer. He's so drunk that I consider making a run for it. There's no way he could chase after me. I'm not even handcuffed. But where would I go?

There are three other men in the car. The man who fetched me from the cell gets into the driver's seat, chuckling happily; he's not interested in why I am here but is clearly enjoying the novelty of collecting me, a rumpled European, from the jail cells. He's just following orders, which are to fetch me and deliver me, but to where?

Over the music, I can hear the drunken laughter and banter from his friends, who are also completely hammered. They shift over, making a space for me between them on the back seat. After the silence of the cell, the noise in the vehicle is bewildering. It's obvious they're enjoying this unexpected outing and offer me a beer, but I decline, sitting back, feeling the torn edges of the sun-damaged fake leather digging into my back.

One of the men hands me his phone, asking if I want to call someone. I take it, but my mind hits a blank and I can only remember one number: home. I punch it in and press dial, but a tinny recording announces that I can't make an international call from this number. In despair, I realise that I don't remember any of the numbers for my contacts in Malabo. Who bothers to remember numbers these days when they are all stored on your phone? Just scroll, select and dial. I realise how pointless my network of contacts is, some of them VIPs, as well as close friends, colleagues and the embassy, when I have no way to reach them. I curse the supposed simplicity of modern technology that's of no use to me now. There's not a soul that I can call.

I hand the phone back, wondering who these men are and why I've been collected by a civilian and his friends. Again, I ask the driver where we are going, and they all laugh uproariously as he looks at me in surprise.

'Don't you know?'

I shake my head. 'No, I haven't been told anything.'

He chuckles and takes a swig of beer. 'Don't worry, you are going to see just now.'

The car fills with pungent marijuana smoke as one of the men lights a joint, which they pass around, offering it to me. I shake my head. It's soon followed by a bottle of beer. Eventually, the driver remembers he has a job to do and puts the key in the ignition. The engine coughs, then starts up with a rattle, and we lurch out of the parking area, accelerating erratically into the oncoming traffic, and barrel down the highway to parts unknown. Feeling thoroughly disheartened, I think that with any luck he'll roll the car and that'll be the end of my journey – perhaps the more favourable option compared to whatever lies ahead.

We zigzag through the traffic and turn onto a coastal road, heading north. The music is loud and the driver swigs from a bottle at regular intervals; all of them are having a whale of a time, while I am alone with my thoughts. I make peace with God, asking for forgiveness for the things I've done, for things I've long since forgotten I did, for things I didn't do. I think of Melanie, my children, my parents. I'm not a negative person, probably right at the opposite end of that scale, but, like animals seem to sense what's coming when they arrive at the gates of the slaughterhouse, I know that this is not going to end well.

17

Destination Unknown
Malabo
18 December 2013

The driver and passengers are oblivious to my emotional state as we race along Kenya Road, the car bouncing as they bop to the beat of vulgar American-style rap blasting from all sides. Another bottle of beer is emptied and thrown out of the window, bouncing hard against the pavement. They crack open the next one and hand it around. I realise that we're close to the Catholic Catedral de Santa Isabel, a monument in the neogothic architectural style and a favourite spot for capturing selfies and special moments, but as I'm not on a sightseeing trip its allure is lost on me.

As we drive on, the sun begins to dip below the clouds, heading towards the horizon, casting long shadows and painting the world in rich golden hues. It's a magnificent scene and I manage to savour it, knowing that I will need reminders of the beauty and tranquillity of the world on the road ahead.

We're approaching the presidential palace, and I realise without a doubt that our destination is Black Beach. My blood runs cold. I've heard about its notorious reputation for human rights violations and know that many who are sent there are never seen again. Even if it was the last place standing after an apocalypse, you wouldn't want to step through its gates, and I've always thought it strange that a place like this lies within the grounds of the presidential palace. Is it a case of keeping your friends close and your enemies closer?

We pass the imposing walls of the palace and head towards a guard hut at the top of the hill. The car labours up the steep incline, its engine rattling and threatening to cut out, and as we crest the rise, the guards wave us through without stopping or searching the vehicle or even asking what we're doing here. I'm not sure what this means, but it's highly unlikely I've been scheduled to meet the president for afternoon tea. At this point, the driver turns to me and announces proudly that the guards know him – he is also a guard and it's his job to drive the prison van, but today he is off duty so when they called him he decided to fetch me in his own car.

From this position on the hill, I can see the prison below on the left, facing the Atlantic, walled in by a hill to the east where the Malabo regional general hospital is located. Although I can't see it, I know that the Río Cónsul river is to the right, spilling into a small inlet flanked by naval buildings. Along the hilltop, a cluster of military barracks surrounds the presidential compound. Below us is the road leading to the infamous prison. Welcome to Black Beach! One way in, one way out.

As we descend, the brakes squeal and a few prisoners in the yard glance up curiously. The car groans in protest and they abandon what they're doing to follow the progress of our struggling vehicle. I need to hold on to my faith. I know that it will destroy Melanie when she finds out that I'm not coming home today. I know that I am about to enter a dark place and begin to pray silently, asking God to give me the strength to face what is to come. The car shudders, the engine wheezing and coughing as we rattle to a stop outside the guard hut.

The driver turns to me with a big smile. 'We're here,' he says gleefully, as if we've just arrived at the gates to Disneyland, and he opens the door with a flourish, stepping out and waving to the crowd gathered at the fence.

He's in his element, enjoying himself immensely at my expense, thrilled to have a starring role in the unfolding drama. The crowd of curious spectators grows as he shouts a greeting to the men who've come out of the guard hut, then he leans in through the driver's window, proudly announcing that it's not often that he has the job of delivering a white man to Black Beach. Nothing like a bit of unexpected entertainment to brighten up the inmates' day.

It appears that my roller-coaster ride has finally come to an end, delivering me at the entrance to a House of Horrors. A dumpsite for the dregs of humanity to be discarded in a dark and smelly cove on the outer reaches of the island. I sit dazed and detached, the tick, tick, tick of the engine cooling filtering through my mind as I gaze through the cracked windscreen at the scene before me, looking beyond the excited crowd clinging to the diamond mesh fence at the cluster of decaying structures that make up the prison.

The cloying stench of rotting garbage wafts towards me and smoke rises from an open area, creating a thick, soupy haze over the buildings, which have a distinctly Mediterranean facade. The walls had at some point been painted an insipid mustard-yellow but now the paint is chipped and spattered with dark streaks of mould and dirt. There are several guard turrets positioned at intervals along the perimeter and we are parked outside what appears to be a guard hut at the top of a steep embankment. A few scattered patches of pale, bleached grass have forced their way out from beneath the barren, hard-packed red earth, emerging in a futile pursuit of existence only to bake in the relentless heat. This is a place of decay, a place devoid of any sense of hope or humanity. I have truly entered the Valley of the Shadow of Death.

PART 2

'We do not remember days,
we remember moments.'

– Cesare Pavese

18

I Am Not That Strong

```
Hoekwil, South Africa
December 2013
```

I wish everyone would go away, just leave me alone. Daniel is missing. How can they all carry on as if things are normal?

They're making coffee in the kitchen. I can hear the tinkle of teaspoons being placed on saucers, the clatter of the cupboard doors closing as they fetch cups and arrange them on a tray. There's a look of concern on their faces when they glance in my direction. I can see the worry and sadness etched there as they fuss about, keeping busy. They turn away to put on the kettle and arrange rusks on a plate, which they place on a tray with the sugar and milk. I think they've run out of things to say to me.

I listen to the low murmur of their voices whispering softly so as not to disturb me. I want to scream at them. Yell. Break something. *Don't they know?* Nothing they do will make me feel any better. Nothing will make the pain go away. I don't want coffee. I don't want rusks. I don't want them here. I don't want to be polite and say the right things. I want to rage, scream, and throw something.

Someone is sitting on the chair next to me watching sport on the television with the sound turned down low; it doesn't seem as if he's really seeing what's happening on the screen. Bubbles whimpers at my feet and jumps up onto the couch next to me, nuzzling my hand. I pull him onto my lap and bury my fingers in his fur. He knows something is wrong and snuggles into me, trying his best to comfort me.

The dominee comes in quietly and walks over to me, resting his hand on my shoulder. He leans down and gently tells me not to lose faith, that God will take care of things. But I don't want to hear about God right now. I don't want to pray. I just want my husband back. God cannot fill the emptiness that I feel inside. Only Daniel can do that.

I shrug the dominee's hand away, push Bubbles aside, and race down the passage to our bedroom, slamming the door shut behind me. Leaning against it, my body trembles, I can't stop shaking and the ache in my chest feels as if my heart has been ripped out. I throw myself onto the bed, sobbing into my pillow. I don't want to breathe any more. I pull the duvet over my head and beat my fists into the mattress.

No! No! No!

I'm consumed by an overwhelming sense of loss, exhausted from trying to run away from the reality that I've been forced to face since Daniel's mother received the call from the embassy. I don't want to think any more. I don't want to imagine what's being done to him. I just want my husband back. I turn onto my side and reach across the bed, running my hand over the spot where Daniel sleeps. But the bed feels empty, too big. What if he never comes back? How can I live without him? My heart is breaking. I don't know how to cope. I can't pray. Why is this happening? What have we done to deserve this? We are good people. It's not right. It's not fair.

My body shudders with sobs that I can't control. Nothing matters except Daniel. I need him. Sighing, I sit up on the bed, hugging the pillow close to my chest, and gaze around the room. Daniel's presence is everywhere. The cap he wore to the wedding in Loxton hangs from the corner of my dresser. A photo of us from one of our cycling trips is on the nightstand. A framed collage of pictures of us with the kids is next to the book he'd been reading before he left. The smell of the perfume he bought me for my birthday lingers in the air. His Bible is on the little table near the door. I swing my legs over the edge of the bed, throwing the duvet off, and walk over to the table, picking up the heavy book and running my hands over its worn cover. He loves this Bible. He loves God so much, but where is his God now? Why did God choose to do this to his faithful follower? I flip through the pages, an infinite jumble of words that are somehow meant to guide you through these moments in life, but I can't find the answers. Right now, it's just a book, and the only thing it represents is the connection to my beloved husband. I know that wherever he is right now, Daniel will not have lost his faith in God. He will believe that God will get him through this. I am not that strong.

I put the Bible back down on the table, walk over to Daniel's cupboard and open it, looking at his clothes hanging neatly, waiting patiently for his return. I run my fingers along the orderly row of shirts and jackets. Touching them somehow makes him seem more real, like he just popped out to the shops, like he will be home soon, like he isn't locked up in some godforsaken prison in a godforsaken country on an island halfway across Africa. Touching the things he's worn makes me feel connected to him. It gives me a glimmer of hope. I need hope; I need to believe that he is coming back. I feel so alone. It's been so long and I am so afraid.

It's hard to stay positive and believe that everything will be okay when I can't speak to him or get any straight answers from anyone. It's hard not to be sucked into the depths of despair. I pull one of his favourite shirts out of the cupboard and rub the soft fabric against my cheek. It's all too much for me and a river of tears streams down my face. I miss him so much. I am not the brave one. Daniel is the strong one. Daniel takes care of things. I cannot cope. I don't want to cope. I don't want to have my faith tested. I don't want to live without Daniel at my side. I need him and he needs me. I want him to come home.

I let the shirt slip out of my hands and it falls silently to the bottom of the cupboard, the ghost of a memory. I feel empty. I tug and yank at his clothes, ripping them off the rail and watching them drop to the floor, the empty hangers rattling and clinking against one another as I climb into the cupboard and slam the door shut, letting the darkness surround me as I drag his clothes into a heap, covering myself with them. I pull his favourite warm winter jacket over my shoulders and push my arms into the sleeves, burying myself in the scent and memories of the man I love.

19

I Will Fear No Evil

Black Beach Prison, Malabo
18 December 2013

Reality beckons as I hear the taunts of the crowd shaking the fence. How long has it been? Seconds? Minutes? Did I black out? I look down at my hands, turning them over. Yes, this is real, I can see the mark from my wedding band, reminding me of home, of Melanie, my love, my soulmate. I am real. This is real.

With a start, I realise that the guard and his companions are all standing outside the vehicle and he's yelling at me to get out. I force myself back to the present, gathering my thoughts as I climb out, leaning heavily against the car, my legs buckling as I slowly make my way back from oblivion. I square my shoulders, preparing to face my new reality. *I will fear no evil: for thou art with me.* I know that what lies ahead will test me, test my strength, my courage, my faith. I have no choice but to face it. No way out but through. I've made a solemn vow to find my way back to Melanie, whatever it takes. God is with me, and Melanie is waiting. She is my world, my everything, my reason for living. Without her, my life has no meaning.

I'm steered towards the guard hut. By now the bush telegraph has spread the news of my arrival and the courtyard is brimming with hordes of prisoners clamouring and shaking the fence, yelling '*Blanco, blanco, blanco!*' I'm shocked to see how many are crammed into this space, women and children too – how is this possible? What kind of wretched hellhole have I arrived at?

The guard escorting me lurches unsteadily, almost falling off his feet and dragging me with him. He chuckles and burps loudly as he leads me towards the guard hut and out of sight of the prisoners. I can still hear them shouting with excitement and anticipation, like hounds clamouring for fresh meat.

More guards are waiting at the prison entrance and seem confused by my appearance. Clearly, I am an unexpected guest, and deciding what to do about it is way above their pay grade. They ignore me, and after a lengthy discussion in Fang, one of them disappears inside. I hear him making a call, trying to figure out what's to be done. They're not watching me, so I look around and quickly realise that I won't get very far if I try to make a run for it.

Down in the yard, the prisoners are still at it: *'Blanco, blanco, blanco!'* The monotonous chanting works on my nerves as I wrestle with my emotions, struggling to subdue the rage building up inside me. Was it only this morning that I stood at the entrance to the aircraft that was to take me home to be reunited with my family for Christmas? I should be somewhere in the jet stream over Africa right now, and yet here I am, still stuck in Malabo, what feels like a million miles away from home. How can one man have wreaked such havoc in my life? How much more do I have to endure? Surely this can't go on? I have to get home to Melanie.

First on the agenda is staying alive. It's not over for me yet; I'm not going down without a fight. Melanie needs me and I need her. Frustration fuels my anger. Angabi has crossed the line and cannot be allowed to win. Even if I have to find my way out of here and wade into the forbidding grey waters between Bioko island and mainland Africa and swim my way to Cameroon, I'll do it, if that's what it takes.

A last glimmer of sunlight breaks through a small gap in the clouds. For an instant, it hangs suspended above the sparkling waters of the Atlantic, casting a shimmering iridescence over the ocean, then abruptly disappears below the horizon. It's just a moment, but it's all I need to calm the turmoil in my mind and silence the rage building inside me. Is God sending me a reminder that I am not alone? At this moment, I feel He is with me.

I know that physically I can cope with what comes next; I am fit and healthy, recovered from my bout of malaria, my body resilient, but to survive whatever lies ahead means that I cannot give in to the rage building up inside me. Everything will be okay as long as I don't let these people get to me. I know that my biggest challenge will be controlling the impulse to fight back, and I must make sure that I don't react to the inevitable provocation coming my way. I must ignore the taunts and insults and stay focused and clear-headed. I cannot allow the rage lying beneath the surface to rise. I cannot allow it to take over. I must control my emotions. My years in boarding school taught me that those with rank or power often thrive on belittling others, and fighting back only spurs them on. I must stay calm and protect myself.

The guard reappears, beckoning me and my escort inside the hut. It's dimly lit, a decaying space, everything grey with neglect. A few lopsided chairs are scattered around and there's a desk at one end. A small lightbulb hangs from the ceiling, flickering as it sways from side to side. They're still debating what to do with me and I wonder just how high up the chain of command they'll have to go to get answers. It seems as though no one told them that I would be brought here today, and if that's the case then the fact that I am here at all can hardly be legitimate. Surely there are procedures? Even the fact that the guard appeared in civilian clothing in his private vehicle suddenly takes on a more sinister undertone. It's clear to me that, once again, the powerful elite, somehow sanctioned by the judge, are behind this latest unscheduled stop on my itinerary.

Through the thin walls of the hut, I hear the monotonous chanting – the prisoners haven't gone away and don't seem to care how long it takes for the main event. I turn my focus inwards, drowning them out, wondering how long I spent in the detention cells at the Palacio de Justicia without trial or being convicted of any crime. Now my fate is being determined by a couple of low-level prison guards in an insignificant, anonymous hut at the entrance to one of the world's most notorious prisons. I try to fit the pieces of this puzzle together. No matter which way I look at it, nothing fits. Except for one piece: Angabi. How did it come to this?

I hear the crunch of tyres on the gravel outside as a vehicle pulls up. The engine shuts off, a car door creaks open and slams shut, followed by the sound of hurried footsteps heading our way. The door crashes open, windows rattle, and instantly the tension rises as a man in military fatigues barges in. His autocratic manner and the star insignia on a red shoulder band tell me everything I need to know – this is their superior officer, most likely the warden, and he's on the warpath. He is short and stocky, and judging by the considerable paunch hanging over his belt, he has a taste for the good life.

The guards avoid making eye contact as he scans the room until his gaze narrows, settling on me, his contempt evident. I take the measure of this man, glaring back, not willing to cower before him even though I'm about to bear the brunt of his discontent. I know his type, and quickly realise that it's going to take everything I have not to sink to his level or retaliate. I've encountered people like him at boarding school. Bullies. Oppressors. Sadistic bastards who get a kick out of controlling others. Abusing others purely to feed their ego.

For him, this is going to be a game. I take a deep breath and vow not to let him win. I must control the rage brewing inside me; I don't want to do anything that I won't live to regret. *Bring it on*, I think. I've made an enemy by my mere existence. Someone higher up in the food chain must have summoned him here to deal with me, and he is clearly not happy about it. Quite frankly, neither am I.

He slams the door and crosses to the opposite side of the room, barking orders to the guards in Fang. I don't need to understand what they are saying – it's very clear that what lies ahead is going to test me. I watch them carefully, my senses amplified as I hear the faint whirring of a small fan that does little to dissipate the heat, the scrape of steel-capped boots across the rough floors and small scuffling sounds from a creature somewhere out of sight. The warden pulls a pack of cigarettes from his pocket and shakes one out, throwing down the pack on the table. I hear the scratch of a match as it flares, the warden's long breath as he inhales. As he leans against the desk, watching me, I feel like I'm being hunted, as if predators are circling like a pack of hyenas moving in for the kill. He takes another deep drag, exhaling a blue stream of smoke that wafts across the room, and nods towards me, issuing a terse instruction. Immediately, the guards close in, pushing me into the centre of the room while he relaxes against the desk, feet crossed at the ankles, ready for the evening's entertainment.

There is no documentation and no protocol. There are no witnesses and no rules. I am at the guards' mercy as they order me in Spanish to strip. Knowing that this is just another attempt to humiliate, degrade and exert their power over me doesn't make it any easier to comply. I can feel rage boiling just beneath the surface. I need to harness it and use it to take control of my emotions, channelling it into a means of survival. Reacting to these people will just fuel their enthusiasm for the game. I am the prey cornered by a gang of feral beasts whose only pleasure will be toying with me, hoping to provoke a reaction so that they can pounce, resorting to brute force if necessary. Do not reward them. Just breathe. Don't think. This is just a game to them. Something to pass the time. Entertainment. The anticipated humiliation fuels my anger, but as much as I don't want to submit to them, I need to push these thoughts aside and just do as I am told. It's the only way it will end. It's the only way I will get through this.

Slowly, I take off my shoes and place them neatly side by side on the floor. The guard moves in and kicks them away. They laugh. Don't react. I reach up and slowly unbutton my shirt. I become detached as I go through the motions, loosening the last button and shrugging it off, placing it carefully over the back of a chair. The other guard, not to be outdone by his comrade, reaches over and picks it up, runs his fingers over the seams, the buttons. Looking for contraband? No. Watching for a reaction, he holds it up in front of his face, sniffs, and drops it on the floor. He looks around at the others, as if seeking applause. This is a game in which they're well versed: degradation, humiliation, appreciative nodding, chuckling with approval at their technique, enjoying the sport.

Don't react. Turn down the sound, drown out the voice inside your head clamouring for vengeance. Separate the actions from the emotions. There is no shame, there is no guilt. I have done nothing wrong. I take off my jeans, drop them on the floor, and, finally, remove my boxers.

I stand naked before them. Let's get this over with, I think. I know that my God is by my side. I will get through this. I await only His judgement. The guards' mocking laughter pushes me to my limits and I close my eyes, breathing out. Stay calm.

I feel the cold touch of his baton on my torso and open my eyes again. The guard motions for me to raise my arms above my head. I comply. He moves closer and tells me to open my mouth. I comply. I shudder with revulsion as he peers into it, almost gagging as the stench of stale sweat coils around me. He runs his fingers through my hair. There's not much there in which to hide anything, and he knows it. This is not about contraband; it's about power and control. His touch makes my skin crawl. He turns my head, pokes his fingers into my ears, and then abruptly steps back and tells me to turn and face the door. My back is now to them, their scornful laughter grating inside my head.

'Lift your foot,' he commands. 'Now the other one.'

I sense movement behind me. He taps me on the shoulder.

'Turn around.'

I turn to face them and look at the warden. He's enjoying the show. Don't react, I think.

The guard nudges my arm and looks pointedly at my groin. I know the drill. Slowly, I reach down and lift my penis and scrotum. The inevitable laughter rings out; perhaps it's the most fun they've had this week. Don't react. Don't make eye contact. Pray. I have to get through this. Don't imagine crossing the room, curling your hands around his neck, squeezing with every ounce of your being…

The guard nudges me: turn around, bend over, spread your cheeks, turn around, squat and cough. He tells me to get dressed, laughing as I scramble to pick up my clothes and quickly pull them on. It's over. I've survived.

I know that they probably do this with all the prisoners, but as I am clearly not supposed to be here, it seems to make it even more satisfying for them. I give silent thanks to God for helping me to get through this without reacting or retaliating.

Mission accomplished, it seems that they have run out of ideas as their jibes and mocking laughter ebb away and they turn to the warden expectantly, awaiting instructions. He nods curtly, satisfied. 'Open the gate,' he says in Spanish, flicking his cigarette on the floor and crushing it with his boot.

20

Bangkok

```
Black Beach Prison, Malabo
18 December 2013
```

The guards grab me roughly by each arm, hustling me towards the main entrance. The warden watches, his expression dark, immutable, distancing himself from the events taking place. My mind shuts down. The only way I am going to face what lies ahead is not to process it. Switch off. Shut down. Stop thinking.

Mechanically, I lift one foot after the other, a puppet controlled by the men at my side. Perspiration drips off me, pooling in the creases of my neck, snaking down my back, exacerbating the hot stickiness of my skin. My loathing for those who conspired to put me here intensifies with each step. The sickly odour of stale urine and rancid sweat mixes with the stench of sewage and rotting garbage hanging over us and I gag, choking down my revulsion.

As we approach the prison, the seething mass of inmates swarms towards the gate like a pack of starved animals, baying for blood, pounding the bars in a frenzy of excitement, shouting, threatening, taunting me. Again I pray, pleading with God to hold me in check, because reacting will only fuel the fire. I know they want to intimidate me, goad me, push me over the edge. The guards yell at them to step back and then open the gate and shove me in. The gate clangs shut behind me, the sound reverberating against the walls, before being drowned out by the roar of the advancing crowd.

Fresh meat! Black Friday special!

Madness descends and I'm swallowed up by the surge of bodies pushing me further into the building until suddenly it's as if I've been spirited outside my body and realise that God has taken control, enveloping me in a protective shroud. It's as if I'm watching from above.

Everyone wants a piece of me, grabbing, pushing, shoving, a crush of bodies against mine. They search my pockets, tear at my clothes, groping, touching everything, even my manhood. I recoil in horror, but I must not retaliate – if I do, I won't survive. I bring my arms up to protect myself, pushing away the hands touching me, tearing at me, squeezing my crotch. Keeping my head down, I pry their fingers away, shoving back with every ounce of my being, muscles taut, fear and rage rising. I must trust that God is protecting me; my life is in His hands; he *will* protect me! Knowing this helps me resist the urge to fight back. Now is not the time to unleash my rage against the injustice of where I am and why.

I have to do what it takes to survive. This is a pivotal moment in my life. I don't understand how I have ended up here, where the scourge of humanity has been abandoned to rot in an overcrowded space of misery and suffering. All I know is that there was Daniel before, and there is Daniel now. I am no longer the same man.

I am not dying here, I tell myself. Not like this. Not today. This is not my time. I shouldn't be here; this shouldn't be happening to me. I'm lost in a chaotic world where survival is everything, there is no sense of reality, or of time, just the persistent crush of bodies, twisting, writhing, pulling, tugging. Abruptly, I sense a change, feeling an intense, oppressive presence as the others move aside, growing quieter, some slinking away. Bewildered, I peer into the gloom and see something moving in the shadows: a man emerges from the darkness, bearing down on me.

His shirtless body is a mountain of muscle covered in scars, and as a sliver of light falls across his face, I look into his soulless eyes, as dark as the depths of hell. Instinct tells me to run for my life, but there is nowhere to run to, no escape. I am powerless as he advances towards me, spurred on by an excited crowd intoxicated by the prospect of a bloodbath. I feel a primal instinct, something deep and powerful taking hold inside me, a pervasive fear that I am about to encounter a dark force that I could never have imagined, even in my worst nightmares. I stand alone before him.

He moves in for the kill, searching for a weakness, an entry point. I am just an ordinary man, a husband, a father, I think as I brace myself in readiness to fight for my life. I know that I cannot show any fear. I know that with this man, I *must* fight back. I must show him that I am not weak or afraid. In the wild, the hungry pack preys on the weak and vulnerable. I am vulnerable, but I am not weak. I will not give up. My weapon is my faith. God is my shield. He will protect me. I refuse to believe that I will die here tonight. I am ready to release the rage inside me. The well is deep, and I have too much to live for.

A crazed intensity and hatred emanate from the man bearing down on me, and yet I feel a sense of control, a reminder that God is my sword and my salvation. I will fight with every ounce of my being to save myself. I trust in the divine protection of my God, that He will shield me from this deranged killer with murder on his mind.

'Bangkok, stop!'

A voice booms down the passage and a tall man emerges, pushing his way through the crowd towards us. He is lanky and sinewy and the two are matched in their unbridled hostility towards one another. In an instant, he moves between us and lunges at my attacker, grabbing his arms and shoving him aside. It's clear that the newcomer has confronted the man called Bangkok before. The tension between them is palpable. Is this man protecting me, or does he want me for himself? I watch incredulously as, after a moment, my attacker mutters in disgust and sullenly moves away, disappearing into the gloomy interior of the prison.

I am bewildered, unsure what dangers I will have to face next. I'm not about to become anyone's prison bitch, so I prepare to defend myself from the newcomer, but he turns, smiling, and beckons me to follow him as he moves away along the grimy wall, pushing the curious bystanders aside. I weigh up my odds for a second, and then decide to take my chances.

We elbow our way into the depths of the prison. I pray for the strength to face whatever comes next, but to my surprise, as we break free of the crush of the crowd, he stops and turns, brandishing a bottle of mineral water.

'Welcome to Black Bitch,' he says with a wry smile that makes me wonder what he did to end up in this place. 'My name is Ugochuku,' he adds. 'Don't worry about Bangkok for now. He is lazy; he doesn't like to have to work too hard for his reward. You must be sure to remember that.'

I've had nothing to eat or drink since early this morning and my throat is parched. I open the bottle of water, gulping it down gratefully. It's gone in seconds. I nod my thanks, not trusting myself to speak as the adrenaline drains away and the horror subsides. My body shakes as the tension dissipates. I can do nothing to stop the tremors and just try to catch my breath. Now is not the time to try to make sense of what just happened. Even though I feel dazed and confused, my energy and spirit have been strengthened by Ugochuku's simple act of kindness and generosity. God's power is infinite, and it has somehow found its way into this dark corner of the world. Somehow, a Nigerian convict has been sent to be my guardian angel.

As we make our way deeper into the hell that is now my home, Ugo tells me that I always need to be on guard against Bangkok. 'He is *loco*,' he says, adding that Bangkok hates Europeans. He says that he should have been put to death long ago and is only here because he is connected to someone high up. Bangkok murdered at least three people before being sent here. He was convicted of murder on the outside and then killed someone at the prison he was initially sent to, so they moved him to another prison, but he killed someone there too. They didn't know what else to do with him, so he ended up here, in Black Beach, to rot or end up murdered.

Ugo explains that Bangkok is like a wild animal caged in a zoo: you can never let your guard down around him, he is always on the lookout for weakness and can snap at any moment. He tells me never to trust him if I want to stay alive. Bangkok has a demon inside him, he says. Most days he appears normal, but in a split second a switch flips and he is out of control. Everyone fears him, even the guards. It doesn't do much for my sense of security knowing that I am already on this madman's radar and there is not another white man in sight. It's hard to blend in when your skin is like a spotlight shining on you.

The oppressive heat and humidity are punishing, and it's impossible to escape the crowd. They follow us from a distance, shouting questions, wanting to know why I am here. Ugo says that the last time white men were here was a few years back when Simon Mann and a team of South African mercenaries were sent here for attempting to overthrow the Equatorial Guinean government. They were tough, savage men who used fear and aggression to intimidate the other inmates, so although I am 'fresh meat', the prisoners are uncertain how dangerous I might be.

It's as noisy and dark as an engine room on a cargo ship as we weave our way through the prison, stepping over sleeping inmates who lie curled up on thin foam mattresses scattered around the floor, oblivious to the excitement of my arrival or perhaps just immune to it. The putrid scent of decaying sewage mingles with the smell of rotting meat cooking on open griddles, and I struggle to control the urge to retch. The floor is slippery and sticky, and I don't want to think about what we are stepping in. A thick layer of slime coats the mould-stained walls and there is very little light, perhaps a small mercy as it cloaks the squalor in a murky gloom, blurring the harsh reality of my new surroundings. A thick cloud of smoke trapped in the enclosed space makes it difficult to breathe, and the acrid fumes of kerosene stoves adds to the overpowering stench.

Prisoners appear from every corner to watch us. Some inmates sit staring into oblivion. I'm not sure if they're sick or high or have just given up. I have entered a savage universe of desperation and anguish. It's hard to process what I am seeing. Blood-spattered men in handcuffs lie comatose in the grime where they've been dumped after being beaten and tortured, their own shit, blood and vomit pooled around them. We step over them. It's hard to digest the fact that these are all living, breathing human beings.

The noise is as intense as on a Friday night at the local shebeen. The rhythms of African music compete with the repetitive electric beats of gangsta rap pounding through the building, echoing and bouncing off the walls, creating a jarring, discordant backdrop to the clamour of too many voices all wanting to be heard in a tightly packed space.

We pass laughing groups of men huddled together around cooking fires; they seem totally at home and I get the feeling that maybe they even enjoy being here. Big fish in a small pond. The smell is getting to me, decaying, rotting. I can't escape it. I feel like I am suffocating. Each breath is like inhaling toxic fumes. I struggle not to puke on the people I am stepping over.

I follow Ugo in blind faith. I don't know where he is taking me, but he is clearly respected in the prison and we have drawn quite a crowd, which he keeps back with a word or a look. With him as my escort, there seems to be less chance that the others will attack me.

As we venture deeper into the bowels of this grim and forbidding place, we make our way through an open rectangular space that extends to the top of the whole structure. Metal stairs lead from the ground floor upwards to a row of cells, with a walkway connecting to another row on the opposite side. A rusted mesh fence has been stretched across the void above us, probably put there to prevent people from jumping or being thrown off, but it has the unexpected benefit of extending the floor space by providing valuable real estate on which prisoners have erected makeshift sleeping nests. I am overwhelmed by the sheer number of people squeezed into a relatively small space.

It feels like I have been thrown onto a post-apocalyptic, *Mad Max*–style film set, complete with all the sounds, smells and feelings associated with a dystopian movie depicting a desperate and savage underworld. Somehow, I have landed the starring role, one I certainly don't want or deserve. I have collected quite an entourage, and it seems that many of the inmates are surprised and amused by the novelty of a white man in the prison; Africa's colonial past has ensured that the boundaries between black and white are still very much established, even here. For a white man to end up in Black Beach, he must have done something really, really bad...

21

The Bench

```
Black Beach Prison, Malabo
18 December 2013
```

Ugo looks everywhere for the Jefe de Castel, an inmate appointed by the guards to oversee the prison from inside and the person responsible for everything that goes on beyond the gate. All new inmates are brought to him, as the guards don't enter during the night, and he reports back to them on anything that happens.

I've already learnt a lot from Ugo, who has pointed out which groups to avoid. Outside, I'd heard rumours about Black Beach, but they pale in comparison to witnessing it first-hand. Murderers, drug dealers, addicts and the mentally challenged are all locked up in one confined space together with thieves, gangsters and the depraved like Bangkok. Thrown into this mix are innocent people who perhaps criticised the wrong person, voiced an unwanted opinion or cannot afford to pay a bribe, who have been sent to Black Beach until their families can raise the money required to secure their release. Even political prisoners, policemen and soldiers who have fallen foul of someone in power are incarcerated here. It's a powder keg, a volatile mix guaranteed to explode with regularity, and I can't begin to imagine the hell endured by the women and children I've spotted lurking behind the pillars.

According to Ugo, the Jefe de Castel will issue me with a mattress and I'll have to find a place to bed down for the night. He warns me that the mattress is just a thin piece of foam, probably filthy, unless I can pay for something better. And as there is no open space, I'll need to find a spot where someone allows me to 'move in'. Apparently, there are daily fights for space and privacy. Ugo points to the wire mesh covering the open expanse between the ground floor and first level of the jail, telling me that most new guys end up sleeping on this rusty 'net'. He also warns me that pickpockets will try to take advantage of me by pretending to be asleep close by. They do this to newcomers especially, using razors to cut through your clothing, and they will steal anything, even if you think it has no value. These are desperate, starving men and boys.

Two-man cells are located on the second level, and that's where most political prisoners and the sentenced are held, but if you have money or influence you can buy yourself an upstairs room. Some of them even have satellite television, a fridge or deep freeze, and some personal items are allowed. But everything comes at a price, as they have to pay for protection at all times and that's not cheap. It seems that even in Black Beach there is a divide between the 'one per cent' and the rest.

Finally, we find the Jefe, but he dismisses us with a wave of his hand, saying he's not interested in giving me a mattress and it's not his responsibility to find a place to put one unless I pay him. Obviously, I don't have any money. Ugo realises there's nothing to be gained from debating the point and we walk away. I see now why Ugo commands such respect in the prison: his confidence ensures that nothing bothers him. He shrugs, saying we'll make another plan, and we head off to the upper section of the prison where I'm introduced to a friend, Old Man Luis, who has a bench outside his cell.

Nobody dares to sit on this bench as Old Man Luis is not known for his hospitality or good nature. He was sent here for a double murder many years back and is the longest-serving prisoner in Black Beach, and he will be here until the end. There is no chance for him to experience life outside these walls again; his days are numbered, as Equatorial Guinea has the death penalty. Every time those with death sentences hear that a date has been set for executions, they become extremely distressed. Old Man Luis has made himself as comfortable as possible under the circumstances and doesn't feel the need to tolerate the companionship of others, but tonight he is feeling mellow and allows me to sit on his bench while Ugo disappears elsewhere.

While I savour the 'privilege' of sitting on a double murderer's bench, I finally have a moment to catch my breath and take everything in. I'm not ready to process all I've been through and find it inconceivable that just this morning I'd been about to board a plane that was to take me home to my family. I am deeply shaken and traumatised by the events that followed, but I know that thinking about what I've been through and where I should be will just drag me down, and I'm not sure if I'll be able to make my way out of the abyss where those thoughts lead. Instead, I focus on the here and now.

Survival means adapting and processing everything moment by moment. It's hard to make sense of the bewildering images emerging from the murky depths of this place, as most of the lightbulbs are either broken or missing. The noise is intense and the overcrowding unimaginable, people tightly packed into every inch of available space screaming at one another, angry outbursts in every direction. I know that these smells and sights will be burned into my mind forever. I try to hold my breath for as long as possible, but the urge to throw up is ever present.

I'm still wearing my long-sleeved shirt and it sticks to my back, soaked in sweat and grime. I wipe away the salty trickle of perspiration dripping off my head, unaware that the privilege of sitting on Old Man Luis's bench is not something to be taken for granted. In here, having a chair is taken very seriously and people go to great lengths to protect these precious items. I will discover later that many battles start over someone attempting to sit on another person's seat.

I notice a man sidling up to me and am instantly on the alert. Can anyone be trusted in this place? He looks fairly amiable, but who can tell – after all, I am sitting on a bench outside the cell of a dangerous murderer in one of the worst prisons in the world. I wonder what the approaching man has done to find himself here and what he wants from me.

He introduces himself as Amadou, a brother from Mali and one of the few devout Muslims in this predominantly Christian country. For some reason, Old Man Luis tolerates his presence, and we sit in almost companionable silence as we watch the wheeling and dealing of a group of young thugs who have laid claim to a corner close to where we are sitting and seem totally at home in this hellhole. What must their lives have been like on the outside that they are content here? They're youngsters, about the same age as my kids, and Amadou tells me that they are part of one of the most violent gangs in the prison. Having grown up rough, orphaned on the streets of Malabo, they have adapted to life behind bars, taking care of themselves and one another by selling weed. It is their sole motivation, their business, their livelihood and their life. They have no fear or respect for the guards, or anyone else. Old Man Luis tells me that when they have money, they smoke their own product and use the money to buy alcohol, a close second on their list of essentials. Food is the last of their priorities. Once the money runs out, they steal from others, and when all else fails even from each other. Thankfully, they don't seem that interested in me.

Ugo returns and tells me to follow him, and we make our way to the other side of the jail. It's even darker here and I can hear singing and clapping coming from one of the cells. It appears that this is where we're headed, and I experience a moment of doubt. I know that many locals dabble in voodoo and black magic and that cannibalism is still practised on the island. I don't want to end up on the menu.

The cell door is closed, but Ugo pushes it open and ushers me inside. As I enter the cramped space, roughly five by five metres with six double bunks along the walls, I encounter a sight that I never would have believed possible: about thirty inmates are crammed into the room, standing together forming a tight circle, their heads bowed in prayer below a roughly hewn wooden cross tacked to the wall. They look up and then rush to surround me, greeting me with hugs, handshakes and an overwhelming sense of love and kinship. God has led me through the darkness into the warm embrace of my new family.

I feel some of the tension leave my body – I am going to be okay. A solemn young man introduces himself as Pastor Fernando, taking my hand in a firm grip and welcoming me in Pichi. I take an instant liking to him as he places his hand on my shoulder and guides me to a spot beneath the cross. We join hands with the others and bow our heads in prayer, and I no longer feel so alone. Weak with exhaustion after the shock of what I've been through, finding this small haven, this holy refuge away from the stinking decay and depravity of this place, brings me close to tears. I'm overwhelmed by the kindness radiating from these people. Who knew that the power of God could reach so deep inside these walls?

Later, after the congregation leaves, Pastor Fernando and Ugo sit with me. Knowing that these men have befriended me gives me faith that I will get through this until the embassy finds out where I am and I am released. I can see that Ugo is something of a leader and well respected; they tell me that in the prison he is considered an elder, having survived here for a long time. Apparently, he was arrested after being found with counterfeit money and was accused of dealing in it. Having worked in Malabo for many years, I am aware that there is a huge supply of counterfeit currency in circulation, but because Ugo is Nigerian, he was given a hefty sentence and has already been here for almost eight years. It seems that everyone here has a story of injustice to tell.

Ugo is the unofficial leader of the Christian group, but because he is a foreigner, Pastor Fernando, who is from Malabo, is the officially recognised head of the 'church'. His sincerity is endearing, and I feel an almost fatherly instinct towards this earnest young man as he tells me about his life on the streets of Malabo where he had no one to teach him right from wrong and did whatever it took to survive. He says that he committed every sin possible, with no consideration for the consequences. Life on the streets was a game of survival, and if you stopped to think about what you were doing, you were dead.

When he landed in jail, he finally realised that he had a choice. If he wanted to respect himself, he had to change his ways, so he abandoned his 'friends' and turned to God. God became his salvation, serving God brought meaning to his life, and when he found peace and forgiveness within himself, he knew that he could help to change others' lives. He believes that his purpose is to lift others up, to turn them away from sin and walk with them along the path to righteousness. His message is simple: we cannot be united with God unless we freely choose this path, and to sin against our neighbours is to sin against God. We must love and respect ourselves in order to find God and escape eternal damnation.

I am moved by his simple mantra and how he has found meaning and purpose in this place, how he has accepted his situation and has absolute, unwavering faith in God's mercy. Without any formal training, just pure determination, he has turned his life around, using his own story to inspire others to seek absolution and salvation.

He goes to a corner of the room where there is a makeshift cabinet stacked with a small pile of books. A few items of clothing, eating utensils and what appears to be bed linen are neatly placed on the shelves. I am impressed by how relatively clean everything is, in stark comparison to the chaos and filth just outside the door, and I remark on it. He tells me simply that having a clean space honours God and is the first step to cleansing the spirit and being set free from evil thoughts and actions.

He takes a book from the shelf and passes it to me. I turn it over in my hands; it's a hardcover Gideon Bible. I am filled with emotion, almost brought to tears as I run my hands over the worn burgundy cover, feeling the deep impression of the flame symbol synonymous with the Gideons organisation etched into the cover. I flick through the dog-eared pages. It's the English version, circa 1956, with both the Old and New Testaments and all the Proverbs and Psalms. I find it almost incomprehensible that because an anonymous guy somewhere in the middle of the USA donated a dollar towards the printing and distribution of this holy book, it managed to make its way here, shining a light in a very dark place in Africa.

This Bible has been used and abused, and yet somehow survived the ravages of time and circumstance, passing through many rough hands searching for solace. Some pages are missing, and I realise that they're likely just the right size for rolling a joint. A short verse catches my attention. Romans 12:12. It's one of my favourites:

> *Rejoice in our confident hope.*
> *Be patient in trouble,*
> *And keep on praying.*

I must not lose faith. Meeting Pastor Fernando and reading these words reminds me that sometimes worshipping God means giving up on chasing what we want from life and learning to use our spiritual gifts for a higher purpose. I must not lose sight of a future worth celebrating, and I must use the power of prayer to bring me through the struggles that lie ahead. God is at my side. This is not the end.

22

The Longest Night
Black Beach Prison, Malabo
18 December 2013

Members of the church group have given me clothing and even food, not that I have any appetite, but the greatest gift is their companionship. The idea that I'm not alone and not everyone is an enemy fortifies me. Most are economic migrants from neighbouring African countries who left harsh living conditions and limited job opportunities back home to seek their fortunes here in the oil industry. As a key producer of crude oil and gas, Equatorial Guinea has attracted global investment, providing much-needed employment in the region. I've spent some time working on the oil rigs off the coasts of São Tomé and Bioko, so I quickly form a bond with some guys from Cameroon and Nigeria who speak English. It's a huge relief when they shed more light on how things work here.

While we pass the time as if we're not locked up, the pressure mounting in my groin is persistent – I need to pee. I haven't mustered the courage to leave the safety of the group, and besides, the smell escaping from the toilet block turns my stomach. According to my new mates, there are clean, functioning private toilets, but you have to pay to join a group controlling access to them, so for now that's out of my reach and I have no choice but to head for the communal facilities.

It looks like the remains of a bomb site. I hold my breath, gagging as I wade through the stinking swamp of urine and faeces. The crumbling walls are mottled green and the tiles, basins and toilets are cracked, broken or missing. I don't want to add to the nauseating stew of excrement pooling around my feet and the horror of the situation quickly becomes overwhelming. I'm forced to use the nearest broken toilet, vomiting up what little there is inside me, retching until I feel like my gut is turned inside out. Slimy muck clings to my jeans, coating them with a thick, soupy slime.

A man walks in, stops short just inside the entrance, faces the closest wall and urinates. I hurry out, making sure not to touch the walls now that I have a pretty good idea of the nature of the mottled smears. I don't deserve this!

A spark of anger ignites inside me as I make my way out, and I tuck the sense of hopelessness into a dark corner of my mind where it'll be difficult to find and harness my outrage at my situation. I need to keep my wits about me if I want to get out of here alive, and I have to focus on getting out of here.

Now the Jefe de Castel turns up, clutching a disgustingly dirty, thin old mattress. I'm appalled and vow that no part of my body will touch it. He has obviously hunted long and hard to find me the worst mattress possible so that I'll be forced to buy a better one from him as soon as I get some money. But despite my initial misgivings, I quickly realise that even this mite-infested artefact is preferable to sleeping on the filthy, slimy floor. And I grudgingly admire his entrepreneurial spirit as he asks me if I'd like to buy some 'white gold', which I interpret to be toilet paper. I take the mattress from him and someone from the church group gives me a bed sheet, reasonably clean considering where we are. Although I am eternally grateful, I can't help thinking how I've gone from sleeping in style beneath the softest percale linen on a luxurious king-size bed at the Hilton to this, all compliments of one man: Angabi.

But these minor details are irrelevant against the backdrop of the living nightmare playing out in front of me. It has my full attention as Ugo helps me find a spot against a pillar and I fold the sheet on top of the filthy mattress, making sure it doesn't drape over the edges and touch the floor or my feet, which are still covered in muck from the toilets. I sit with my back up against the pillar, grateful that I only need to watch for predators from three directions.

Most prisoners have bedframes, and I make a mental note to get my hands on one as I sit down on the mattress. I'm grateful for my Levi's jeans which are comfortable and offer some protection from the filth surrounding me. I'm worn out and emotionally drained; I've lost track of time in a nightmare that never ends, but sleep is the furthest thing from my mind. How can I sleep knowing that I'm being watched all the time? I feel like a live goat thrown into a crocodile-infested swamp. It's not a question of if they are going to eat me, but when …

I hang on to the Bible, my only possession, a link to God and a source of strength and hope. The air is thick and clammy and there is no escaping the relentless heat, even though it's the early hours of the morning. I feel like I'm slowly suffocating, every breath a challenge. My nearest neighbours are all murderers, but they don't seem to mind my presence here. Ugo says they'll offer me the best protection against the likes of Bangkok and the teenage gang members who prey on other inmates for sport. I gaze around the room, realising that when I do eventually fall asleep, I won't suffer any nightmares as I am living one right now.

Blocking it all out is not an option. I'm forced to watch one of the men sexually assault a female inmate on the pallet bed not too far from me. It's clear that she has been forced to do this before and has no choice but to comply. I struggle to grasp the daily horror that female inmates must endure to survive behind these walls. My shock and revulsion compete with my instinct to intervene, but one of the murderers resting beside me touches my arm and shakes his head, warning me not to get involved if I want to live.

No matter which direction I turn, the onslaught is relentless. A man lying nearby looks close to death, his skin grey, his body shaking uncontrollably. I have no idea what's wrong with him. What if it's contagious? The last thing I need is to get sick in this place. A mosquito buzzes around my head and I'm reminded that the threat of malaria is ever-present. I swat it away, but it dodges my hand and quickly resumes its attack.

A loud argument erupts somewhere out of sight, something about Barcelona not getting a penalty against Real Madrid. Across from me, a fight breaks out over a board game while someone sits stirring a pot of rice over a paraffin stove. A little way away, I can hear the group of teens I encountered earlier laughing loudly, full of self-importance and adolescent bravado. Just beyond them is a guy sitting alone, totally indifferent to everything going on around him. A man walks towards the bathroom area with a bucket of water to wash himself, pauses at the entrance, disgusted by what he sees inside, shakes his head and makes his way behind the wall. I understand his reluctance to go in there. Another man walks past with headphones on; I can hear the throb of the music, turned up to the max, blasting into his ears, drowning everything out.

There is no personal space anywhere, but no one seems to care. Opposite me, a young man is trying to read the Bible by torchlight, his concentration intense, as if he is physically feeding his hungry soul. I run my hands over the cover of my own Bible. There's not enough light to read by, but I'm grateful to have it and bow my head to pray, keeping my eyes open, feeling once again like Daniel thrown in among the lions at the whim of a politician. I started the day in high spirits and ended it in the depths of hell. I don't know when I finally fall asleep, but total exhaustion eventually overcomes me.

23

A Place to Call Home

Black Beach Prison, Malabo
19 December 2013

It's morning, and after little to no sleep and the trauma of the night's events still weighing heavily on my mind, I am nudged by the persistent prodding of a boot. The Jefe de Castel has ordered his minions to come and find me, and I am given the gruesome task of assisting the others as they gather up the sick and dying. We carry them outside, dumping them in the baking sun at the prison entrance to wait for an ambulance to arrive. Even if they receive urgent medical attention, I think it will take a miracle to see them pull through.

During the daylight hours, the prison is marginally more bearable, like a filthy, scaled-down imitation of a busy African village. Loud music comes from all directions, a discordant background hum that sometimes obliterates the sounds you don't want to hear. Layered over the monotonous drumbeats and tinny disco are the voices of the teenagers, who all seem to be aspiring rappers. Apparently talent is not a prerequisite. In the background is the incessant shouting and dialogue of a few hundred people speaking different languages.

Some time later, I walk past the entrance; shocked to discover that the ambulance still hasn't turned up, and judging by the waxen expressions and the grey discolouration of some of the stiff, swelling bodies in the sun, rigor mortis has set in. Nobody seems to care, certainly not the guards, and I am concerned with keeping myself alive and don't have time to mourn the passing of these strangers who are already at death's door. I'm sure that most think the dead are probably better off...

Time passes in a blur. Somehow, I manage to get through another day and night drinking only water, eating nothing, living in the perpetual twilight of the prison. The lack of food leaves a hollow ache in my stomach and danger is ever-present. If I want to stay alive, I must not fall asleep. I need to be vigilant and alert at all times, which is not helped by the constant onslaught on my senses and the persistent drone of mosquitoes eating away at my sanity. Cockroaches, mice and other vermin scuttle in the dark, sometimes running over me. I feel them biting my toes and wake from half-sleep in a cold sweat, shaking them off.

Sometimes it's hard to distinguish these moments from reality, and with the relentless, smothering heat and humidity, it is almost impossible to get any rest at all. It seems that criminals prefer to live in the obscurity of the shadows and the prison officials have given up replacing the lights, as they're quickly stolen or broken by the inmates. If you want a light, you need to buy your own bulb and look after it.

Guilty thoughts rise with the moon. Nightmares are common, inmates screaming as they face imaginary beasts, and some spend the night pacing, pacing, pacing, doing their best to keep the demons at bay, staying awake at all costs. The wicked and depraved skulk in the shadows, pilfering whatever they can get their hands on – everything is a commodity and has value, either as a potential weapon or as something to eat or sell. Other than that, preying on the weak, raping and abusing the women and children, takes up much of their time. It's hard to look the other way, but I am powerless to stop any of it, barely able to keep myself alive. Lights out is at 11 p.m. and there is supposed to be silence after that, but things usually only quieten down in the lonely hours before dawn, if we're lucky. A few prisoners live their lives in a reverse cycle, rising as the sun sets and living like nocturnal creatures on a permanent nightshift.

Even after having been here for a couple of days, I find it impossible to ignore the disgusting smell of this place, and what with the heat and humidity, broken toilets overflowing with urine and faeces, smoke from the cooking fires, sweat, weed and trash, not to mention the stench of over four hundred sweaty, unwashed bodies crammed into a space smaller than a soccer field, I spend a lot of the time gagging, puking and feeling like I'm slowly suffocating. It's as if I'm inhaling a toxic gas that will ultimately kill me, if one of the inmates doesn't get me first.

For those living in the cells, life is not as perilous. They can avoid most of the hazards that plague the general population as the cells can be locked from the inside. However, they're reserved for the really dangerous criminals, who spend their first month confined inside them. Political prisoners are also assigned cells and must remain there for the duration of their sentence, except when the Red Cross comes to visit, and the cell is opened in an attempt to demonstrate that these prisoners are afforded the same 'rights and privileges' as the rest of us. The prisoners are informed well in advance that they need to behave while the Red Cross is visiting and the consequences of not heeding this warning are dire, so everyone plays along and is on their best behaviour. It's hard enough living here without drawing the unwanted attention of the guards.

On the upper floor, each cell has an 'en-suite' toilet and shower, and a double bunk. These cells were designed to accommodate one prisoner, but they all contain at least two inmates, with some housing four occupants. None of the showers or toilets work and there's no running water; prisoners have to collect water from outside during the day and wash with a bucket. However, if you have influence, you can buy a cell for yourself, and get a TV, a fridge, a fan, a woman ... All the comforts of home.

Amadou, the Malian brother who I met on my first night here, is facing a death sentence and has a cell upstairs that he shares with another guy who is also waiting for that day ... He has an extension cable that he uses to boil his kettle for tea and to run his barbershop business. There are no power outlets in the cells, but the inmates often make illegal connections to the light fitting in the ceiling or directly via the passage lights. But these solutions are unreliable, as the guards regularly rip out the wires, or someone connects and trips the entire prison's electrical system and we end up without power for a few days until it's repaired.

Outside the cells is a passageway that reminds me of the underside of a bridge on the wrong side of town where delinquents, the homeless and society's discarded and unwanted congregate. Although it is open to everyone, certain areas are staked out and draped with plastic or old sheets, creating little tent-like structures where people have a certain degree of privacy and real estate. It's here that I decide to eventually set up my own camp.

I've quickly learnt that to survive you need allies. As the only *blanco*, I'm something of a novelty, which I use to my advantage, especially as there is no shortage of applicants for the job of being my friend. Most are looking for ways to extort money; this is prison after all, and I represent an opportunity as someone to exploit. In the past, during the heyday of colonial Africa, the white man was perceived as wealthy, and this way of thinking has lingered long after the oppressors left, so it's not surprising that some of the inmates just want to see what they can get out of me. They find it hard to believe that I have nothing to offer them and return time and again to make sure that my situation hasn't changed since their last visit, ever hopeful of making a deal.

I understand their desperation. The odds are stacked against you if you don't form alliances with people willing to help you; if you get sick in here, you'll probably die without someone to take care of you. It's not like I need a reminder of how fragile my mortality is in this place.

Networking is key to survival. The guys who befriend me show me the ropes, advising me about who, and which areas, to avoid, and they're willing to share their limited resources with me until I can get help from outside. Ugo, despite being recognised as a leader, is not immune to the punishments meted out by the guards, and Pastor Fernando readily admits that he went down the wrong path that ultimately led him here, but, having paid the price in time and suffering, he has chosen to change the course of his life and help others to change their lives too. People like them are rare in this hostile place. And then, of course, there are the innocent, people like me, who are here because they have powerful enemies. Most, apart from the political prisoners, have accepted their fate and do what's necessary to survive until they can get the hell out of here. This place will break you, physically and psychologically. The biggest challenge is staying mentally strong. My determination not to let Angabi get the better of me strengthens my resolve.

In my short time here, I've seen tough guys walk in with no fear, full of bluster, only to sit in a heap a few days later when they've given up. I'm sure that's why weed use is prevalent, ignored by the guards as it helps dull the senses, making the inmates more manageable. Alcohol is also plentiful, if you have money, but it creates havoc in the prison. I've never been much of a drinker and don't smoke or take drugs, so these options don't even occur to me. My needs are simple: survive until I can get out of here.

It's tough adjusting to living in the perpetual chaos of this place, so even though it's scorching hot outside, I find myself spending more time on the Esplanada, a concrete platform where prisoners congregate to escape the insidious decay of the dark hovel where we spend our nights.

Old Man Luis, who shared his bench with me on that first night and has been confined to Black Beach for decades, at some point constructed a makeshift corrugated-iron shack on the Esplanada that provides shelter from the persistent heat and torrential downpours that occur regularly during the rainy season, and an escape from the 50° C oven inside the boarding block. The prisoners refer to the block as 'Djibloho' or 'the coffin', a reference to the name of a Russian-built research vessel used for geological surveys that is often seen en route to its anchorage at Luba to the south of the island. Its similarity to Black Beach is obvious: a rusted, decaying two-storey structure with a single access point through massive iron double doors. Although there by choice, I think the men on the ship must experience a hell similar to ours.

Old Man Luis's shelter is a popular gathering spot for the older, hardened criminals, who play draughts and tell stories while they watch the younger, more energetic prisoners burn off excess energy playing soccer. Black Beach will be Old Man Luis's home until he dies, whether from natural causes or by firing squad is anyone's guess, and I think the futility of his life and how it's likely to end weighs heavily on his mind, leaving him bitter and acrimonious. Nevertheless, I visit his shack frequently. Stomaching the smells of my new surroundings is easier out here in the open on the Esplanada among the traders, their tables littered with wares, the banter of my new friends providing a distraction and making it easier to come to terms with life here. Despite their crimes, which range from rape and murder to cannibalism, the more time I spend sitting with these men beneath this ramshackle shelter, hiding from the sun, the more I realise that you have to find a way to cling to the essence of being human in here. I hold on to the hope that this is just temporary and that there is a different ending for me than what Old Man Luis has to contemplate.

'Blanco!'

I look up, realising I am being called. It hasn't taken long for me to adjust to my new prison name.

'Blanco, abogado visita.'

A young boy is making his way through the crowd towards me. Is what he's saying true? I have a visitor? As the boy nears, he gestures, telling me to hurry up. He's been sent by the guards and feels very self-important. I do have a visitor! I jump up and rush after the boy, wondering, wishing, hoping … Am I going to be released?

I can see a man standing near the fence, but I don't recognise him until we get closer, and when we do, my heart sinks. His arrogant smirk is obvious, even from a distance, his cheap suit and shoes displaying the calibre of man he is – a social climber and my sworn enemy. It's Angabi's gofer, Mariano, who I last saw at the Palacio de Justicia on the morning the judge ordered my release.

Mariano smiles smugly, looking me up and down. I can only think that he must have risen in the ranks to be given the honour of coming to check up on me, or maybe Angabi knows how much I dislike the man and wants to add insult to injury. I glare at him in disgust. His only skill seems to be turning up at just the wrong time, and I can tell how much he is enjoying this moment. I wonder if there's any chance Angabi has had a change of heart and decided that I've been taught a lesson and is authorising my release. But the longer I stand listening to Mariano's mirthless chuckle and snide remarks, I know that he is merely an emissary sent to make sure that I am enjoying my stay in hell.

24

Breakfast of Champions

Black Beach Prison, Malabo
December 2013

Sleep happens by accident, the strain of constant vigilance leading to total exhaustion. A few moments of oblivion and escape, and then I wake up, surfacing from an empty black void, confused as to where I am until the festering stench and inescapable noise remind me.

It doesn't get any easier. My shirt is filthy and clings to my back and I'm covered with itchy, red welts from the mosquitoes, bedbugs and other critters that have taken up residence in my mattress. I'm weak and dehydrated, and it feels like I'm slowly starving to death. There is nothing nutritious to eat and anything vaguely nourishing comes with a hefty price tag. As at Guantanamo, the arrival of a white man in the jail has led to an unexpected surge in enterprise, and the entrepreneurs among the inmates turn up with regularity, offering me a cellphone, clothing, food and water. The rates are exorbitant, and as I have nothing to trade, it's all out of my reach, but they don't give up easily, returning often to see if I've changed my mind or magically found some money to pay for their goods.

At this point, all I'm hoping for is to get someone to take a message to the embassy. I wonder if Thandi or Sengani have had any contact with my family. Melanie must be beside herself knowing that I have disappeared. She's probably terrified that I am dead. The frustration of being totally cut off, with no way of communicating, makes me angry, and until I can reach someone outside, my life depends on the goodwill and kindness of these hardened convicts.

I need to feel like I have some control over my situation to stay strong physically and mentally, so I explore the prison to get my bearings. Unbelievably, there are no kitchen facilities. It boggles the mind, considering that there are over four hundred prisoners who need to be fed. The authorities have found a way around this problem by designating a specific area as an informal, makeshift cookhouse, located next to what is known as 'the green zone' which houses the prison offices, a courtroom and a pharmacy, all inaccessible to the prison inmates unless under guard. There is no running water in the cookhouse, so water is collected and pots are washed on the ground outside. The first time I watched prisoners preparing food here, my stomach churned and I vowed never to touch any of it, let alone eat it. But that was three days ago. A lot can change in three days.

Hungry, tired and irritable, I head off to find out what's on the menu, even though anything I eat will eventually lead to a trip to the bathroom, a place I am avoiding at all costs. There are so many sick people here, and with us all living on top of one another it'll only be a matter of time before I catch something.

I pass the crowded Esplanada where two enormous garbage chariots exhale a putrid stench of rotting food as flies buzz around them in a frenzied lust. The entire area is blanketed in a shroud of smoke rising from the cooking stoves. Much as I don't want to eat what's on offer, I know that I need fuel, so today's goal is to find some food that hopefully won't be any worse for being prepared in this disease-riddled, vermin-infested environment.

Each morning the guards serve breakfast and a team of inmates are responsible for handing out a piece of bread (usually a few days old) and a cup of milk warmed in dirty pots and which tastes different each day. It's risky to drink as most of the time you end up with a bad case of diarrhoea. But here I am: day three, hungry and out of options.

Our daily routine is underpinned by the deafening boom of the 'gong' – a massive sheet of thick metal that the guards strike vigorously to announce breakfast, lunch and dinner, and at the end of the day when we are locked in for the night.

As a newcomer, when the breakfast gong sounds and I join the food line, I am sent to the back. The kitchen staff tell me that I have come from the city, my belly is full, I can wait, these men have been here for years, they must get priority. In some ways this makes sense, but by the time I get to the front of the line there are slim pickings. As foul as the food is I need it to keep my body strong though.

Corruption is rife. Apparently the warden receives his monthly budget to buy rations in cash, so it's no surprise that only a limited portion of these funds is actually used in the procurement of food for the prisoners. Meat, always past its sell-by date, is obtained cheap from logistics companies, and when it comes to staples like bread, yesterday's bread is free with a small fee paid to a 'friend' for delivery. Some prisoners sell their meat to get money to buy cigarettes or alcohol and others will trade stuff like soap for things they feel they need more.

The government has a contract providing four million CFA francs (around R100 000) a month towards food and beverages for the prison, but as with any government-run operation it's common to find that when they acquire a new contract, they immediately learn the importance of 'economising' and will handle it in a way that most benefits them. Eat some, keep some. Or, as the locals say, where the goat is tied is where he feeds.

Corruption from the top down is built into the structure and fabric of society in Equatorial Guinea. It probably doesn't occur to the public that there is another way, as it's such an integral part of daily life, even though this means that the poorest of the poor, who will never afford to participate in these private arrangements, are excluded from the inner circles, affecting their ability to rise above the poverty line.

Police corruption and impunity are a big part of the problem, and abuse of power starts way down among the lowest-ranking officials who extort bribes from citizens and immigrants or use their power to get rid of rivals in business, love and everything else. The courts are powerless to stop it at the higher levels of power and government. Many judges are courageous enough to withstand the tyranny up to a point, but often the mechanisms to investigate allegations of abuse and corruption are poorly handled, with intimidation playing a big role in whether the case will ever come to trial before the accuser 'disappears' for good.

It's not surprising that within the micro-culture of the prison, this hierarchy persists. Those who have more, get more. Those with power rule. In Black Beach, these are the unwritten laws we live by.

There is no system for cleaning or hygiene. Nobody cares, and right now that includes me as I prepare to take my chances joining the line of prisoners waiting to collect something to eat, trying not to think too much about what it is that I will be putting into my body. I've always prioritised a healthy, balanced life, so I find it difficult to stand in this line, waiting to be served a piece of stale bread, but you do what you must when your options are limited.

While I wait, I look around and see Bangkok up ahead at the serving tables. He's spotted me too and I can see he is watching my progress down the line. Even though I know what he has done to earn his spot in here and have faced him once before, I stare back defiantly.

Today he has put himself in charge of the food line.

'*Blanco!*'

I'm really not in the mood for him today.

He yells again. '*Blanco*, what are you doing here? You cannot eat this food.'

What is he saying? Is he denying me food or pointing out the obvious fact that this food is not fit for human consumption? Hunger fuels my sense of outrage, making me reckless and up for the challenge. I'm not planning on starving just because Bangkok doesn't want me to eat.

I glare at him but say nothing. He starts towards me … Am I going to have to fight Bangkok to get my hands on a piece of mouldy, stale bread and a cup of sour milk? Right now, my priority is food, so I'll take my chances and defend myself against him if that's what it takes to get my rations, unappetising as they may be.

He bears down on me and as he gets closer, he calls again: '*Blanco*, if you eat this food, you will die. This food is for animals.' He grabs me by the arm, and I am about to try to shake him off when he says, 'Come.'

I remember Ugo's words from the day I arrived, that most of the time Bangkok is 'normal'. What is *normal* in this place? But Bangkok does seem different today – he's belligerent but seems calm. I decide that if I'm going to be stuck here for a while then I need to show him that he doesn't scare me, so we head to his cell where he tells his cellmate to serve me a bowl of food. The room is small and dark, but surprisingly quite clean. A fan oscillates feebly in a corner. I look at the pockmarked, blackened pot of food bubbling on the table-top stove. I have no idea what it is or what the origins or nature of the ingredients are, but if Bangkok and his cellmate are eating it, how bad can it be? It certainly beats what's on offer in the kitchen.

Bangkok's cellmate spoons some of the contents of the pot into a bowl and hands it to me. It's my first real meal since I tasted freedom on the day I left for the airport. Haute cuisine, no doubt, served compliments of Bangkok. I consider the irony that my first meal in prison has been presented to me by my sworn enemy. Ugo was right: Bangkok is unpredictable. Is it possible that somewhere inside this violent brute is a human capable of compassion? *If our enemy is suffering, we should try to meet his need.* I take the bowl and dip in the spoon, raising it to my mouth as the two men watch expectantly. I am grateful as it goes down and stays down.

25

Hell's Kitchen

```
Black Beach Prison, Malabo
December 2013
```

It's all about survival in here: scavenging and begging for food and water, never dropping your guard for a moment. Hungry people are dangerous, and desperation can build into a simmering rage in the most patient and easy-going individuals, driving them to any means to get their hands on something to eat or barter. Luckily, my new friends share what they have if I'm willing to risk a meal prepared with expired meat, chicken or cheap fish. Rice is our main staple, available in abundance and effective at keeping hunger at bay. It's starchy and possibly the cheapest, worst rice in the world. I have no idea when it came over to Africa from the East, as it's infested with weevils, but a friend tells me that we do not know what the elephant ate to get so big, so, with this logic, we boil the weevils with the rice and they serve as a source of protein.

Money changes everything: you can buy raw food from the kitchen and cook it yourself, which is safer and more hygienic, but there are many times, especially in the early days, when my only source of sustenance is what my friends share with me, and I can't risk offending them by declining. I learn quickly that it's best not to ask what's on the menu. In any case, the general response is 'bush meat'. In my experience, the term refers to food hunted in the forest – cane rats, bats, snakes, monkeys or birds – but here in Black Beach, 'bush meat' is what my friends say when they don't want me to know what's really boiling in the pot. Mostly, I'm better off not knowing. Sometimes the 'chicken' I am served has fish bones in it, and I once have a bite of something I'm told is cat. I'm also given delicacies such as 'elephant meat', apparently hunted in the western jungles of mainland Equatorial Guinea. Because we're on an island, fish is a regular staple, and I risk my friends' disapproval if I don't want to eat it with them. I hate fish! Some years ago, I had a really bad experience eating a seafood pizza in Luanda, and more often than not, the memory results in a mad dash to void the contents of my stomach.

Although I'm starving most of the time, it's difficult to completely ignore where the food I'm eating comes from because once it's been caught or hunted, it's hung outside or thrown on top of the roof and left to 'age' for a few days. On a rare, good day, it could be a pigeon, but mostly nobody asks questions, especially when it's clear that it has four legs and a long, low-slung body. The question of how many days a carcass can spend maturing in the scorching heat and humidity before it's butchered and boiled in a stew is best left unanswered.

Everything is disguised with a liberal sprinkling of chillies, and if you're lucky a few rotten vegetables are thrown in for good measure. On rare occasions, vegetables are for sale inside the prison. They may be organic, but these specimens would not make it onto the swanky dining tables of Raw Food restaurants. Still, by adding an old, rotting tomato or onion and the requisite chilli, everything suddenly seems more nutritious and appetising.

I work hard at being grateful to my friends, trying to forget where the meat comes from. Luckily, when we eat 'bush meat' it's usually in a stew, so there are just a few tough, chewy morsels floating in a thick, grey soup with fiery hot chillies to disguise the taste. When it's been a week or so since your last piece of protein, this will most certainly do just fine.

Today, my friends have bought some chicken and are excited as they run to find me, brandishing it proudly, dangling it by its feet. I catch a whiff, notice the sickly yellow-green colour, instantly gag and have to rush off to find somewhere to throw up. When I come back, they laugh, patting me on my back, and invite me to watch them prepare the meal. I'm not sure what Gordon Ramsay or even Bear Grylls would think of their methods, but when your choice is to eat or starve, it's easier to focus on the fact that the dead creature in front of you will provide you with fuel to survive another day.

We cook the chicken for a really long time and then, to make sure it's thoroughly dead, kill it again by submerging it in hot oil, hoping the germs die in the process. The result is a tough, chewy and stringy chicken biltong. *Survive before thrive.* It fills the emptiness in my stomach, giving me the strength to face life in Black Beach. Whatever it takes.

With very little ventilation in the prison and having to live on the floor crammed in with so many others, I'm constantly worried that I'm going to get sick, especially as I don't eat regularly and what I do eat doesn't provide much nutritional value. Extreme heat in these conditions is life-threatening, so finding enough clean drinking water to stay hydrated is a full-time occupation.

It's the dry season and the island can go for weeks without rain. I'm living on the edge. Existing is exhausting, and I simmer in the salty sweat that pours into the nooks and crannies of my body. Sometimes the heat outside is too intense and I am forced to take cover within the walls of the prison. The constant itch from sweat and insect bites intensifies, and I long for a change of clothes and a cold shower, but this is a delusion as there is no running water, just the occasional dripping tap. The reality of having to wade through a slimy trail of faeces and urine to get there takes the joy out of dreaming about this simple pleasure.

In this season, there's no chance of standing outside in the refreshing downpour of a tropical thunderstorm. I pray for rain as the days merge into a blur punctuated by a few moments of oblivion when I fall asleep from sheer exhaustion. I wake up, my body slick with sweat, forced to repeat the grim task of finding something to drink and scavenging for food. The official breakfast is once again a piece of stale bread served with a milk powder mix that my brothers have warned me will make me sick. But this morning the ache in my belly makes me desperate, and I join the queue outside the kitchen.

One of the inmates has gifted me with a spoon, which he tells me belonged to another white man – the notorious Simon Mann. I've spent some time grinding the handle down on the cement to form a makeshift knife and someone else has given me an enamel plate and dented tin cup. Bangkok is not serving breakfast today, so after waiting in the chaos where everyone pushes and shoves to get their share, I finally walk away with my prize: a portion of sour milk and stale bread.

I've always been partial to a milkshake and swallow the milk down quickly. It's nothing like the sweet satisfaction savoured after a hot day out cycling in the mountains, but my hunger is temporarily deferred and I join my brothers on the Esplanada where they're sitting in the shade of Old Man Luis's shelter watching an animated game of draughts. I marvel at these hardened men, criminals of the worst order, passing time in the punishing heat like they're enjoying an afternoon in the park. How have they accepted and adapted to such a hostile environment, existing day by day in an inhospitable place with little contact with the outside world? At times like this, it's hard to imagine that my nightmare will ever end. Some days are worse than others, and it's a struggle to shrug off these feelings of despair, but sitting with these men boosts my spirits. At least it's better than sitting in the coffin, alone on my mattress, thinking too much.

As time passes, it's clear that my breakfast is not sitting well. My stomach lodges an official complaint, bubbling and grumbling, apparently very dissatisfied. As the sun marches across the sky into the afternoon, I break out in a cold sweat, my stomach churning. Regret is a cruel master. Facing the consequences of my impulsive decision will soon be unavoidable, my reckless defiance rewarded with a trip to the bathroom. I dread the thought of having to go anywhere near there, but as the cramps intensify, I know that if I don't hurry soon I won't have a choice. Now I understand why my friends are so adamant about not eating the in-house breakfast…

My stomach is most definitely angry with me. I haven't eaten much since I got here and have consequently managed to avoid using the toilets too often, but now a trip to the latrines is inevitable. You learn quickly in this place, and experience has taught me that the more traditional squat toilets are the best option when you can't avoid the call of nature any longer. There is no direct contact with the seat, which in most cases is broken or missing, leaving the filthy, jagged edges of the ceramic bowl to perch on. I certainly don't want to risk infection by getting a scrape or cut on my thighs or backside, so the squat toilets with their larger bowls and run-off straight into the drain are the obvious choice.

Although it's difficult to miss a clearly demarcated hole in the ground, many still fail to hit the target and end up dumping their noxious load along the perimeter, so besides avoiding the puddles of urine, I will have to practise the art of not stepping in fresh faeces while squatting, while making sure I don't miss either. When you consider what we're eating, it's no surprise that the stench in here is unbearable, and as toilet paper is a luxury most cannot afford, excess waste is wiped off with fingers and the walls are smeared with the slimy greenish-brown remnants of whatever has been deposited into the cesspit. It's not a place where you'd want to spend any time thinking, reading or checking emails on your phone.

None of this crosses my mind as I race through the slime, barely making it in time to pull down my pants and squat over the hole, trying to avoid stepping on faeces as this morning's breakfast explodes out of me, spray-painting my legs and feet in a putrid slime, a disgusting reminder to pay more attention to the wisdom of my fellow inmates. The relief of having expelled this vile substance from my stomach is quickly replaced by the realisation that I don't have any toilet paper, and I now understand why they refer to it as 'white gold'. Until now, my mind has been focused on surviving all the other horrors I've had to face, and toilet paper has not been a priority. Only sentenced convicts are allocated any, but you can barter or buy some if you have money. Right now, I'm out of time and have no money, so my only pair of underwear must be sacrificed for wiping up the mess as best I can. Once this grim task is completed, I pull up my pants and realise that they have not survived the onslaught either. I shudder in horror to think what has become of me, standing here in my own shit in a filthy cage, civilisation just minutes away but beyond my reach, with little hope of salvation.

In the wash area, there's a slow dribble of water from a broken tap, but with two guys already queuing to fill their buckets, I know it's going to be a long wait, longer than I can bear, so I slink outside, attempting to look casual while I look for another water source to try to clean myself up. I find a trickle, but it's not enough to wash myself with. The best I can do is to clean my hands and rinse away some of the humiliation.

Later, once we're locked in for the night, I still have no way to clean myself and going to the bathroom at night is far too dangerous. I work hard at swallowing my outrage. For once, it seems as though even the mosquitoes are avoiding me as I lie itching and smelly in the heat and humidity, my legs still stained with the evidence of my shame.

Lessons learnt:
1. Always know where to find toilet paper if you do not have your own.
2. Always have a bucket of water to wash with.

26

Slow-Roasted

Black Beach Prison, Malabo
24 December 2013

December is one of the driest months in Equatorial Guinea; the sea off the coast is a balmy 28°C, warm as bathwater, creating a persistent sticky humidity. Our day begins under a dense cloud of fog, our discomfort growing as midday temperatures soar upwards of 40°C in the shade. The 'real feel' is at least 48 to 50°C, and finding enough clean drinking water is a constant struggle. There is little chance of relief. The dry spell will continue until February, and I hope to be long gone when the rainy season starts in March.

We're all irritable, tired and restless, with no respite from the merciless heat, and cranky prisoners are dangerous. 'Hot and bothered' really is a thing; the weather affects everyone, and although most are too drained to do much, for some it intensifies their already aggressive state, fuelling violent disagreements that the guards are too lethargic to end.

The guards seldom set foot beyond the gates, and if they do we're treated like dangerous animals in a zoo, herded into the courtyard and locked in while they deal with the problem. So far this week, there have been five really bad fights and two beatings. At moments it's been terrifying but I am relatively unharmed. God has sent an army of angels to protect me.

Sometimes, thugs try to hassle me for money or push me around. I know how to handle them, but many don't, and it's not unusual to have to step over limp bodies lying battered on the floor. If they don't move for a few days, the Jefe de Castel orders them to be carried out and they're dumped at the entrance, to be dealt with by the guards. After a while, you become immune to stepping over broken and bleeding bodies. You can't help them, and getting involved puts you at risk, so you avoid the slick wet patches that are probably blood, although it's difficult to tell as the stains blend into the filthy floor.

I stay out of harm's way and try not to draw any unwanted attention to myself, which is difficult when there are hundreds of people crammed into a space designed for a fraction of this number and I'm easy to spot in the crowd. But in this heat, even the teenage delinquents who cause the most trouble are too sluggish to move, preferring to stay inside the sweltering oven of the sleeping area, listless on their mattresses. When the sun sets, night brings little relief.

Disease is a constant concern. I still avoid using the toilets. Thankfully, because I eat so little, I haven't needed to make a trip there more than a few times. Hygiene is a problem, but my brothers have shared a bucket with me which I take outside to fill with relatively untainted water and then head for the showers. Using a small cup, I douse myself with water to rinse off some of the grime. My daily 'shower' is a highlight as I am temporarily revitalised after it, but as soon as I curl up on my thin and mouldy mattress, the insects resume their trek over me, and dirt sticks to the fresh layer of sweat coating my body. The mosquitoes are persistent and malaria is a constant threat.

I'm starting to understand the hidden rhythms of this place and can tell something is up today. I'm inside, hiding from the infernal heat – even for a sun worshipper like me, spending any length of time outside at the moment is suicide, like stepping into a furnace, so I begin most days by reading the Bible and writing little notes to my mother and Melanie on scraps of paper that I've scavenged. Pens are also difficult to come by, so I spend some time looking for places to conceal my secret stash where hopefully they won't be found if the guards conduct a search. Even though my words are unlikely to find their way to my family, writing provides a welcome distraction from the familiar ache of an empty stomach and delays my inevitable search for something to eat that won't kill me. I lie on my mattress, reading my Bible and trying not to think of home, unaware that I'm about to have the worst experience so far in the misery of my new life in hell. The horrors of my first Christmas behind the walls of Black Beach will top the charts.

There is an air of anticipation in the sleeping quarters. It's not the usual arguments and shouting that I've grown accustomed to. Prisoners are making their way in and out, chattering excitedly. Curious, I decide to brave the outdoors and head into the scorching heat. Any change in the atmosphere of the prison is unsettling, but this is different – the buzz seems almost festive and everyone is happy, for a change. As I traipse after the others towards the main gate, I realise that outside in the real world, tonight is Christmas Eve.

The warden is away somewhere on the mainland and his second in command, Paul, is making hay in his absence. Paul is a tall, slim guy, very laid back and relaxed, who is always in the background. He knows everyone, knows everything that goes on, but seldom gets involved. Wardens may come and go but Paul is always there, working behind the throne, staying out of the limelight, in charge and feared by all. Everyone wants to befriend him, as he can do much to make life easier here. Today it seems he has stepped out of the shadows to throw a party for us.

I hadn't realised how much money actually circulates here, and tonight those with funds are planning on spending it on beer and cheap liquor that Paul and the kitchen manager have been delivering to the prison over the past few days. Everything is a business in Black Beach, and if you have money, you can buy anything, including your freedom. Initially, the steady supply of liquor and drugs into the prison was a surprise to me, but money changes everything and the warden turns a blind eye to people like the kitchen manager, a prisoner with special privileges who can come and go as he pleases. Some are paid to look the other way or to facilitate the procurement process, all living well off the proceeds of illicit trade.

Over the past few days, I've witnessed the brisk trade going on behind the prison walls as inmates bartered what little they had to raise the funds needed to buy a bottle or two to celebrate Christmas. Finding things to trade has been their sole focus lately and, as more and more crates are offloaded, it seems that many have been successful.

The parking area is a hive of activity, a steady stream of vehicles pulling up outside the kitchen area. As I watch from behind the fence, I don't give much thought to the consequences, until I see crates of 500-millilitre glass bottles being offloaded and realise that this is a really bad idea. As the pile of crates in the courtyard grows, I'm pretty sure that our Christmas Eve celebration is not going to end well. I've never seen so much alcohol in my life, and it's all destined for a bunch of criminals. When you consider that most have nothing to live for, you understand why they drink as if there is no tomorrow – they probably don't care if there is one.

Alcohol is usually prohibitively expensive, but Paul and the kitchen manager have clearly realised that they are onto a good thing and have dropped the price for a one-time-only hot Christmas special, ensuring that a luxury usually out of reach for most is now attainable, depending on what you are willing to do or sacrifice for it. Today it seems as though many of my prison brothers have succeeded in exchanging their worldly possessions for the temporary distraction found at the bottom of a bottle.

Paul watches dispassionately from the shade of one of the buildings. He clearly has no issue with us celebrating Christmas behind bars, especially as his pockets are filling with every case that is offloaded. After all, what is a party without beer? He doesn't seem to give a damn about the consequences.

My stomach echoes with a familiar emptiness. I notice that they're not delivering any crates of food, which would have been better appreciated by most of us who exist on a few scraps here and there. Black Beach hardly seems like a place where one would celebrate the birth of Jesus, and there will be no religious service held here tonight. It's merely a convenient opportunity to make some cash, to get drunk and forget about your sins. The alcohol will be consumed until there is nothing left. It won't be a case of sitting around the campfire, sipping a beer and enjoying the camaraderie of a shared celebration, but rather a desperate 'down the hatch, there is no tomorrow' spree by a bunch of violent, out-of-control prisoners with nothing to lose looking for a way to vent their frustration. My sense of dread grows at the thought of these testosterone-fuelled thugs drunk and uninhibited. I've seen what they're capable of without alcohol.

This 'party' is going to lead to a whole heap of trouble for everyone, and living on my small mattress in the general population, there'll be nowhere to hide, no way to protect myself or my meagre belongings.

It's early afternoon and the trucks are still disgorging their contents, so I head inside, gather up my Bible, sheet and mattress, carry them up to the first level and ask Old Man Luis if I can store them in his cell. He agrees and returns to the task of unpacking the beer he has bought to sell to the other inmates. He has a stock of about five crates and is placing them in his personal deep freeze. Although the appliance doesn't work due to the intermittent electricity, he's had the foresight to ensure that a supply of ice has been provided to keep his stash cool.

I pack my things away and watch him offload the last few bottles and stack the remaining ice blocks around them. Once satisfied, he digs down to the bottom of the freezer and pulls out an ice-cold beer, offering it to me. I accept gratefully – anything cold to drink is pure bliss; all I've had since arriving here is tepid, mostly tainted water, sour milk and my Malian friend Amadou's dark, earthy tea.

I wrap my hands around the bottle, enjoying the cool sensation of chilled glass against my skin, and twist off the cap, catching a whiff of hops and freedom in the fizz that escapes as I take my first sip. *Mmmmm*, liquid gold. I gulp it down, the cool, refreshing amber liquid bringing a surge of memories, a temporary distraction from the horrors of the here and now. I savour the bittersweet taste as it transports me to my life in Namibia where beer is considered the local water. Happier times. The moment is fleeting but intoxicating as time and space converge, a part of me lost in the memories of the vast deserts of my youth, while physically I am trapped, locked up in the dystopian world of Black Beach.

Never in a thousand lifetimes would I have imagined that I'd be 'celebrating' Christmas Eve behind the decaying walls of a prison on an island beneath the sweaty armpit of Africa, my companions and neighbours the scourge of society – murderers, drug dealers and rapists. As I savour the last sip, I understand why my brothers have traded everything they own in an attempt to find solace at the bottom of a bottle, even if just for a moment …

27

Feliz Navidad

```
Black Beach Prison, Malabo
24 December 2013
```

As the afternoon wears on, tempers flare and the courtyard erupts, everyone fighting to claim their share of the Christmas bounty. For those ravaged by guilt for the deeds that led them here, this 'party' is a chance to forget where they are and why they're here. The simple concept of joy is absent behind these walls; misery and suffering are endured by everyone, no matter their crimes and whether or not they are guilty. I understand their need to find an escape, no matter how fleeting. In a way, this Christmas Eve 'celebration' creates a connection to life outside and memories of happier times spent with family and friends.

As the sun sets, most of the booty has been carted inside. The gates are slammed shut and the guards disappear to their stations. We have not yet been locked in for the night, so I head away from the chaos, grabbing my last opportunity for some fresh air outside the sweltering, claustrophobic sleeping quarters. The ocean is just a few steps away; I can't see it, but I know it's there. I turn my face to the cooling breeze wafting in from the sea, imagining for a brief moment that I'm wading into the water, feeling the waves wash over me. *Heaven.*

Inside these walls, there is no sign of nature, everything has been stripped bare, and the only way to experience anything untainted by the seething mass of humanity is to look up at the sky. It's unusually quiet out here after all the action this morning, and I imagine those in the free world heading off to celebrate with their loved ones. In the distance, beyond the prison walls, I can hear sounds of revelry, cars hooting and people singing.

There are around four hundred of us behind these walls and most nights there are just three guards on duty who seldom set foot inside. Tonight will be no exception. I stand at the fence and dream of home. Usually, it would be too dangerous to be out here on my own, but right now the vibe is electric, my fellow inmates jubilant, preoccupied with gathering their stash and getting drunk inside. Soon the Jefe de Castel will lock us in.

I gaze up, wondering if I'll be able to spot the Christmas star. The sky is fairly clear, the evening tinted with the rich, velvety hues of fading twilight as darkness closes in. I breathe it all in. Hearing a door open, I look up to see a guard heading out of his hut and climbing into his car. He starts it up, revving the engine before racing off. There are now just two guards left to handle the chaos that is sure to follow.

I go back inside, pushing past the drunken party animals, and head to the bench against a wall where I usually sit in the evenings with my friends. They shift up, making a space for me and I take a seat, careful not to lean back against the mould-covered wall stained with little black dots of shit from the plague of cockroaches – another evil that emerges to feast at night. We settle in for the evening's entertainment.

Noise levels rise and it feels like the roof is going to cave in as the seething mass of revellers surges past like a multi-headed Hydra emerging from the swamp. We hear shrieks of pain as some disappear, swept underfoot in the stampede. No one cares. It's Christmas Eve, and they're having the time of their lives.

Less than two hours after the door was slammed shut, locking us in for the night, the first serious drunken brawl flares up. At the centre of it is a girl. The men have been taking turns with her, and there is some disagreement over who is next in line for her favours. The distinctive sound of a slap rings out, which would usually put an end to the argument, but unfortunately in this case the recipient is Tadeo, known as Rocky, a violent, dangerous man put in here after being convicted of killing his wife during an argument. Legend has it that when the police came to arrest him, he injured one and killed two others with his bare hands.

Rocky is waiting for his death sentence to be carried out. It could be any day now, so he has nothing left to live for. He is not someone you want to piss off: built like a gorilla, with muscular arms and a massive barrel chest, he is without a doubt the strongest man in here. He makes Bangkok look like a Pygmy. Right now, he is enraged, massaging his ear, which is no doubt stinging from the slap. He shoves his opponent. Big mistake!

His challenger staggers back, regains his footing and, fuelled by alcohol, takes the fight up a notch, grabbing a knife, leaping forward and slicing it through Rocky's shoulder. Blood spurts and Rocky roars in fury, pouncing like a cat on a mouse, retaliating with his fists, driven by a lethal alcoholic rage.

I hear the crunch of breaking cartilage as he punches his attacker in the face, then quickly steps aside, waiting for the man to regain his footing, deftly dodging the fists flying at him, and dances back, drawing the other guy in closer.

We're in the danger zone as the fight moves towards us. Rocky has the upper hand, but the other guy is too drunk to give up, even as Rocky pummels him mercilessly, smashing his face to a pulp before delivering a final 'Superman' punch, lifting his opponent off his feet and smashing him into the ground. The guy rolls onto his stomach and tries to get up, blood dripping from his mangled face as he crawls across the floor. He reaches out, but there's nothing we can do to stop the carnage as Rocky comes in for a final blow, kicking him in the back and sending him flying in our direction. Rocky then reaches down, picks him up and hurls him face-first into the wall, picks him up again, and, holding him by the scruff of his neck, smashes his face into the wall over and over, finally dropping him to the floor. We're frozen in horror. Rocky is beaming, enjoying the hunt, enjoying the game, watching his prey trying to escape.

The crowd closes in around them, joining in as Rocky plays with his new toy, the woman at the centre of the conflict forgotten in his lust for blood. We lose sight of them as another group of demented inmates push their way past, singing loudly as they dance barefoot through the broken bottles discarded on the floor, bopping to the rhythms of makeshift drums being beaten by their pals following close behind. Some of the younger guys are already totally plastered, lurching and stumbling over the empty crates scattered around. Another fight breaks out and I duck as a beer bottle flies past my head, crashing into the wall in a shower of broken glass.

It's like watching a petrol tanker leaking fuel everywhere and everyone you see has a burning match. The night wears on. Hundreds of prisoners are now totally deranged, running amok, breaking glass, hurling beds and crates, their fists flying as they careen through the prison, mowing down anyone in their path. The alcohol has flipped a switch and utter savagery has been unleashed.

All around us, bodies lie comatose on a bed of broken glass, and as I look at some of them I wonder if, after tonight, there will even be a tomorrow for them. It's impossible to tell if they'll ever get up again. For many, it's clear that they will not. Others are dazed, wandering around in vomit-and-blood-stained clothing, their eyes sunken and vacant, their actions frenzied or clumsy as they look for more alcohol, pulling bottles out of crates and guzzling them down, flinging them aside and then scrambling to grab another, beating away their friends, punching and kicking one another into oblivion. Sleep is inconceivable as the revelry continues unabated. Tonight, while the world celebrates Christmas, we fight for our lives.

As the dawn light softens the sky, things finally quieten down a little. None of us has emerged unscathed. Those of us still able to stand make our way out, stepping over the fallen, our feet crunching through glass. It's like the aftermath of a war as we slip on a floor slick with blood and vomit. A few of the hardiest drunks are still awake and stagger about, rummaging through the discarded remains for a bottle that may have survived the night.

Disgusted, we push past them and head outside, only to discover that not even our guardians to the gates of hell are immune to the perils of this place. The two guards who were on duty lie in a pool of blood at the entrance. Dead. The third guard, the man I saw leaving last night, lies nearby, mortally injured from a self-inflicted gunshot to the head, his gun discarded on the ground beside him. We can't tell if he is still alive or not, but if he is it won't be for long.

Merry Christmas, from Black Bitch...

28

Mi Familia

```
Black Beach Prison, Malabo
December 2013
```

I'm in shock following the massacre at Christmas and the repercussions reverberate through the prison in the days that follow. Now more than ever, I'm determined to get out of here. Being cut off is maddening, and I find it difficult to control my frustration not knowing what progress is being made. I can't help feeling like an innocent man on death row. It now seems clear to me that Angabi may well leave me to die here. I know the threat is real. The South African government needs to apply pressure before it's too late, and although it will be an uphill battle, I have to believe that I will get out of here. It's all I have.

The warden keeps tight control over us after the Christmas rampage and the atmosphere inside is subdued. Many inmates are taken to the torture room, which happens to be where we sometimes hold our church services. When we sing and praise God, I try not to dwell on what goes on here, but the bloodstains on the floor make it hard to forget the presence of those in power over us. Mostly, the threat of torture or suspending privileges ensures that everyone toes the line. Inmates who temporarily forget pay the price and their battered bodies serve as a reminder to the rest of us.

There are no happy days here, or even good days; it's all about survival, no time to think about tomorrow or the future. My focus is on surviving from one moment to the next, doing my best to make sure that when tomorrow dawns, I'm still breathing. My daily routine consists of scavenging and begging for food and water, always vigilant and aware of what is happening around me. You can't drop your guard without being robbed or finding yourself in the middle of a dispute or fight. There are too many here with nothing to lose. They have no fear of punishment; the worst has been done to them several times already.

The warden has taken a particular interest in me since my arrival, making sure that I don't receive any special treatment. He has eyes everywhere, so I keep my head down and stay away from trouble. When any one person or group become too powerful, they are quickly destroyed. I can tell that he won't hesitate to show me exactly how things work here if I don't cooperate.

In African cultures there is an underlying respect for one's elders, but in Black Beach the younger generation think they know it all. For many, life outside is not much different from a life behind prison walls, trapped in a constant battle for survival. Many are homeless, orphaned and forgotten by society, their only companions other poverty-stricken kids with no prospects. Unemployment and a lack of education bind them together on the streets where they do whatever is necessary to survive, forced to eat out of garbage bins, with no access to shelter, clean water and sanitation. Meanwhile, their political leaders live a charmed life, parading past in flashy limousines or jet-setting around the world in private planes, living off the riches that should be shared with all the citizens of Equatorial Guinea. In a country with billions in oil reserves and a relatively small and young population, poverty should be non-existent, but greed and self-interest have ensured that the incredible wealth remains in the hands of the few, people like the president and Angabi.

It's no wonder that the Lost Boys – the *delincuentes* – in the prison have no respect for their elders. Growing up rough, they lacked parental guidance and don't even have the sanctity of religion to turn to, meaning that they have no moral compass to guide them. Many are superstitious, believing in black magic. They don't have the benefit of faith, of believing in something bigger than their suffering, something to give them strength and a feeling of support. All they have is each other and the escape provided by bullying, drugs, alcohol and sex.

Fortunately, I have God to turn to. I've been welcomed by my fellow Christians and we work together, helping and supporting each other, putting our faith in God to get through the daily torment of our existence. The Muslim community is also a tight-knit group. Mostly French-speaking foreigners from Senegal or Mali, they are quiet and stick together, taking care of one another.

Besides Amadou, my tea-drinking companion who has also become my barber, I have formed a friendship with Ali, the main leader of the Muslim community in the prison, and I often visit him in his cell to chat. He understands English and it's great to be able to speak my native language, even though he mostly replies in French or Spanish. He looks out for the other Muslims that come in, giving them food and clothing, providing protection and helping them to find a place to sleep. Like me, these men keep to themselves and avoid getting involved in prison politics.

The drug rings control certain areas, defending their turf and surrounding themselves with young delinquents who are submissive and easy to control. Being welcomed into the 'family' has immense appeal for these boys, as most have grown up without a mother or father.

Each gang consists of around eight or ten guys between the ages of sixteen and twenty. They follow the oldest in the group, quickly acquiring new skills and tricks necessary for a life of crime – how to steal, where to steal, and how to get weapons. Bravado is everything, and they are brutal and indifferent to the suffering of others, raping women and young children incarcerated with us at every opportunity. Many are back within a month of being released. One incident in the outside world involved a group of them who had been drinking and partying at the beach. They'd decided to try to impress a girl by fighting her boyfriend; the attack soon turned into a frenzy as more joined in, and they kicked him to death, laughing as he lay dying in the sand at her feet.

Then there are the 'untouchables', important people on the outside with a 'temporary problem'. Nobody messes with them, knowing that these prisoners don't stay long and will soon be 'forgiven' or will buy their freedom. These types don't forget and are guaranteed to retaliate with a vengeance that knows no limits. One of them was a senior policeman. Whenever new inmates arrive, we all cluster together, crowding the entrance to watch the action, and I am always reminded of the night I was brought here. But anything that alleviates the monotony is a welcome distraction. When the police officer was brought in, everyone cheered, shouting and calling for vengeance. He was known to many, notorious for his use of excessive force, beating and torturing 'suspects' and even killing the ones who 'just don't listen'. But once the gates closed, nobody touched him. He kept a low profile, and a day later he was released to resume his tyranny on the streets of Malabo. Apparently, he'd beaten the wrong guy, someone protected by the elite – a mistake he will surely not make again.

29

Ubuntu

```
Black Beach Prison, Malabo
December 2013
```

Weekends are a highlight on the Black Beach social calendar. No visitors are allowed during the week, so everyone looks forward to Saturday and Sunday, hoping to see their loved ones and friends, and to stock up with supplies brought from home. I watch enviously from a shady spot in the courtyard crowded with prisoners pushing and shoving for a space at the perimeter fence. Feeding time at the zoo. There's chaos as the scavengers circle, ready to grab what they can.

I'm on the lookout for someone I can approach to see if they would be willing to pass on my handwritten notes to the embassy. Most are too afraid to get involved, so I've retreated to a spot where it's not so crowded and watch jealously as packets of food, cool drinks and other essentials are handed through the fence. The warden has ensured that I don't receive any privileges or favours, presumably following orders from high up the chain of command to make my stay as unpleasant as possible.

My family must be distraught, desperate for news, wondering if I am still alive or if Angabi has been true to his threats and arranged for me to disappear permanently. Apart from Mariano, I've had no visitors or calls, but I'm not giving up. At the very least, the weekend has brought a welcome distraction from the monotony of daily existence, and as long as I am breathing, my goal is to get out of here. Never give up, never surrender, never say die.

Just then, a youngster shouts to me, pointing towards the fence: '*Blanco, ha visita!*'

I look up curiously. Surely he's mistaken. It's hard to pick out anyone I know from the throng of people gathered in this tightly packed space, but I stand on tiptoes, craning my neck, and vaguely make out two official-looking men and a woman. I'm not sure who they are until I push my way through the crowd and realise it's Sengani from the embassy, looking every inch the diplomat in a pair of tailored Bermuda shorts, a stylish golf shirt and a Panama hat, like he's on his way to the country club for lunch. My eyes widen in surprise when I realise that his beautiful wife, Masala, is with him. I don't know many women willing or brave enough to come to Black Beach on a Sunday afternoon, but she seems completely unfazed by her surroundings, smiling and waving when she spots me making my way through the crowd. Relief washes over me at the sight of someone I know, and not just anyone – South Africans, and embassy officials at that.

I shove my way into a spot at the fence, grinning from ear to ear. My first real visitors! I'm overwhelmed with emotion. Finally someone from outside, someone from the real world, someone who can tell my family that I am still alive, someone who can help get me out of here. I'm not one for public displays of affection, but right now I want to reach through the fence, grab hold of them and never let go. The last time I saw Sengani was when Angabi pushed him out of the office at the airport when I was supposed to have left for South Africa.

I can only imagine what they are thinking as they greet me warmly, ever the diplomats. My clothes are filthy, despite my attempt to wash them yesterday, which involved leaving them to dry in the heat of the tropical sun while I guarded them and 'worked on my tan'. I've lost weight and I can tell that despite my visitors' broad smiles, they're shocked by the state I'm in.

Sengani tells me that the embassy has been working non-stop trying to find me and had heard rumours that I'd been brought here but couldn't confirm anything through the official channels. He says that today they've snuck in 'unofficially' but now that the guards know who they are it's unlikely that they'll manage to come again. He introduces me to another man with them, a local diplomat who showed them a way of working outside the 'system'. I'm grateful and offer a silent prayer of thanks to God for sending them to renew my hope and lift my spirits.

Sengani says it's been a traumatic time and not being able to give my family answers has weighed heavily on him. He tells me that he had no choice but to try to gain access to the prison through unofficial means. Reading between the lines, I realise that he risked everything today so that he could confirm that I am still alive. I reach through the fence to shake his hand, humbled by his spirit of ubuntu – the compassion and humanity that unites South Africans as a nation.

Sengani says that, from a political standpoint, there is little the embassy can do, as they have been unable to locate any formal documentation stating that I've been charged with a crime or incarcerated at Black Beach. Officially, I am not here.

To me, this seems to be further proof that the order came from the top of the pyramid. Nobody disappears without official sanction for fear of reprisal from the judiciary, the president, or Teodorin, whose official role is minister of armed forces, police, prisons and detention facilities.

Where do you start in a situation like this? Sengani tells me that it's tricky navigating the red tape of bureaucracy as they are bound by strict diplomatic protocol and have to tread carefully. They know I'm innocent, cleared by the courts, and that there is no sane or legal reason for me to be here, but because there is no paperwork stating that I am here, there is nowhere to start the process of getting me released. Even though I am standing right in front of them, it's as if I don't exist.

After more discussion, Sengani asks me what I need to be more comfortable and returns a few hours later with three bags of groceries and some bottled water, a pair of shorts, two shirts, a towel, a toothbrush and, of all things, a fan! The electricity supply here is erratic, but this gift will be a godsend, keeping the mosquitoes at bay and providing some relief from the sweltering heat and humidity.

My VIP guests have drawn a lot of attention from the other inmates, who cannot disguise their curiosity and swarm around me. For the first time since my arrival, I now have a big problem: I have *stuff*!

Everyone suffers behind these walls, and suddenly I have things that they want. It's like throwing a piece of food into a cage of starving animals as I struggle to hold onto my new bounty. In the chaos of getting my bags over the fence, I have to place things on the ground beside me, pushing away the hands reaching into the bags as they try to grab what they can. I realise that I probably have a very slim chance of getting all my new things to my mattress, and once I do, it's going to be a mission to hang onto them long enough to enjoy them.

I finally manage to secure everything, and it's an emotional goodbye as my visitors leave. I'm overwhelmed by an aching sense of abandonment knowing that there's a good chance they won't manage to visit again. I watch them go and then focus on trying to get my few home comforts back inside, pushing away the emptiness brought on by their departure and clinging to the strength their visit has given me to keep going. My heart swells with an immense sense of pride to be a South African, from a country where people take risks because they care. The spirit of ubuntu knows no boundaries. I walk away focused on the joy of having something decent to eat and the relief that soon my family will know that I am still alive.

My brothers rush over, eager to help me carry my prizes inside and curious to know more about my important visitors. They can't believe that people from an embassy have taken the time to come to see me and are even more amazed by their generosity. I look at my new friends; these men are some of the worst criminals, yet they have shared what little they have with me and have likely never experienced any form of charity from anyone in authority. I take my things to Old Man Luis's cell, grateful that I have somewhere to keep them safe, even though I have to give him something in return.

Later that night, my faith and spirit of ubuntu are tested to their limits. For the first time in many days, I have something decent to eat and an ever-expanding circle of brothers who are all expecting to share the food. Suddenly, all I want to do is look after number one! I am a Christian; I know I am supposed to share; I know I should be grateful to these men who have helped me when I had nothing to give in return, but it's hard to watch as the food, which would have sustained me for days, disappears in minutes.

But this is how it works here: you have your 'pack' and you work together, taking care of each other; you share when you have something, and they share when they have something. In its way, this too is the spirit of ubuntu, and it dawns on me that perhaps I do have a purpose here; perhaps God has other plans for me, delivering me an opportunity to learn patience and work on my failures, learn from my new brothers and also show them a different approach to life. *Tamos juntos*. We're in this together.

30

Incommunicado

Black Beach Prison, Malabo
January 2014

It's like swimming with sharks in here: if you don't bleed, they just circle you, going for the one that does. I sleep in shifts, rarely surrendering completely to the exhaustion that overwhelms me as predators lurk in the dark. They know that this is the best time to attack. The stolen moments of escape, when I am able to fall into a state of oblivion, are all that sustain me.

I have learnt the hard way not to keep anything of value with me. At one point I had some money and kept it with me, believing I could keep it safe, but I quickly suffered the consequences of that mistake.

Luckily, even though he is unstable and convicted of a brutal murder, Old Man Luis is as close to a trusted friend as I can have here and allows me to keep my few possessions in his cell. He's given me an old pair of flip-flops which I've mended with wire and I wear them most of the time. My clothes are hand-me-downs from previous prisoners, things nobody wants. My philosophy is that if I have nothing to protect, then I can focus on controlling my mind and keeping my body as strong and healthy as possible. If you can control your mind, your thinking, you can overcome almost any situation.

The passage area where I live forms the main confluence of the sleeping quarters. There are small, tented structures staked out everywhere, like temporary shelters erected in the rubble following an earthquake. During one of the riots, my brothers ripped out the internal surveillance system; the wiring for the cameras was installed inside PVC pipes that we quickly harvested to use as tent poles around our mattresses, tying old sheets together to provide some privacy and hanging up a much-needed mosquito net.

Thankfully, I missed the 'big riot' that took place some months before my arrival, but my brothers talk about it often. The prisoners had been angry over something trivial; a few started throwing stones at the guards and then went on a rampage. The situation escalated, even worse than at Christmas, and the elite special forces had to be called in to restore order. They abseiled down from a helicopter, beating and shooting the prisoners into submission. There were no negotiations like you see on television. Shots were fired at random, killing an unknown number of prisoners, with many critically injured, and then it was all over, apart from the beatings that followed.

Every day there is a long queue of prisoners begging the warden for a quick phone call. If he feels like it, he gives you his cellphone or takes you to his office. Most return disappointed. For me, the outside world no longer exists, unless I find some money with which to bribe the guards. There is one effective method of getting an opportunity to make a call, though, and that is to report to sickbay.

Step One: You need to convince the Jefe de Castel that you are indeed unwell, and, if you're lucky, he'll put your name on a sick list for the next day.

Step Two: By the Grace of God a medic shows up, usually drunk.

Step Three: You are called before him and the warden to report your symptoms and convince them that you are sick.

Step Four: If you make it past this stage, then you, together with the other inmates who have made it to this point, are escorted to the medical station where you are probed and checked. If there is medication available, you are given something for your ailment. Once your examination is concluded, you wait for the others to be seen. And if the warden is in a good mood, he will allow you to make a local call.

This is certainly one of the warden's most powerful weapons to keep us at breaking point. I always look for the good in people, but in his case there are no redeeming qualities. He's a sadistic bastard and I stay out of his way. While the other foreign prisoners are allowed to call their families once a month, I am never afforded this privilege. At one point, I am permitted to make a local call, but this turns out to be more of a curse than a blessing as I don't want to put my local friends in danger. Another time, I attempt to call the embassy, but the prison authorities cut the call. After that, my local phone call privileges are stopped. The warden never actually says 'no' outright, he just tells me 'maybe tomorrow' or 'later' – another form of control, making me beg. After I realise this, I stop asking.

One day, the warden offers me his cellphone, saying I can call my wife. I don't trust him, so I thank him politely, telling him it won't be necessary as I know my family are well. He stares at me long and hard, realising that he no longer has any power over me.

As the days turn into weeks, I write and send many letters, smuggling them out through the drug dealers' channels or trying to get weekend visitors to take them from me. I rush to the fence with my notes, ever hopeful that someone has come to see me. I ask anyone willing to listen to send messages for me and, if possible, give me a reply by the next week, but most are too afraid and unwilling to take the risk. I don't give up and just wait for the next weekend, and the next, and the next.

Eventually, my perseverance pays off as the bush telegraph system works well in Africa and news of my incarceration finds its way to some of the men who've worked for me in the past. They risk everything by turning up over weekends, bringing me whatever they can and smuggling my letters out. I pray that at least some of my notes get to my family to give them hope and confirmation that I am still alive. Seeing these old friends restores my faith in humanity, making me realise just how important having a network of support is.

Unfortunately, it seems that if the guards know something is for me, they confiscate the items before they make it past the gatehouse, and I am none the wiser. Even my attempts to get letters out are fruitless as the guards are always watching and most of my letters are intercepted when my visitors leave, so I've adapted my strategy. On Friday evenings, I take the letters I've written during the week and hand them to a few friends on the inside who I know receive visitors every weekend. I am pretty sure most will not reach Melanie but I will never give up hoping that by a small chance some of them might make it through.

The guards don't have it in for everyone, though; some of the inmates are even family or friends. The guards bring them things and even give them a cellphone to make calls when the warden is not there. This situation facilitates most of the illicit trading and the supply of drugs, alcohol and other 'essentials' into the prison.

Sometimes, inmates go to extraordinary lengths to cause problems for me with the guards. One afternoon, while I am sitting in the shade with my brothers, I am summoned to the guard hut. For reasons unknown, I've been reported by a fellow inmate for starting a fight. The guards know that it's bullshit, but they enjoy this opportunity to harass and threaten me. They all hate me for one reason or another, and I've grown accustomed to their threats. Sometimes they draw their weapons and point them at me, pretending to take aim and fire; other times they drag their fingers across their necks, mimicking the action of slitting my throat. This time they seem disinterested and just hassle me verbally, but I'm never quite sure how far they will go.

I don't know if I will ever come to terms with what is happening to me, but my focus is on getting out of here, not why I am here, so I look forward to weekends when there is a chance that I will be able to make some contact with the outside world. Using scavenged bits of paper, I continue to write notes to my family, with Melanie and my mother's telephone numbers included – the only numbers I can remember. I am still cursing modern technology for making storing information so easy that nobody needs to remember contact details.

To make sure that Melanie knows the messages are genuine, I address them to '*Fuffyloops*', which is my pet name for her, and sign it with love from '*Waterdraer*' (my birthday is in February and my sun sign is Aquarius, the water carrier). Even though writing these messages is a painful reminder of where I am and what I am missing, it keeps me connected to my life outside these bleak walls, and it feels like I am doing something to get out of my situation. At the very least, I am providing them with proof that I am still alive.

Little do I know that these phone numbers are pointless, as any messages sent to them will be lost in cyberspace. Back home, Melanie no longer has access to the cellphone number I have written down as Vodacom has cancelled my contract and all our numbers have been discontinued.

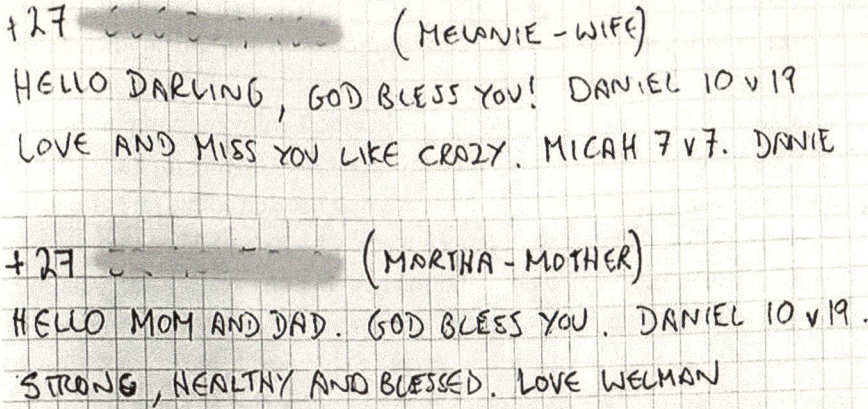

31

Close Shave

```
Black Beach Prison, Malabo
January 2014
```

Time passes slowly behind these walls. There are too many hours to sit and wonder what's going on outside. I'm used to driving projects forward and making things happen. It's hard not knowing what, if anything, is being done to get me out of here. *How* am I going to get out of here? When? What can I do to get out sooner? Is someone pushing the embassy team? Are my family being informed of their progress? There are too many questions unanswered and no contact with the outside world. A man can go crazy wondering…

It's like being in the devil's playground: the thoughts spinning round and round bring doubt, anger and frustration into a place that is already hostile and devoid of hope. Being patient and trusting that God is in control is something I have to remind myself of each day.

Luckily, on this hot and sticky morning, Amadou turns up and distracts me from my thoughts, telling me that I need a haircut. We head off to his 'barbershop', and he brews us some of his special tea, pouring the warm, bitter liquid into a cracked cup, and ladles in a generous amount of sugar. I'm glad Amadou is able to provide these small comforts. He's very organised, with an old sheet to drape over your shoulders, and he even has spirits to clean the shaver, which he burns to disinfect it.

Despite the differences in our religious beliefs, I enjoy his companionship. He is a humble man, facing a death sentence for a terrible mistake that he acknowledges with regret, and he has resigned himself to his fate and takes each day as it comes. Unlike the Western world with its anti-Muslim prejudice, it seems that behind these walls religious beliefs don't really affect relationships. You'd be hard-pressed to find a Muslim and a Christian sitting side by side drinking tea together in many parts of the world, but we have much bigger things to worry about in Black Beach. I know that as a member of the small Muslim community, he has some level of protection, but I don't have the benefit of any protectors sleeping nearby. God's angels are working overtime taking care of me.

In his former life, out in the real world, Amadou was a driver for a local construction company, enjoying his job, proud to be providing for his family back home in Mali, until he found his way behind these walls a few years back by stealing the payroll and beating and strangling his Moroccan manager to death. He will never see his family again. Like most, he doesn't talk about his crime, but in a rare moment of admission he tells me that he doesn't understand why he did it as he had never felt any murderous or criminal tendencies before that fateful day. Does the devil lurk inside every one of us? He acknowledges his guilt and has great remorse for what he did, accepting that his punishment lies at some unknown point in the future when he will face the firing squad.

He lays out his equipment: a razor blade, a cloth and a bottle of clear liquid, and then sits me down. I tell him I am after a Bruce Willis look and he promises to oblige. We chat just as if I'm sitting in a regular barbershop, although our conversation and the situation are somewhat different: I'm discussing the pros and cons of escaping from one of the world's worst prisons with a convicted murderer wielding a razor blade, trusting that he won't slip as he follows the contours of my skull, stripping the hair in long, even strokes.

'Escape'! A word only ever discussed in hushed tones. Just talking about it is dangerous, so it's seldom mentioned, and only then in the company of your most trusted companions. Sometimes, inmates joke about someone trying to escape, but for the most part the subject is taboo. Just recently, four guys were called to the guardroom and only returned a few days later, badly beaten. I never heard exactly why, but the rumour was that they were hatching an escape plan that involved one of the guards, who subsequently disappeared.

I'd be lying if I said that the thought of escape hasn't crossed my mind a few times, but I know that if I do attempt it, there will be no going back. I will have to be willing to kill or be killed. I know that if I am caught, there will be no mercy for me – a case of shoot first, ask questions later. And if by chance I survive, I'll be beaten until I wish they had killed me. Besides, being the only white guy here makes it difficult to leave without being noticed.

I've heard a rumour that Amadou is one of the few who has managed to pull off an escape, and today offers a rare opportunity for discussion as we are alone in his cell. I broach the subject cautiously, curious to know more, and, surprisingly, Amadou obliges with a reply. I suppose that as he is waiting for his death sentence to be carried out, he has no fear of telling me about his escape attempt; what can they do, kill him twice? Shrugging his shoulders, he tells me that his escape was one of very few successful attempts from Black Beach, but his freedom was short-lived: once he made it outside the prison walls, he had nowhere to go, no money and no options, so he headed to a friend's house. It wasn't long before the police came knocking.

Escapees who do make it past the walls often hide out in the unpopulated mountainous rainforest area to the south of the island. But living in the forest is harsh and most escapees end up making their way back to family or friends in Malabo and are quickly hunted down and returned to Black Beach, with a few trips to the torture chambers for a little attitude adjustment.

The fact that we're on an island makes escape even more difficult; the closest mainland is Cameroon, more than thirty kilometres away across shark-infested waters. If you do successfully escape from Black Beach, you'll have to find your way off the island pretty smartly, otherwise you'll be back behind bars in no time, often putting your friends and relatives at risk of joining you behind these walls. Malabo is not a good place to get on the wrong side of the law.

Constructed when the island was still a Spanish colony, the prison was built to house up to eighty prisoners. Its design is based on traditional Spanish prison architecture generally used in the Mediterranean and entirely unsuitable for tropical conditions. During the rainy season, which is about ten months of the year, storms lash the perimeter towers, exposing the guards to torrential downpours. Amadou says that whenever it rains, you never see the guards as they take cover under a tarpaulin inside the tower.

As he continues to slide the blade across my skull, it feels as though my skin is being stripped away layer by layer, but Amadou seems to be perfectly satisfied with his work. He goes on to tell me about three inmates who managed to cut through the iron bars across the window of their cell and then waited for just the right moment during a thunderstorm before attempting their escape, knowing that the guards would be sheltering from the rain. They removed the bars, threw down their mattresses and abseiled to the ground with a rope made from their bedsheets. They then carried their mattresses over to the barbed-wire fence and used them for protection as they climbed over and walked out of the grounds, free men! The entire process took minutes and went completely unnoticed by the guards who were sheltering from the elements under the tarpaulin.

The guards are held responsible for any escape that takes place under their watch, so there is a powerful incentive to apprehend the runaways as quickly as possible so that they don't end up on the wrong side of the fence themselves. As usual, the fugitives were caught within a day and returned to Black Beach.

Amadou sets the blade aside and shakes a liberal amount of liquid from the bottle onto the rag and rubs it thoroughly over my head. The sharp sting of alcohol burns into my skin and it feels as though he's set fire to my skull. I yelp, but he ignores my protests, continuing the conversation and explaining that if I wanted to escape I'd need help from outside and a boat to get me to Cameroon. These are not options that I could arrange or even discuss with any of my weekend visitors, as you never know who is listening in that crowded space. I have to accept that rampant corruption makes buying my freedom the only viable option if diplomacy on the part of the embassy fails.

Buying your way out is considered the only 'legal' solution to gaining your freedom, and it's a topic for lively discussion every day on the Esplanada, with many offering advice on how to do this, when to do it, whom to approach and what the going rate is. In fact, it's so common that some professional career criminals keep a portion of their ill-gotten gains aside for the sole purpose of buying their way out of Black Beach.

One of the guys I met in the early days of my arrival, who left soon afterwards, was back again within a short time and he told me that he would only be here for about six months, explaining that as long as you do not kill anyone, it's easy to buy your freedom. You just need to wait until the dust settles and most have forgotten about you, then your lawyer pays the judge, your folder disappears, and you walk out a free man. When he left us for the second time, he returned the following Saturday to visit, bringing food and money for his prison friends. Later, we heard that he'd been shot and killed trying to rob a warehouse in Malabo.

Many of the people here are awaiting-trial prisoners. One of the most incredible stories I've heard is about a bank robber who had been here for nearly a year before finally getting his day in court, where he was subsequently sentenced to fifteen years. He returned to Black Beach on a Friday, and the following day, as visitors were coming and going, he just walked straight out the gates. Apparently, he'd used his 'slush fund' to pay the guards to look the other way. We heard via the bush telegraph that soon after that he left for Spain. *Hasta la vista…*

32

Welcome to News Hour
Black Beach Prison, Malabo
January 2014

I've managed to borrow an old portable radio from a brother. After harvesting a few strands of wire from the fence to fashion a homemade aerial and a long and drawn-out search for batteries that still have some life in them, everything is in place. I'm finally ready to tune in to the radio waves from around the world as I sit on my bench on the Esplanada, shirt off, working on my tan.

I adjust the headphones and start tweaking the dial, trying to pick up a signal – anything will do – but the dial is loose and wiggles in its slot. It feels like I am doing brain surgery as I twist it gently this way and that, trying to coax a signal strong enough to hang on to. There's a lot of static, with the odd short burst of music or a voice that quickly disappears, and then, just for a brief moment: *'Good afternoon. You're listening to the BBC World Service. Welcome to News Hour, coming to you live from London. Here are the latest headlines ...'*

I have goosebumps, thrilled to have news from the other side, a connection to a world bigger than these walls that I am trapped behind. The signal is elusive, but I hold my breath, manipulating the dial gingerly until the voice emerges again, crystal clear in that distinctive British accent, every utterance charged with sincerity and authority, gliding smoothly down the airwaves and transporting me away from the chaos of my reality.

What a moment. At times it's been difficult not to feel forgotten and abandoned; I've stopped hoping for updates from the embassy and, starved for information, experiencing my first link to the world outside of my claustrophobic existence makes me feel quite emotional. Some days it's hard to remember that I am still part of something bigger than this cage I am living in. To be able to shut out the hubbub that continues unabated day in and day out and listen to the news making headlines around the world read out in calm and comforting tones is an amazing escape. I can only hope that the batteries I've found last long enough to listen to the entire broadcast.

It appears that not much has changed in the world out there. Muslim

WELCOME TO NEWS HOUR

extremists have captured the headlines. In Syria, Islamist rebels have infiltrated the ISIS headquarters in Aleppo, killing more than 270 people. The next report is somewhat closer to home as a correspondent tells of the growing conflict in Bangui in the Central African Republic, where a Christian mob have burned two Muslims in the street while French and African Union soldiers struggle to contain the sectarian violence that erupted after Muslim rebels took over the country.

As I sit here, in prison, surrounded by men from all over Africa of various races, religions and political affiliations, I realise just how pointless the conflict in the outside world really is. When will we ever learn to respect one another's beliefs and choices? When will politicians stop fuelling the fire by using our differences to drive a wedge between us?

The news anchor moves on to the weather. A severe ice storm has hit Canada and parts of the USA, causing widespread power outages and destruction, the worst experienced in half a century. I consider the absurdity of sitting here in my shorts, with no shirt on, baking in the 40°C heat while listening to reports describing the complete opposite.

I turn my attention back to the news report, relieved that the batteries have lasted so long. The presenter has moved on to the sports headlines and the next story is something that I know will affect my brothers locked up in here with me. They're crazy about soccer and many fights begin as innocent disputes about whether a referee has been fair in making a call in a match they're following. The news that local football hero Eusébio da Silva Ferreira has died is not going to go down well. Eusébio was one of the first world-class African-born players, nicknamed 'the Black Panther' and considered by many as one of the greatest footballers of all time, known for his speed, technique and ferocious right-footed strike that made him a prolific goal scorer. He inspired many to dream of following in his footsteps.

The final report on the show leaves me stunned and saddened to hear of Michael Schumacher's skiing accident. I can't believe that such a fit and healthy man, a legend among us, lies trapped in a coma. Although I am in vastly different circumstances, the fact that I, like him, am cut off from the world is not lost on me. I realise that as bad as it is in here, at least I am still a functioning human being; I can walk, talk and think. I still have the option of believing that I will one day get out of here and hold my wife in my arms again.

I'm sure that Michael's family are praying for him as they hold vigil at his bedside, willing him to return to them with all their might, and I am profoundly touched as I listen to his wife, Corinna, appeal for privacy, calling on the media to 'let the doctors work in peace'. For a moment, my mind wanders, imagining that the Schumachers are offering the same bargaining chips to the universe as I am, making promises to change their lives, to do things differently, to spend more time together focusing on the really important things, if only to have him back the way he was. I know how they must be feeling, as I have spent my time here praying fervently every day for just one thing: to return to my family, my wife, to wrap my arms around them and never let go.

33

Sick

Black Beach Prison, Malabo
January 2014

I am drowning in sweat, trembling, shaking with chills. There is a tightness in my chest making it difficult to breathe. I feel my muscles contracting, my body twitching. I'm breathing too fast, but my lungs feel empty. I can't fill them. A voice inside my head is telling me to breathe, breathe, breathe, but I feel paralysed.

I'm helpless.

Later, I emerge from the depths feeling weak and disorientated. I retch, feeling my body spasm in an urge to throw up. My lips are dry and cracked. I vaguely remember someone dripping water into my parched mouth, but I don't know when that was or how long I've been out. It's too exhausting to think as I slip back into a feverish dream world. Vivid scenes from moments in my life flash by too quickly to grasp as the world around me blurs, racing faster and faster, like I'm on a carousel, then fades into a monochromatic backdrop of emptiness that seems to transcend space and time.

I open my eyes, staring straight ahead, and see nothing but indistinct shapes, a blur of shadowy grey. I blink, trying to make sense of it. How did I get here? I need to find my way back. I close my eyes again. There is no before. There is no after. There is only now.

I must escape. Melanie is waiting. I push against the blackness of the abyss, but it swirls around my body, merging with the shadows, dragging me down into the depths of an ocean. I like it here; I want to stay. It's peaceful. I relax into the ocean's warm embrace, drifting slowly back up towards the light. As I near the surface, I hear the gentle sigh of water rushing over pebbles, tumbling, rising, falling back in an ancient rhythm against the shore. I lie back, luxuriating in the warmth of the sun on my skin and watch the clouds drift by, tinged with rose-gold hues, and soak up the salty freshness of the sea, drifting with the current as it carries me into the shallows where I reluctantly step onto the silky golden sand, the water lapping softly at my feet. I turn and look back out towards the horizon and raise my hand to block the sun. Is that

Melanie I see in the waves? Where am I? How did I get here? It's so good to be free …

Shards of light flash like laser beams into my eyes, penetrating deep into my skull. Slowly, reality dawns. There is no Melanie. There are no waves. No rose-tinted clouds or fresh air. No cool waters to wash away the filth clinging to my sweat-soaked body. I am still trapped in the real-life nightmare of Black Beach. I try to sit up, but my muscles refuse to cooperate, aching with bone-deep tiredness. The effort is too much and I sink back against the mattress, throwing my arm across my face to block out the light that's filtering inside my 'tent' and making my head pound. A crippling spasm hits me and I roll over in agony, clutching my stomach as I break out in a fresh sweat. Sharp, stabbing pains run down my right side. It's all too familiar as I lean over the edge of my mattress, dry retching, acid bile burning my throat. Malaria.

With no access to medical care, I'm in serious trouble. How can one tiny creature cause such agony and suffering? These minute bloodthirsty vampires are responsible for millions of deaths each year and I'm worried that I might be next. Cerebral malaria is the most dangerous form, and having had it before I don't need a doctor or blood test to confirm my diagnosis. It's hardly surprising, considering the hordes of buzzing bloodsuckers tormenting me night after night. The way I feel right now, I'm pretty sure that I am staring death in the face, but I'm too sick and exhausted to care, and I curl up on my mattress, closing my eyes against the light.

Someone shakes my arm. It's too much effort to emerge from the dark, but they're persistent, so I open my eyes a crack, blinking, bringing the world back into focus. A young boy is peering down at me. His name is John, a street kid around seventeen years old who, like many others, shouldn't be in this place. John has grown up on the streets with no guidance and limited education and does what he must to survive. Surprisingly, he speaks a little English, and I've spent time chatting with him and listening to his stories. Now it seems that he is taking care of me.

He raises my head with one hand, pouring some water into my mouth, and then helps me to sit up. The effort is draining, but he props me up and hands me a sheet of paper and a pen, telling me that the drug dealers said I must write a note asking for medicine and help from the embassy. My grip on the pen is weak, but I manage to scrawl a short note and sign it, knowing that smuggling out the note will be tricky. Clearly, even the most hardened criminals here realise how sick I am if they're willing to send out a message together with their 'prescriptions' for the day via their crude washing-line system from the guard tower to the toilet window.

John tells me that the others have been checking up on me and say it's not just malaria – I have typhoid too. It's only treatable with antibiotics, which I definitely won't find here. He heads off to deliver my note. Next door, my neighbour is moving about in his tent, groaning and vomiting onto the floor in the space between our mattresses. It stinks and I shudder as the urge to throw up resurfaces, adding to my misery. I roll over and stick my head out of the tent, overcome with nausea as my stomach clenches and I retch, feeling like my insides are being torn apart. Nothing comes up and the exertion makes my skin prickle as a fresh layer of sweat runs off my body.

I fall back against the mattress, shivering, and drift off into a fevered, delirious sleep, disappearing into a void that straddles the divide between life and death. My lucid moments are punctuated by hallucinations of people calling out to me, but I'm stuck at the bottom of a well and in my weakened state I don't have the power to make my way back to a reality that is just a continuation of the nightmare.

Days go by as I drift in and out of consciousness, occasionally emerging from the dark thinking that I am going to die, and then, as the darkness descends once again, I pray that I do. At some point, I'm vaguely aware that someone is giving me medicine, dripping water into my parched mouth and washing down my body with a bucket of cool water.

As my fever breaks, there are fewer moments of oblivion, and each time I resurface, I become more aware of my surroundings. I am weak and have lost a lot of weight, but I'm surprised and relieved to have made it through to the other side. Although I can barely stand, I make it off my stinky mattress and stagger on shaky legs, leaning heavily on John as he helps me to the bathroom where I splash myself with water. The effort is draining but invigorating and I feel slightly better.

Each day it gets a little easier, until eventually, with my friends propping me up, I make my way outside and, for the first time in days, experience the simple joy of 'fresh' air, revelling in the warmth of the sun on my skin which lifts my spirits and provides much-needed vitamin D to aid my recovery. I feel vaguely human again basking in the sun, looking up at the miracle of a clear blue sky. I praise God that I have survived, overwhelmed with gratitude to John and the others who have taken care of me.

I have no idea if my note ever found its way to the embassy and don't know where the medication came from, but it's clear that one of my brothers is responsible for getting it for me. I am constantly amazed that these dangerous men are the ones showing compassion and fellowship, supporting me through my weakest, most vulnerable moments, even though I have nothing to offer them in return.

I hear that while I was locked in my personal vault of suffering, the warden decided that writing or receiving letters is forbidden, and to underscore this message he has also banned pens. Paper is now even more scarce and must be smuggled in. Crazy times, and I have slept through it all! Luckily, my friends know how important writing is to me and pen and paper materialise so that I can write more letters that may never be delivered. It's important that my family is spared the details about the depths of my suffering on the off chance that my letters ever find their way to them, so while I'm sitting outside with my shirt off, I write to tell them that I'm relaxing at the tanning salon. Keeping it light-hearted, I add that I've joined the Weight Watchers club and have just been made 'Member of the Month' due to my consistent weight loss. I add that this exclusive weight-loss club guarantees you amazing results, unlike all the fad diets on the internet.

On the first afternoon that I feel strong enough, I collect my takkies from Old Man Luis's cell. Even though putting them on takes effort, I accomplish the task and manage to do a couple of stretches and walk up and down the stairs twice. By this point I'm exhausted, but I know I have to push on. Once I get my breath back, I pick up my newly acquired 'skipping rope' – a cable from the surveillance cameras. It's perfect for the job, and although skipping doesn't come easily, what I lack in talent I make up for in determination. On my first attempt and in my weakened state, I can barely manage about five turns of the 'rope' before becoming too lightheaded and giving up. Next, I attempt some sit-ups. The effort is gruelling. I get to six with a lot of grunting, straining every inch of my body, much to the amusement of my fellow inmates who have gathered to watch, discussing my feeble efforts with laughter and derision. In my next letter home, I announce that I have joined the Virgin Active gym.

Over the next few days I am sick again as the after-effects of malaria hit me hard, but as soon as I can, I'm back to 'the gym' and start taking regular walks outside in the sun, building up my vitamin D reserves. It's slow going, but I vow to rebuild my strength, even though exercising is frowned upon by the guards. If you are caught doing anything physical, they accuse you of trying to get fit in order to overpower them and escape.

My gym equipment is all homemade and rudimentary. During the last riots, some of the prisoners broke off concrete blocks to throw at the guards, and a few of these lie discarded around the courtyard. I manage to find one block of around twenty kilograms – perfect for building muscle and strengthening my arms. After a few weeks, the exercise starts to yield results; my body is recovering and adapting to the new routine. I push harder, eventually managing to skip for thirty minutes, despite the sweat dripping off in bucketloads. I lift the concrete blocks like dumbbells and feel better with each passing day – more positive, mentally stronger and, most importantly, healthier. A few others have been inspired to join me and have started calling me 'Thunder', a new jail name coined by a friendly street thief who has been watching me do sit-ups with weights. It's done great things for my ego, and I much prefer it to 'Blanco'.

As the days go by, I feel stronger and have worked up to creating a circuit for training. Each day, I collect my shoes and, after a couple of stretches, run up and down the stairs twice, then head out of the sleeping quarters into the courtyard to do a few laps. The guards confront me about exercising and confiscate my 'equipment', but this Virgin Active has an abundance of new materials to replace whatever has been seized. Although exercise is a crime, football is permitted, but it has its hazards and is better suited to the younger crowd. The older guys prefer to sit on the sidelines and place bets rather than participate in what often turns into a bloody battle as the youngsters are quick to resolve disputes with their fists and there are no referees to caution players for dangerous or reckless play, unsportsmanlike behaviour or infractions of the rules.

One of my favourite pastimes is to walk outside in the rain, which gives me a chance to escape and reboot. Back in the real world, golf was always an enjoyable way to relax, and in South Africa there's an abundance of world-class courses, such as Oubaai, designed by sporting great Ernie Els, Pinnacle Point in Mossel Bay, and Simola, the first golf course in Africa to be designed by the Golden Bear himself, Jack Nicklaus. There are no wide-open spaces here, and certainly no beautifully tended fairways and greens, but I am always on the lookout for something to take my mind off the harsh reality of this life. Fresh, untainted water pouring from the heavens rejuvenates me and I enjoy it almost as much as the sunshine.

One of the inmates has given me a broken umbrella, which I've managed to put back together. As I walk around the empty courtyard (my brothers don't share my enthusiasm for the rain), I glance up at the side of the hill and find myself thinking, *Hmmm, it's about 160 yards and would take a good five-iron shot to land there.* I fold up the umbrella, holding it like a golf club, and set up mid-stance with an imaginary ball, slowly taking the 'club' back and swinging. I imagine the ball flying through the air and can almost hear the soft 'plop' as it lands on the green ... *Boom!* Right next to the flag.

I focus hard on my next shot, playing the various courses that I am familiar with, traversing the contoured greens of my memories. For a short time, I am able to keep my mind busy, focusing my thoughts on walking the links, breaking free from where I am as I relive the courses I've played: Fancourt, and then Pezula with its windswept panoramic ocean and lagoon views from the Knysna clifftops. I have no idea what the others think I'm doing. They're watching me from beneath the shelter of Old Man Luis's shack, chuckling as I stand in the downpour swinging my closed umbrella then cupping my hand over my eyes and peering off into the distance.

It's a real disappointment to return to reality as the rain subsides and the sun returns in full force, reminding me that where I am there is no nineteenth hole in which to end the round. Sadly no Pro Shop either ...

34

Until We Meet Again
Black Beach Prison, Malabo
January 2014

Over the past few days, the mood at Black Beach has been tense, and I'm filled with a sense of foreboding. My brothers who have spent years behind these walls tell me to prepare for the worst, certain that a riot is looming. Everyone is on edge, and I struggle to suppress my feelings of uncertainty.

My recovery has been slow, and although I am much stronger and getting better each day, I know that to recover fully I will need more medication, better sanitary conditions and a few decent meals. The odds of me surviving a riot are slim. You have to fight to protect yourself in a riot. The warden and prison staff are indifferent to my cause and have done nothing to aid my convalescence, most likely as per their orders from above. I know that in my present state there is no way I can fight off an angry mob, so I decide that in case things go horribly wrong, I should at least write a last will and testament, which will hopefully find its way through the prison network to the embassy in the event of my death.

Sitting in the gloom of my tent, I stare at the blank page for a long time, wondering how to put my final thoughts and emotions into words on a scrap of paper torn from a notebook. How do you say goodbye to the ones you love, the ones you have shared your life with? My wife, my children … My parents have already suffered so much, losing my brother when he was just a toddler and my sister as a young adult, and now perhaps me too. Surely this is more than one mother, one father, one family should endure?

The burden of the pain I have caused my family and the importance of surviving my ordeal sometimes overwhelm me, and, as always when I find myself faltering, I turn to my Bible for guidance and reassurance. As I flick through the pages, I'm drawn to the Psalms and search out one of the most iconic passages, in Psalm 23:4:

> *Yea, though I walk through the valley of the shadow of death,*
> *I will fear no evil: for thou art with me; thy rod and thy staff they comfort me.*

There is no doubt that I am existing in physical and spiritual darkness, separated from everything I know and love, and yet even here behind these walls, God has found his way to me, providing comfort and divine protection. I'm reminded that no matter what lies ahead, I won't be facing it alone, and I begin putting pen to paper, writing my name at the top of the page and addressing it to the South African embassy.

I begin with the practical issues first, advising them that in the event of my death I want to be buried in Malabo. There is no point in adding financial and bureaucratic strain to my family's pain and suffering by getting my remains all the way back to South Africa. I add that they will meet me again someday in heaven. I include a message of unconditional love and gratitude to Melanie, my children and my parents for being a part of my journey in this life.

It feels better to have made a start, and writing it ultimately takes longer than I anticipated. I pause often to reflect on the life I've had with my family, the times when we'd just talk and laugh, doing the mundane things that everyone does. All the important moments, too: getting married, seeing my children for the first time, their first day at school, school prize-giving, our dog Bubbles, bike rides in the mountains, Christmases, birthdays and holidays ... There are so many precious moments that are woven together to form the tapestry of our lives, reminding me just how much I cherish every one of them. Once I've finally finished writing, I fold up the document carefully and push it between the grubby pages of my Bible, hoping that they will never have to read it.

I head out of my tent. If I hurry, I can join the church group in time for morning prayers and then do a mid-morning gym session at 'Virgin Active', followed by tea with Amadou in his cell. Although I never truly feel safe and don't drop my guard for one moment, my life behind bars is slowly evolving. It seems that no matter where you find yourself, life takes on its own rhythm. More and more, I am discovering that finding structure in the little tasks and appointments undertaken each day brings a sense of order in a chaotic world.

But today is different. I can't seem to shake my feeling of unease as I make my way to the cell where the church services are held. Something just doesn't feel right. I go in and find everyone settling in for prayers. I join the circle, linking hands with the others, and bow my head, and together we recite the

Lord's Prayer. As the prayer comes to an end, we share a moment of silence, offering up our own private communion with our saviour.

The stillness is shattered by the clear sound of a name being called. Usually, a single voice would go unnoticed amid the clamour and commotion of Black Beach – the prison is so noisy that usually nothing can be heard above the din – but a strange silence has fallen across the entire prison. As I hear the name called again, my heart plummets. We look at one another in shock and the person to my left tightens his grip on my hand. They are calling for one of our Christian brothers, a man sentenced to death for witchcraft and the brutal slaying of his wife.

From the moment the first name is called, we realise what's going on. Throughout the prison, the silence is absolute. For the first and only time since my arrival, everything stops and the inmates talk in hushed whispers. Everyone is still, contemplating their own fragility against the dark forces that control this evil place.

The next name is called and I go cold. *Amadou*. My barber, my tea maker, my friend. A prickling sensation runs like a million spiders over my scalp, shivers race down my spine and my skin tingles as goosebumps erupt on the back of my neck and ripple down the length of my arms. I sink heavily onto a bench, feeling weak all over, tasting bile in my throat as I struggle not to throw up. There is no way to explain the depth of my emotions. I know that Amadou has been stoic all along, accepting his fate and telling me that he is ready for his punishment, but I can't imagine how he is feeling as he faces the reality of it in this moment, standing somewhere in the prison, hearing them calling his name and knowing that this is the end. Today will be his last on this earth.

I've heard that firing squads are the preferred method of execution in Equatorial Guinea and AK-47s are the weapon of choice. This shoulder-mounted semi-automatic assault rifle is simple to use and, in Africa, a popular option for the military and terrorists alike. The common AK-47 magazine holds thirty rounds. I am familiar with it on an all-too-personal level, having grown up on the continent.

My mind is a dark place picturing Amadou standing alone in front of a squad of soldiers, weapons cocked and loaded, waiting for a hail of bullets to rip through him, puncturing, mutilating, killing him. I can only pray that his death will be quick and that he won't suffer too much.

We abandon the church service and hurry outside to join the crowd at the fence to watch as the men, seven in all, are lined up and handcuffed at their hips – a method reserved for the most violent prisoners. The guards are taking no chances as they march them out of the gate and hand them over to a group of soldiers.

As I watch the prisoners leaving, I spot Amadou. Directly behind him is Tadeo (aka Rocky), the man who almost beat another prisoner to death right in front of me on Christmas Eve. Their faces are blank, devoid of any emotion. The last thing I see as they are shoved into a truck is their eyes, downcast, as the door slams shut and the truck winds its way up the hill.

We're all in shock. These are the first 'official' executions since 2010, when four political opponents were sentenced to death by a military court for treason and attempting to kill President Obiang, who himself came to power after his uncle was executed. Those men had their sentence carried out in secret within an hour of the court delivering its verdict, depriving them of their right to seek clemency or appeal to a higher court. They were denied the right to see their families, to say goodbye, just as these men that I know, men who have shared their meagre possessions with me, cut my hair and whose wisdom and generosity have kept me alive, have today been denied. Although they have done terrible things, they still have families and have been given no warning, no opportunity to communicate with them or their lawyers, no last goodbyes.

Later, as information starts filtering through the bush telegraph, we hear the gory details and are especially shocked to hear that Rocky did not die easily. The prisoners were taken to the naval facility nearby, led into the compound and lined up against a wall. At an officer's command, the soldiers had taken aim and fired, a system bound to fail as the firing squad was untrained, over-excited, and at least a few of them were drunk. Apparently, even after being hit several times, Rocky did not go down until, finally, the officer in charge delivered the fatal shot by walking up to him and putting a bullet in his head using his standard-issue pistol. Their bodies were then loaded up and buried by soldiers at the Malabo cemetery.

A subdued atmosphere settles like a fog over the prison, and I feel an intense and overwhelming loathing for this dark and wretched place and the men that police it. It's a cage that serves no purpose other than to breed more hatred and rage against each other and the injustices of the system, a soulless pit of sadistic cruelty and oppression where the men in charge literally have our lives in their hands.

As we turn and walk back inside, I'm distinctly aware of the heavy silence hanging over us. There is no music, no pots clattering on the cooking fires, no shouting or arguing, no youngsters playing football on the Esplanada, just an endless hush that continues throughout the day as we reflect on the fate of our friends and what it really means to be trapped behind these walls.

This is not a place of behavioural rehabilitation or skills development, unless you count apprenticeships in drug dealing, prostitution, stealing, rape and murder; this is a place of fear, torture, abuse and humiliation – a toxic mix guaranteed to poison minds and souls. As I sit huddled in my tent, struggling to come to terms with the brutal and unexpected slaying of these men and trying to make sense of things, I am willing to risk anything to get out of here.

35

Happy Birthday to Me
Black Beach Prison, Malabo
February 2014

It's February 2014. My birthday has come and gone, and I don't even realise it until sometime after the fact. There is nothing worth celebrating here, but I stick to the ritual of writing letters, knowing that if I stop, it will be a downward spiral. Black Beach is a bottomless pit, and it doesn't take much to drag you into its depths, so today I am doodling little Valentine cartoons for Melanie, remembering that it is a special day we always set aside for celebrating our love. If they ever reach her, she'll have a good laugh at the little images I've drawn. It makes me smile remembering our life together, and the Lord knows that reasons to smile are rare in this wretched place.

Black Beach is haunted by the ghosts of countless tortured souls who spent their last days on African soil chained and confined before being shipped off to parts unknown, destined to endure a life of suffering as slaves working the sugarcane fields of America and the West Indies. Early European traders launched their transcontinental slave routes using Bioko (then called Fernando Po) as a key trading port and link to the African mainland. They preferred the relative safety of the coast, and tales of black magic, cannibalism and witchcraft made them wary of venturing too far inland. Coffee, cacao and timber were key assets traded by the locals until the Europeans set up their own plantations here, after which labour was in short supply. The indigenous Bubi population refused to work for them and were eventually pushed inland, their numbers decimated by alcohol addiction and diseases brought in by the European traders. The labour problem was solved by shipping Nigerian migrant workers across from the mainland. Later, when sugar and other crops were cultivated in the Americas, Bioko became a popular base for ships to anchor and secure full cargoes and a steady supply of captives from the interior. Slavers added guns to their portfolio of goods to trade from the fort that served as a collection point for slaves, gold, ivory and wood brought in from Central and West Africa.

For centuries, Europeans exploited the region, exporting more than six million souls as slave labour, which had a profound impact on the population and destroyed the local culture and history. Along the African coast, pidgin languages flourished as a lingua franca, facilitating trade relations and becoming embedded in the cultural fabric that endures today. Even Angabi prefers to converse in pidgin.

According to my friend Ugo, the name 'Black Beach' is simply derived from the colour of the sand where a creek running alongside the prison joins the river leading to the ocean, staining the sand dark with effluent. It's a swampy area frequented by crocodiles that emerge from the murky waters to bathe in the sunshine on its banks, creating another very effective barrier to freedom for anyone considering escape. Beneath the prison 'hospital' lie the remains of a small facility built by the slave masters to house and torture the most 'stubborn' slaves. If they died, their bodies were thrown into the creek, either to be eaten by the crocodiles or washed out to sea.

How many lives have been lost on this soil before my time here? Innocent men, women and children lie buried beneath me. I don't want to join these forgotten souls who were brought to this island on the first step of their journey into slavery. Those who survived were taken from the shadows of this coastal enclave as captives in chains, loaded onto small vessels and transported to slave ships anchored offshore. Most died on the voyage, but those who survived faced a life of struggle, suffering and hard labour on the vast sugar plantations that had begun to be cultivated in the 'Land of the Free', while European traders and New World landowners grew rich on the spoils of their wanton exploitation and plundering.

After the Spanish took over from the Portuguese, they made use of the facilities left behind by the slave masters to detain anyone who was suspected of a crime or who'd made a nuisance of themselves. The place remained much as its former slave owners had left it. There were no ablution facilities, so sewage ran straight into the creek and out to sea. Occasionally, the river would dry up and there would be no fresh water at all, so Black Beach remained a stinking pit until independence in the 1960s when Francisco Macías Nguema, the uncle of the current president, came into power and the need for a secure prison facility meant that the same pattern continued from the days of the slave trade and Spanish occupation.

Later, a new facility was constructed and 'Black Bitch', as the locals refer to it, rose upon the graves of those that had gone before, providing a place for yet another generation of masters to carry out ever more cruel and vicious methods of torture and misery on behalf of the new regime. Anyone unfortunate enough to find his or her way down the hill into this cove behind the presidential palace knows that their life is in jeopardy, that there is no such thing as human rights, that while you are here, your suffering will know no end, and should a general or superior order you killed, their orders will be carried out expediently, no questions asked. For many, if you are brought to this place, your family will forget about you. It's as if you are already dead.

I hear a pot crash somewhere in the building and am jolted from the fog of these dark thoughts. I sigh and force myself to refocus. I realise that it's highly likely that I will conveniently 'disappear' at some point; I will just have to do everything I can to avoid it. Around here, things change in an instant. I must be strong and not let the darkness overwhelm me.

Just then, there is a movement outside my tent and someone tosses in a small scrap of crumpled up paper. Curious, I reach for it, it's fragile but I can see there is writing on it so I begin to gingerly unfold it, smoothing out the crinkles to reveal a jumble of words painstakingly transcribed by someone whose first language is not English. Initially it's difficult to decipher, all in upper case and the letters so tightly packed together that it's hard to separate the tangled words until finally I make sense of it and tears pour down my cheeks as I read and reread the words I've been longing to see. A message of love to me from my best friend, my soulmate, my reason for being… It's my first message from Melanie, telling me she loves me, telling me she's waiting, telling me she is praying for me.

    Thank you God.

PART 3

'Life without liberty is like
a body without spirit.'
– Kahlil Gibran

36

Butta My Bread

Black Beach Prison, Malabo
February 2014

It's early evening and I'm sitting on the Esplanada watching the younger prisoners enjoy an animated game of football when the gong sounds. I reluctantly pack up my things and make my way inside. I collect my bucket and toothbrush and head for the 'showers', and then return to my tent and try to get comfortable on my thin, grubby piece of foam, curling up under my well-worn sheet, reflecting on the tenacity of the human spirit and how I have adapted to my surroundings. Even so, I dream of a future where I'm enjoying a refreshing hot shower with steaming water cascading over my body before climbing into a soft, comfortable bed, wrapping my arms around my beautiful wife as we snuggle together under the billowy folds of a luxurious feather comforter, Bubbles tucked in beside us. Little do I know that a simple clerical error is about to change everything for me.

Suddenly, the sheet draped around my bed is roughly pulled aside, snapping me back to reality. I tense up, ready to defend my meagre possessions, and am surprised to see the Jefe de Castel peering in at me. He grunts a terse greeting and tosses a shabby brown prison uniform onto the mattress, announcing that my name is on 'the list' and I am to appear before the judge at the Palacio de Justicia in the morning.

I'm astonished. Is it possible that after months of suffering and hardship I'm going to court? Praise God! Dare I hope that I may even be set free? I get up before dawn, too excited to sleep. I pull on my spiffy new outfit. The brown overalls are not particularly clean and I prefer not to think about the stains and smells on them; I've heard that they take uniforms off the dead and hand them out. I pop my small Bible into the pocket, along with a scrap of paper on which I've written the embassy's number, just in case, and then quickly gather up my possessions and head off to find someone to take care of them while I am away.

I've seen prisoners leave for court each week; most come back again, so even though my stomach is churning with excitement at the possibility of being released, I don't want to get my hopes up just yet. I still don't have much worth stealing – just my fan, the crappy foam mattress, a bucket and two threadbare, hand-me-down sheets – but if I do have to come back here, my life will be unbearable without them. My shoes and clothing are safely stored with Old Man Luis in his cell, so I stop by briefly to tell him my news and then make my way outside to join the line waiting for the meat wagon to arrive. *God don butta my bread*, as they say in Pidgin. God has answered my prayers.

I hang around in the sun, my new outfit giving off a ripe aroma that even a vagrant would find distasteful, but for once I don't care. Nothing will distract me from the hope that I may be getting out of here.

Eventually the gates open and we walk in single file past a guard who checks our names against his list, and then we gather outside the guard hut to wait for our transport. The others waiting with me say that everyone who is sent to Black Beach must make a court appearance within ninety days of their arrival for 'proof of life' or for charges to be brought against them. Some are hoping that their charges have been dropped or are counting on their family and friends to have come up with the bribes needed to secure their release. It seems that although I've not been found guilty of anything, and for all intents and purposes I am not even here, my name has somehow made it onto 'the list'. Someone in the admin department is going to be in a world of trouble when Angabi finds out, but I can only hope that I am long gone, en route to South Africa, before that happens.

One by one, our names are called. When it's my turn, I enter the guard hut where I am subjected to the humiliation of a thorough search and then handcuffed to another prisoner. The guards are not taking any chances as many of the prisoners accompanying me are hardened criminals who may be willing to grab an opportunity to escape or attack them.

The vehicle is stuffy and baking hot inside. We're crammed tighter than sardines in a can and the small mesh windows don't allow in much fresh air, but I don't care. I am thrilled to be leaving the hellhole of a prison, even if just for a few hours.

As the truck starts up and lurches out of the compound, we're flung against one another, but no one seems to mind, and once the vehicle gets up to speed and smooths out, the guard seated in the back with us hands his mobile to the prisoner next to me who calls his family to tell them he is on his way to see the judge. He finishes the call and hands the phone to me. I can't believe my luck. Finally, a means to make contact with the outside world! I take out the scrap of paper with the embassy's number on it from between the pages of my Bible and quickly dial before the guard has a change of heart and demands his phone back.

The phone rings. As soon as it's answered I speak urgently in Afrikaans, telling them my name and where I am going to be. I tell them to write down the details and find someone who can meet me at the judge's chambers immediately. I don't feel like I am exaggerating when I say that it is a matter of life and death, and my hands are shaking as I end the call and return the phone to the guard, letting out a long sigh, my heart racing as a surge of adrenaline floods my body. It's as if I've already pulled off a daring escape. I hope the embassy understands just how desperate my situation is and sends someone to help me. After all the disappointments over these past months, I am terrified that the message will be ignored and no one will show up. This is my first and probably only shot at freedom. I pray it doesn't evaporate because my message is lying forgotten on someone's desk.

The other prisoners are all in high spirits knowing that their family and friends will meet them at the courts. For some, if their relatives have raised enough cash for a bribe, today will be their last behind the walls of Black Beach … until next time. I drown out the noisy chatter by praying with all my might, wanting but not daring to hope, praying that someone from the embassy is on their way to rescue me. Black Beach turns even the most optimistic person into a realist, and I've spent enough time fighting the 'system' to know that my chances are slim.

We arrive at the Palacio de Justicia and the van drives straight into the underground parking through the side entrance. I know this place well by now, and I'm hoping that things will be different this time as we're offloaded and marched to the holding cells where I was taken after being abducted from the airport. As the door shuts, I begin to prepare myself mentally for the claustrophobia that I know will overwhelm me, but before I even get a chance to take my first deep breaths, my name is called and the cell is unlocked.

I can't believe that I have been called first. Suspicious, I follow the guard, wondering if this is yet another one of their tricks. What if, by calling me first, they're ensuring that the embassy people don't arrive in time to intervene on my behalf? As these thoughts race through my mind, I wonder how I might be able to stall my appearance before the judge to give them time to get here.

The guard escorts me to the secretary's office, pointing to a chair and telling me to sit, and then handcuffs me to the seat and walks away, leaving me in the company of the judge's secretary, who pays me no attention as she busies herself with the dockets and folders on her desk. Her chair creaks as she swivels around and drops a heap of files into a box on the floor. She is compact and buxom, her peroxided hair immaculately braided, and I get the feeling that she relishes the power she wields, knowing that she holds the fate of every one of us in her hands. It's clear to me that her soul is in the early stages of decomposition, obviously helped along by the piles of cash lying scattered on the desk. I watch in silence. It's hot and stuffy and my hands are clammy. The handcuffs are pinching my wrists, so I flex my fingers and squirm in my seat, trying to alleviate the tingling sensation in my arms. But despite the discomfort, I'd still rather be sitting here than in the cells. I chance a hopeful glance towards the passage leading to the public area of the building.

Footsteps approach and I look up expectantly, but the man who enters barely glances in my direction and heads straight to the secretary's desk. He's wearing a light-coloured jacket with tailored trousers and a pink shirt and is carrying a folder and an envelope. I can see that the envelope contains wads of cash and gather from the ensuing conversation that he is a lawyer paying a fine on behalf of his client. The secretary takes the folder, writes a note, peers into the envelope, slips it into the folder, puts it aside and waves the man away.

As time passes, a steady stream of attorneys make their way to her desk, all delivering dockets and envelopes filled with cash. She listens with an air of boredom, nods, checks each envelope to make sure that there is money inside it, scribbles a note, adding it to the growing pile on her desk, and then sends the attorneys off with a promise to sort it out. I wonder if these are really fines that are being processed.

It seems that this is the only way to get yourself out of trouble in this place, which leaves me feeling decidedly uncomfortable. I feel as though paying a bribe would basically be an admission of guilt. I have done nothing wrong, so hopefully if the embassy intervenes I won't need to explore this option, especially as I am developing an intense dislike for the woman seated in front of me. She represents everything that is wrong with the system. Her arrogance and superiority is obvious and, sitting here cuffed to the chair, I have seen how all the attorneys have treated her with the utmost respect; they know that she is in control of their clients' fates. Her condescending attitude and indifference is infuriating; she clearly has no empathy, and I am pretty sure that it's all about how much money is in the envelope and if she is having a good day and wants to help you or not.

I hear someone walking down the passage in our direction and glance up to see an important-looking well-dressed gentleman striding purposefully into the office. I can tell that he is angry. He glances quickly in my direction and nods brusquely.

'Hello, Danie, don't worry, I am here to help you,' he says in Afrikaans as he marches straight towards the secretary.

I have absolutely no idea who he is, but hearing his words in my home language and the authority in his voice fills me with confidence. Have my prayers finally been answered? Is it possible that I might be going home?

37

Free

Palacio de Justicia, Malabo
February 2014

The secretary ignores him, not even bothering to glance up as she continues with single-minded focus to shuffle through the papers on her desk. Another man enters the office and greets her, saying he is a translator, and then turns to introduce the man beside him as Ambassador Rambau from the South African embassy. I straighten up with a jolt, completely taken aback and gawk at them in awe. I am speechless! The ambassador, no less!

Can it be true that the South African ambassador has turned up in person to sort my problem out? Even though I am astonished, apparently his importance is lost on the secretary, who makes no move to greet him or the translator. I watch in anticipation as I can see that this has hit a nerve; the ambassador is not used to being treated with such disrespect. A muscle twitches in his jaw as he draws himself up and moves towards the desk, suggesting in a low but authoritative voice that she immediately stops what she is doing and pays attention. He tells her in no uncertain terms that she should, at the very least, understand that as the official representative of South Africa he has her president's number on speed dial. It seems he finally has her attention, and she jumps hastily out of her chair as he glowers at her, demanding to see the judge immediately. Soon, she is tripping over her words in an attempt to apologise and call the judge at the same time.

I think the anger the ambassador seems to be struggling to hold in check is directed at the systematic abuse that exists throughout the halls of justice, no matter where in the world you are. While waiting for the judge to appear, he demands to know why I am being treated like a common criminal. The moment the judge appears, full of apologies, he turns on the secretary, angrily shouting for my handcuffs to be removed. I'm really enjoying seeing the tables being turned. In a twist of fate, it turns out that the secretary had followed the law when adding my name to the list for today. If it hadn't been for her 'mistake', I would never have been called before the judge. So, I actually have her to thank for the fact that I am here today.

After summoning a guard to bring the keys for my handcuffs, Ambassador Rambau puts the key into the lock and releases me. I stand up shakily, rubbing my tender wrists. I still can't believe the turn of events as he pulls me into a bear hug and looks me up and down, asking if I am all right. Filled with emotion, I nod, not trusting myself to speak, but words aren't necessary. He understands how I'm feeling and gives me a reassuring pat on the shoulder before turning to the judge and firing a barrage of words at him so fast the translator has trouble keeping up. 'Why is Daniel under arrest? And why is he being treated like a common criminal? Why have we not been informed of this hearing? Is it not law that you need to inform the embassy?' He ends the volley with a simple demand that I be released immediately, saying that he will personally take responsibility for me.

Wow! What a performance. I want to clap I'm so excited! The judge has been rendered speechless, mumbling something unintelligible. Finally, he nods and says that if the embassy can provide a formal letter requesting my release, it will be done immediately.

Satisfied, Ambassador Rambau turns to me, saying that everything is under control, that I have nothing more to worry about and that he will get the letter to the judge within the next few hours. Soon, my ordeal will be over.

The ambassador leaves and I'm placed back in the holding cells, this time without handcuffs. The prison van arrives sometime later to collect those of us who have not been released and we are returned to Black Beach. As the meat wagon trundles down the hill towards the prison, the reality of what has just happened starts to sink in. Is it possible that I may be set free, maybe even by as soon as tomorrow morning?

Lying in the dark in my tent as the night drags on is the longest and loneliest time of my entire stay at Black Beach. Knowing that there's a very real chance I could be free tomorrow is something I'm too terrified to believe. I've been betrayed so many times that I don't want to dare to hope or dream that this could really be happening.

I'm on edge. Every sound I hear might be someone coming to put an end to my existence. A convenient prison spat resulting in my death – a sad but unavoidable occurrence, according to the authorities – is one of the scenarios playing on repeat throughout the long night, but a part of me realises that this could potentially cause an international incident now that the South African ambassador is involved and has absolute proof of where I am. So, in a small corner of my heart lies a tiny glimmer of hope that grows larger as the minutes tick by and night turns to dawn.

I am up early, pacing around the yard. I can't sit still; it's like the thoughts racing through my mind are driving my feet to pace up and down the courtyard. At some point, I glance up towards the presidential palace and notice the blue meat wagon coming down the hill and stopping outside the guard hut. The driver climbs out and looks over at us from the other side of the fence. He spots me in the crowd and nods. No words are necessary. I stop pacing. It's over.

I hurry inside to Old Man Luis's cell and get dressed. I gather up my precious possessions – my mattress, my fan and clothes I no longer need – and give them away. Hugging my brothers, I promise not to forget them and to do what I can to help them.

My pockets and hands are filled with hastily scribbled notes shoved at me by these desperate men as I walk outside, still numb with disbelief. I feel as if I'm walking on air, that the ground is about to disappear from beneath my feet. I wonder if I am trapped in a dream and none of this is real. Am I really walking out of here alive? Damaged, traumatised, broken, but alive?

The gate opens and I float outside with a few other prisoners. The driver smiles and holds the door open for us to climb in. There are four of us being released today and the others tell him where they want to go as they climb into the vehicle. I follow them into the back of the van and settle on the cold steel bench beside them.

'Take me to the South African embassy,' I say as the driver closes the door.

As we begin our slow journey up the hill, I catch one last fleeting glimpse of my brothers still locked behind the walls of Black Beach with little hope of escape. I will probably never see them again.

And just like that, my nightmare has ended.

38

House Arrest at the Bordello

Malabo
March–May 2014

I am lying on a bed in an air-conditioned room watching CNN when the next announcement catches my attention. President Obiang, under pressure from international human rights organisations, has issued a temporary moratorium on the death penalty. Too late for my friend Amadou and the others who were brutally slaughtered just weeks ago. I feel sad remembering the role they played in keeping me alive at Black Beach.

Without official documents, I am unable to check into a hotel, so Gift, the new consul who has taken over from Thandi at the South African embassy, has arranged that I stay at an embassy apartment until I can leave the country. I get to know Ambassador Rambau, and he tells me how, decades ago, he suffered in his fight against oppression and inequality during apartheid. When he saw the way I was being treated, it struck a nerve. For him, fair and just treatment are personal and worth fighting for.

Although I've received the medication I need and have been eating well, I realise that the healing process will be long, and as for my mental health, I'm not sure if I will ever fully recover. I have frequent panic attacks and don't sleep very well. Sometimes it still feels unreal, like it didn't happen, but then I rub my wrists and feel the scars from the handcuffs. They are a permanent reminder to be grateful every day for the freedom we take for granted, and I work hard at staying positive and thank God for getting me this far.

About a month after my unexpected release, a good friend offers me a place to stay at his small hotel, located conveniently close to the embassy. So, I move to Hotel el Castillo, a rather ostentatious name for what is really just a small inn at the corner of a busy street in Caracolas, near downtown Malabo. It's clear that the name has its origins in the exterior architecture of the building, which has a facade resembling a castle, but sadly this is where the illusion of grandeur ends. The hotel doesn't usually cater to long-term guests, focusing on the lucrative short-stay market by providing a private space where the mostly inebriated clientele can escape with the lady of their choice to indulge in pleasures of a more carnal nature. I am under 'house arrest' here as Angabi still has my passport and I doubt he has plans to return it any time soon.

Because the threat of abduction is still very real for me, I am relieved to know that at least within the walls of the 'castle' I am as safe as I am ever going to be in Malabo. Because of the high turnover of clients at the inn, mainly on an hourly basis, staff are on duty twenty-four hours a day and security is essential. But despite this, I am still anxious and hypervigilant, and I struggle to sleep as the noise from energetic pleasure-seekers often carries on deep into the night, but I am grateful to have an en-suite bathroom and would be more than happy to give the inn a five-star rating on Tripadvisor when compared to where I've been recently.

It's risky going out in public without a passport or official tourist permit, which must be carried by foreigners at all times. President Obiang is a suspicious soul; not surprising considering all the coup attempts on this tiny island. Heavily armed security forces are ever-present on the streets of Malabo. All it will take is one police security stop and I'll be thrown back in prison. Until the bureaucrats sort out the papers needed for me to go home, I must be patient. Going for a jog around town is out of the question, so I've settled into a routine of visiting the embassy for updates and taking a taxi to a restaurant owned by another friend on the other side of Malabo where I have my one meal of the day. It's always risky heading across town, as it would be almost impossible to avoid being stopped by the police on the trip there and back if there was a roadblock, but it's my only option at this point as I can't go to any shops to buy things I need. In some ways, I am in another form of prison, trapped with limited options, but I am grateful for the friends who are risking everything to help me.

My biggest struggle after food is staying in contact with my family back in South Africa. The internet at the 'fine' establishment where I'm staying is intermittent; clearly, the customers don't come here for Wi-Fi. In the evenings, I slip out of the inn and talk to the neighbourhood security guards. Most of them are from Ghana and speak English and they always seem to know where the police have set up their checkpoints. Armed with this information, I slip into town, even though I know that walking around Malabo at night is dangerous, but the risk is worth the reward: a chance to talk to my love.

Thankfully, I've managed to evade the police thus far by navigating the back streets; they prefer the busy roads where they can stop more people.

Economics 101. Feeling a little like Batman, I prowl the streets under cover of darkness, sticking to the back alleys and ducking behind pillars and refuse bins if I spot a policeman or an official-looking vehicle heading in my direction.

On one of my nightly forays, I stumble across a bawdy Chinese bar and restaurant, a popular venue for a night on the town with a 'lady'. It's smutty and noisy, but their security is good and a bonus is that if you order a meal or a drink, they give you the Wi-Fi password. Most customers are here for the booze and the variety of eye-candy available to sample by the hour. As a one-woman man, I'm not interested in these services, but having discovered that the internet connection is consistent and fast, I've become a regular here, managing to download some movies and books to distract me during the long, lonely hours. The highlight, of course, is being able to log in to Skype and chat with Melanie.

The first time seeing her beautiful face after months was almost too much for me, and I could barely hold back the tears as she reached out to me, pressing her fingers against the screen, sobbing, smiling, laughing. Now, I look forward to this moment every day, even though it's bittersweet as I don't know when I will be able to hold her in my arms again, but I am willing to take the risk and slip out most evenings and head to the bar. Sometimes, management gets annoyed with me for just drinking a Coke or a beer, so I am occasionally forced to spend what little money I have on a burger and chips. It's worth it to have contact with my beloved.

I can't believe that in the eight months since I left for what was supposed to be a five-day trip, I've been holed up at Guantanamo, seen a torture chamber, been arrested at gunpoint by the Rapid Intervention Force and sent to Black Beach. It seems unreal. Talking to Melanie reminds me of all the things I've left behind, helping me to focus on staying positive and giving me the strength to face another day. We laugh as a steady stream of gaudy, theatrically seductive and heavily made-up 'local talent' approaches me while we're chatting, enthusiastically offering their wares, relentless in their determination to take care of *all* my needs. Melanie and I agree that they're all just a little too flashy for me. There is only space for one woman in my life; there is no way any of them are ever going to make it onto my menu, no matter how 'special' their services are!

The trip back to the inn is always easier, my heart singing with love after talking to Melanie. Darkness is my friend as I walk along the back streets of Malabo, keeping to the shadows until I arrive at the inn. Once inside, I head past the bustling bar to my room and settle in for the night, feeling the persistent dull thud of African music throbbing through the building until the small hours of the morning. I sink back against the pillows and try to sleep, wondering what tomorrow will bring.

39

Malabo Stray
Malabo
June 2014

Freedom is something I can't take for granted. Every day I visit the embassy, where the South African flag waves cheerily, welcoming me as I walk in. I never give up hope that this will be the day I'll hear the words 'Daniel, you're going home!'

It's been four long months since my release, Melanie's birthday has come and gone, and we're no closer to resolving the issues that keep me trapped on the island. I can't really blame anyone, besides Angabi, but I have to accept that without a passport I'm not getting off this island and there are forces stronger than mine at work behind the scenes.

The embassy team have tried their utmost to come to an equitable solution with Angabi's lawyers, but as soon as we make headway, the goalposts are moved. As in a hard-won tournament, I know I must continually rally the team and make a strong comeback. But it's hard to hold back that little kernel of doubt that this will ever be resolved. I do my best to bury these thoughts so deep that there is little chance of them making their way into my conscious mind.

Today, in a last-ditch effort, we've managed to get Angabi and his lawyer to meet us at the Hilton Hotel. A sense of déjà vu sweeps through me as we push through the revolving doors and make our way across the lobby. I doubt Angabi will stick to an agreement, but maybe today is my lucky day.

I spot him puffing away on one of his signature Cuban cigars, the wispy tendrils of smoke curling around him and drifting across the room. He lumbers to his feet as we reach the table and I see the thinly veiled anger in his eyes as he announces that he's not interested in doing any deals with me and stomps off, leaving us staring helplessly after him. His lawyer shrugs and doesn't bother to arrange another meeting.

I can tell that the embassy team is feeling defeated and don't know what more can be done. Disheartened, we leave the hotel, the mood in the vehicle subdued on the ride back. As we pull up outside the inn, I'm told that the team has one last arrow in their quiver. The annual African Union summit is set to take place in Malabo, and the president of South Africa, Jacob Zuma, and his entourage will be here soon. The Equatorial Guinean government has spent millions on the event and the embassy is hoping that it may be an opportunity for someone from higher up in the South African government to plead my case. Plan B is to place my issue on President Zuma's agenda for discussion with President Obiang. I'm dubious about this, but I'm also fresh out of ideas.

After the Hilton meeting, Angabi ignores my calls and his lawyer is nothing short of hostile. He threatens me and I see the writing on the wall and start making arrangements for outside support should I end up in Black Beach again. Having learnt how to make life a little easier inside the prison, I know that I will need cash and someone on the outside to check on me, bring me essential supplies and carry messages. At this stage, the embassy is still adamant that President Zuma will step up and save the day. Reading between the lines, I know they're just saying what they think I need to hear.

A few days later, my Malabo friends pop by to pick me up. They've realised that I need some cheering up, and there is nothing better than a good, old-fashioned South African braai to remind me of home. We gather around the fire, drinking beer, and I mention the embassy's plan, but they have little faith that President Zuma will put in a good word for me. They insist that the only solution is to make a run for it, telling me that it's the only way I'm getting off this island. I know I can count on them to help me, but I don't want to risk it.

It's exhausting listening to their opinions and well-meaning advice, and, feeling under pressure, I go inside for a breather. Fleeing the island illegally is a risk I don't want to take. I am innocent. Why should I run? I'd be endangering myself and them too. I don't want to spend the rest of my life looking over my shoulder. I know they mean well, but it's all weighing heavily on me and it's getting harder to silence the voice of doubt in my mind.

Feeling thoroughly despondent, I head to the bathroom. I stare at my reflection in the mirror and know that the person looking back at me could never run. But how do I explain this to my friends who mean well but are not helping the situation? Back in the living room, I catch myself looking straight into the sad button eyes of a fluffy white toy dog lying on a bookshelf. There are caramel-coloured patches around his eyes and his ears are long and velvety. I stop dead in my tracks; he reminds me of Bubbles, who would watch my every move just in case it involved a treat or a trip in the car somewhere. The way this toy dog is looking at me mirrors exactly how I'm feeling. He looks lost and alone, so I pick him up and sit down on the couch, absent-mindedly stroking his ears, thinking about what escaping entails, wishing for just a moment's peace where I don't have to think about any of this.

As foolish as it seems to my friends, I believe that I am in the right; even the courts have acknowledged my innocence. If I do make a run for it, it'll blow my defence right out of the water. I have to see this through. And besides, I've given my word to Ambassador Rambau that I won't attempt an escape. There are so many people fighting for me and all of them believe that I have done nothing wrong, but how will that change if I run? Would people start to question my version of events? Would they wonder if there was some basis to Angabi's allegations? I need to leave here with my head held high and my integrity intact.

While I sit holding the cuddly dog, I hear the muted laughter of my friends. Resting my head back against the couch, I close my eyes, putting all thoughts of escape and Angabi out of my mind, trying not to think about tomorrow or home, trying to keep it together and hang on to my sanity.

My friends make their way indoors carrying a huge platter of meat. Dinner is served. When they spot me with my new friend on the couch, they have a good laugh at the image of big, tough Daniel, survivor of Black Beach prison, sitting in the soft evening light with a child's cuddly toy cradled in his arms.

We gather around the table, enjoying the meal and the topic of my escape is set aside. I ask about the Malabo 'pup' and discover that he was abandoned here by an unknown visitor and his owner has never been found. I officially adopt him, taking him back to the inn and finally managing to get a good night's sleep, snuggled up with my Malabo stray and dreaming of happier times.

40

Boats, Planes and Automobiles
Malabo
June 2014

I've been reaching out to the community of local friends and expats I've met over the past decade while working in this region, trying to create a loose network of people who I know I can count on should I end up back behind bars. The bush telegraph is abuzz with my story, and I am kept busy fielding calls and discussing options.

A few nights after the failed meeting with Angabi at the Hilton, my phone rings. I went to bed around 9 p.m., dozing off while watching a movie on my laptop. It takes me a moment to gather my wits. I'm not used to getting calls at this time of night and I sit up, rubbing my eyes. I check the time. It's 11 p.m.!

Thinking that a call at this time of night can only be bad news, I answer hesitantly, my stomach in knots, but it's just a South African friend, a charter pilot working for one of the local VIPs. I heave a sigh of relief.

'*Oom Danie, kom gou*,' he says, with urgency in his voice. '*Ons gaan huistoe!*'

I'm still a bit groggy after waking up so unexpectedly and not quite sure that I understand what he's saying. I must come now because we're going home? Without waiting for me to respond, he elaborates quickly. He's flying to South Africa tonight to service the plane and can smuggle me onboard. He's downstairs right now, parked in a white bakkie next to the inn. I almost drop the phone; my mind's first reaction is YES! Praise the Lord! I'm going home!

He outlines the plan, which sounds almost too good to be true: we'll drive to the airport where I can wait in the vehicle while he does the pre-flight inspection, fuels up and gets the engines running, and then, on his signal, I can join him in the cockpit. It's a foolproof plan, he says. I won't even have to go through customs! But by now I am fully awake. Even though all I want in the world is to go home, I've resigned myself to sticking it out. Reluctantly, I tell him that I'd love to take my chances, but I can't ... I am innocent and escaping the country illegally is just not an option. I have to make sure that when I leave, it's on my terms and I am free to do so.

I can hear by his tone that he thinks I'm nuts, and a part of me feels like I am dancing on the devil's doorstep if I don't grab my things and leave now. His parting words – that an opportunity like this won't come around again any time soon – echo in my mind. I know he's right. As I lie back on the bed, listening to the sounds of the night, mulling over his call, I wonder if I am making the biggest mistake of my life.

As the days pass, I try not to think about the fact that if I'd left with my pilot friend, I would be home in South Africa right now. When I am able to venture out at night, I call Melanie from the Chinese bar and try to subtly prepare her for what might lie ahead, making sure never to mention the escape offer in case she questions my decision. God is in control; I need to have faith and keep hoping and praying for a solution. One afternoon, sitting in the shade on the terrace, a tugboat captain and good friend calls, saying he's going to swing by and pick me up. Lunch is on him.

We drive to Pizza Place, a nearby restaurant owned by a Lebanese expat. It's a sprawling venue with a sports lounge, big-screen TV and a popular shisha bar on the terrace, and a favourite hangout among the expats and locals. While we eat, I'm on high alert, vigilant to the point of obsession, always on the lookout in case I spot someone following me. The paranoia is real; I live in fear of being abducted again. Angabi is never far from my mind, and if I'm taken again, this will be where my story ends. I'll never be seen again and my family will never know what happened to me.

Deep in thought, I hardly notice that my friend is talking until I hear him saying my name repeatedly. I realise that I haven't heard a word. He raises an eyebrow quizzically and says that he's invited me here today to talk about a plan to get me off the island by sneaking me aboard an oil supply vessel. The oil companies have their own jetty, operating 24/7, for sending provisions to the rigs. It's ignored by lazy officials who aren't keen on working long shifts or after the sun sets. Even if they did, they would put minimal effort into patrolling this area unless it was an opportunity to line their pockets.

As with my pilot friend's plan, the strategy is simple. All we need to do is drive to the oil compound where I can pull on an overall and a hard hat while still in the vehicle, then board the vessel and stay in the captain's cabin while they prepare for departure. Once we're out of Equatorial Guinean waters, the vessel will head towards Limbe, a small seaside city in southwest Cameroon, where I can disembark. My friend says he'll give me some money and arrange for a vehicle to take me on the five-hour-plus journey inland across Cameroon to the South African embassy in Yaoundé where I can seek shelter and help.

Although the plan has its allure, I decline. My friend is not amused.

Later in the week, another friend calls with yet another foolproof scheme. He runs a business buying vehicles in Europe which he then sells locally, delivering them to the mainland every fortnight. The ferry between Bioko island and Bata on the mainland is not strictly controlled as all movement is facilitated beforehand with 'payments' made to the right hands. He says I can drive one of the vehicles onto the ferry and once we're in Bata, he'll drive through immigration control to Cameroon legally while a guide takes me on foot across the border. We'll meet up again at a prearranged location and drive to the South African embassy in Yaoundé. I chuckle, thinking that this sounds just like a movie plot involving Mexicans trying to get into the USA. Again I decline.

Even though I am in a desperate situation, I love the sense of adventure and camaraderie as he tries to convince me that this plan will work and that I'd be crazy not to take him up on the offer, but I have my sights set on going home in the comfort of a cattle-class seat aboard an Ethiopian Airlines Boeing 777 flying from Malabo to Johannesburg via Addis Ababa.

After I end the call, I sit on the terrace daydreaming that in a few short days, thanks to President Zuma, I'll be walking through Malabo airport, passport in hand and settling in for the long flight home, my conscience clear, and landing in South Africa with my head held high and my reputation and integrity intact. I know that my friends are getting frustrated, thinking I've lost touch with reality, but as foolish as it sounds, I must believe that justice will prevail and that I will be set free without having to resort to the methods my friends are advocating. Life is an emotional roller-coaster with highs and lows – mostly lows at this point – but I know that dwelling on the injustice won't change anything, so I focus on making plans that don't include escape. I've been meeting regularly with embassy officials who are positive and committed to getting my problem resolved at the highest level.

The town is buzzing with excitement as dignitaries arrive for the twenty-third African Union Summit where South Africa's Nkosazana Dlamini-Zuma is the official chairperson. According to the embassy staff, everything has been arranged for the meeting between President Zuma and President Obiang.

The roads leading in and out of Malabo are filled with limousines spiriting heads of state and other dignitaries from their luxury accommodation to the event venue. I watch the news highlights on television, and in one report I spot President Zuma making his way to the podium and wonder if someone in his entourage is carrying my file. I listen to his words with scepticism. For so many years I've watched these seasoned politicians and supposed supporters of democracy saying all the right things with such passion and conviction that one almost believes that they mean it. I know it seems cynical, but after years of experiencing the divide between the political elite and the poverty-stricken masses, it's hard to believe that meaningful change will ever take place when there is so much money to be made.

This year the focus of the AU Summit is agriculture and food security, although they also touch on the conflict, civil unrest and terrorist activity that is taking a toll on stability across the continent. As I sit watching the highlights on the news, I pray that the powers that be will spare just a moment to determine the fate of one Daniel Janse van Rensburg. The embassy team had earlier met with the minister of foreign affairs with my file in hand and returned feeling optimistic that my predicament would be discussed at the heads of state meeting later this evening. All I can do is wait. Sleepless with anticipation, I keep checking my phone, but I hear nothing and start to get a bad feeling. Something is not right.

I'm up early and take a quick shower before heading to the embassy for an update. Even though part of me is hopeful, I have a heavy feeling in my gut that I can't shake, and as soon as I arrive there, I can tell something is wrong. Usually I'm greeted with warmth and enthusiasm, but today everyone is conspicuously busy, heads down, avoiding eye contact or even talking to me. My heart fills with dread; this is answer enough. It seems that plan B has failed. I think the team are as disappointed as I am, but they don't have an enraged bureaucrat with connections in all the right places on their tail, they get to go home any time they want to, they can leave the country, they can walk around Malabo without looking over their shoulders. I am gutted when one of them finally admits that my case was not discussed at all.

It's a crushing blow, and I know that later I'm going to have to tell Melanie that everything we've pinned our hopes on has failed. The rest of the day passes in a blur. Later, I make my way through the back streets to the Chinese bar so that I can break the news. It's excruciating to put on a brave face as I watch Melanie's beautiful smile dissolve as floods of tears stream down. I want to reach across time and space and hold her close as she falls against our daughter Abigail, sobbing inconsolably into her shoulder. The pain of watching them fall apart engulfs me and I struggle to hold back my own bitter tears of anger, frustration and defeat. The guilt I feel for causing them such heartbreak is almost too much to bear.

I tell them to prepare for the worst and try to encourage them, saying that they will be all right no matter what happens to me. Melanie is heartbroken, and as I make my way home to my 'castle' I am haunted by the sound of her mournful cries when I said goodbye, not knowing if I will ever see my family again.

As I walk along the dark streets in a small town on an island far away from home, the world suddenly seems ominous and unforgiving. I hope that I have loved my family enough and given them enough as a husband, son and father to carry them through the long days ahead until we meet again at our Father's door.

41

Land of the Free, Home of the Brave

```
Malabo
4 July 2014
```

I arrive back at the hotel and drag myself to the room, closing the door and leaning against it, feeling utterly drained. I take off my jacket and fall across the bed, wondering if I've been a fool not to have taken the chance to escape. I could kick myself! Life is about choices, and I could have chosen any one of the escape plans suggested by my friends. I was given not one but *three* opportunities to escape. Were my friends right? Was I supposed to escape and resolve my innocence later? Will I even live long enough to regret it?

I don't remember much about the rest of the night when I wake up fully clothed, still sprawled across the bed, head pounding as if I had a night out on the town. It takes me a minute to realise that my phone is ringing. I haul myself off the bed and follow the insistent sound until I find it in my jacket pocket.

It's the embassy. They waste no time in telling me that they've received an official letter advising that I must appear with Ambassador Rambau before a judge this morning. My heart sinks. This is not good news, and I try not to let fear overwhelm me. It's the same judge who signed the order that sent me to Black Beach in December. Things did not end well then, and my gut tells me that this time will be no different. It's incredibly unlikely that I'll be going home any time soon, if ever.

Giving in to false hope, I briefly consider that I've got it all wrong and somehow, by the grace of God, the judge is going to return my passport. But if so, he wouldn't need the ambassador to be there, I think, so it's about as likely as Angabi saying it's all been a huge misunderstanding.

I feel the tension mounting in my body as I step into the shower. My stomach is in knots and a killer migraine is taking grip. I try to lose myself in the steamy spray, but despair is a treacherous beast; it sneaks up on you, lurking in the shadows before leaping into your soul and devouring all hope. Standing under the torrent of water, I recognise the fear and anxiety, and know that I need to do everything in my power to slay the beast. Self-pity will get me nowhere; negative thinking won't keep me alive, nor will it get me home to Melanie. Confronting my demons with my head held high is the key to survival. I know I can't give in to the fear. I have to face it head-on.

I make peace with the fact that it has been *my* decision to stick it out here. I could have taken my chances and tried to escape but didn't, so I must face the consequences. I have no one to blame but myself. Giving up is not an option. I just have to keep moving forward. God has brought me through it before, so I must keep the faith and fight to get home. I must do this, for Melanie, for my mother, for my daughter, for my family. I know how much they need me. Feeling braver and stronger, I switch off the taps, climb out of the shower and dry off, brush my teeth and get dressed. I know the embassy staff are gravely concerned and want to resolve the situation, but I've come to realise that they're helpless. It's clear that diplomacy is doomed to fail; we're far beyond that point. There is no honour here, no set of rules or procedures to follow, and certainly no protocol for dealing with a situation like this.

I square my shoulders and head downstairs to meet them. Ambassador Rambau has a prior engagement at a Fourth of July function at the US embassy, so Gift and one of the other diplomatic representatives are to accompany me until he can get to the court.

The drive is short. Too short. Moments after our arrival, we are approached by the police officer posted at the entrance to the Palacio de Justicia who tells me that I am under arrest. He apologises while handcuffing me but offers no explanation. I'm not even given a chance to speak to the judge as I am led away while the two embassy officials watch in dismay, powerless to stop the policeman and hopelessly ill-equipped to take charge of the situation. It's clear that there is nothing they can do to help me or to prevent any of this from happening. It must be demoralising to know that even with all your powers as a foreign embassy, following the rules of diplomacy has been rendered completely ineffectual in the face of pure hatred, malice and abuse of power, and that this has nothing to do with right and wrong. They watch, helpless, as I disappear into the holding cells.

I lose all sense of time until finally the door opens and I'm escorted to the judge's chambers where Ambassador Rambau is waiting for me, and this gives me strength. He berates the judge for detaining me, demanding an explanation, but the judge stands firm, offering nothing, mumbling something about putting me in 'safe custody' while the matter is being resolved. The ambassador is enraged, but his words fall on deaf ears, and I am returned to the holding cells to await my fate.

Locked up in this tiny box, cut off from the world, there is no way to describe the sense of desolation, the misery and defeat that threatens to overwhelm me as the hours pass. I swing between violent rage and deep despair. Somewhere in between is me, the real Daniel, trying to hold it together, trying to breathe, trying to survive.

Nature calls. I know that there is a bottle of piss somewhere in my cell; I can smell it. In the gloom, I spot it in the corner of the cell, half full of the previous visitor's contribution, but I have no choice and use it, doing what I have to do. Luckily, my hands are cuffed in front of me, so at least I can reach for the bottle and unzip my pants without too much difficulty. Thank God for small mercies.

Black Bitch! Can I face it for the second time? Reality fades in and out; sometimes I'm in control, but mostly I exist in a murky haze, emerging briefly, disorientated and confused. As I rise from the depths and consciousness returns, I struggle to imagine a future where I am still alive and reunited with my family. I fear that Angabi has no intention of allowing that to happen, and I'm fairly sure that any orders from him will be carried out with alacrity.

I have little faith in the warden's ability to think for himself, and if a direct command comes from on high, he won't question it. He is incompetent and clearly not qualified to hold a position of authority over a teeming mass of unhinged drug addicts, violent felons and the downtrodden, the forgotten dregs of society cast into the prison on the whim of a politician or one of the members of the social elite. He undoubtedly attained this position by accident of birth or through friends he has cultivated over time. Cowards with the right connections rely on puppets like him, one rung below, who are willing to carry out their wishes, no matter what that entails. As I know, his team of guards are sadistic thugs, henchmen who relish the opportunity to make the lives of inmates unbearable, a misguided sense of self-importance driving their enthusiasm for causing pain and suffering.

Sitting alone in the dark with these thoughts, knowing where I am going, makes it difficult to silence the negative voices in my mind. I am almost relieved to hear the rattling of the keys in the lock, realising that I have no choice but to face what lies ahead.

I struggle to my feet, my arms numb after being handcuffed for so long. The steel has chaffed my wrists, undoubtedly magnifying the existing scars. The door opens and I blink quickly against the sudden sharpness of the light cutting through the gloom. The guard is in shadow, but I see him beckon me to come out.

Once in the corridor, the other cell doors are opened one after another and their occupants join me as we make our way down the passage. At the entrance, we are cuffed to one another in pairs at our wrists and ankles, and begin a slow, shuffling march to the meat wagon parked in the undercover area outside the holding cells. As we climb into the vehicle, I recognise two of my companions, repeat offenders I encountered on my first stay just four months ago. In total, eight unfortunate souls are heading for the same fate. I think of the vicious cycle of corruption, sin and retribution, as old as humanity itself. When did it all start, this power of one over the other? When did we need to be governed, controlled, policed?

Black Bitch awaits.

The ride from the Palacio de Justicia seems too quick, a blur of sights and smells: buildings, cars, street signs, noises, people, RIF officers with their weapons casually draped over shoulders. It all fades as we turn in behind the president's official residence and the vehicle makes its way around the now familiar building, lurching forward to begin the slow descent towards the prison gates, brakes squealing like tormented souls being carried into the depths of hell.

Black Bitch has not changed at all since I left, and her power to strip me of all hope is absolute. The first thing that hits me is the smell. Nothing can prepare you for the stench of more than four hundred people existing like scavengers on a rotting carcass while the humidity hangs overhead in a shroud, trapping the odours, intensifying them in the heat where they stagnate, bringing disease and decay with them. I am abandoned. Alone. Beyond help. Bile rises in my throat as we pass through the last security boom and pull up outside the entrance, the courtyard filled with a thronging mass of curious onlookers waiting to see who is on the menu today.

It's 4 July 2014. I have been stuck in Malabo for 277 days, seventy-two of them illegally detained behind bars at one of the world's most infamous prisons, and now I'm back, chained like an animal, even though I've committed no crime. A cheer goes up from the courtyard as the inmates crowd the fence to watch us hobble towards the no man's land between the guard hut and exercise yard that's used as the informal communal kitchen and sometimes as a place of worship for the Christians and Muslims, depending on the time or day of the week. These are things I know. They are things only an insider would know. And that's not where it ends.

I know what's coming. Even though I've tried to suppress the memories, now that I am back here they bubble swiftly to the surface. All the work I've done over the past weeks to push the memories into the furthest reaches of my mind, to dull the fear, is undone in an instant. I never really expected to be back here, and I know what's coming. I can't run. I can't hide. I feel dizzy and want to keel over, but instead I channel all my energy into putting one foot in front of the other.

By some small mercy, I manage to shuffle slowly in unison with the other prisoners, entering an almost hypnotic state. A fog of nothingness envelops me, and I disappear behind the veil to a place where a kind of numbness takes over and I stop thinking, sinking into a state of suspended animation, going through the motions, doing what needs to be done, following instructions without really being there.

When I emerge from the fugue, I find myself standing at the entrance to the prison, knowing that I've been subjected to a thorough search but without any of the memory of humiliation to torment me later.

There is one more hurdle to cross: Bangkok. I look around warily, but I don't see him in the crowd. I feel a flutter of hope – maybe he's been released? In all my time working and living in Africa, Bangkok is the only person I've encountered who hates me for the colour of my skin. Back home in South Africa, there is still a certain degree of racism that taints the relationship between citizens, thanks largely to the legacy of apartheid and stoked by racially charged discourse that has little to do with reality, but, for the most part, I've always felt that ordinary South Africans try their best to work together.

In Black Beach, with the exception of Bangkok whose loathing for me borders on psychotic, as far as most of the other inmates are concerned, I am just a novelty, the only white man behind bars with them. I stand out in the crowd because of my skin colour and because the others believe I'm better off financially than they are, and they're probably right as most are poverty-stricken, starving in a land of plenty, a country that is the richest, per capita, in sub-Saharan Africa. I know that they are driven to a life of crime through desperation, but not all are innocent, many deserve to be here, such as those who believe in the powers of black magic and kill without conscience.

I hear the familiar chant, '*Blanco, blanco, blanco*', and prepare myself for the turmoil that awaits amid prisoners excited to have something to break the monotony of their lousy existence. The guard unlocks the gates, and we step through. I peer into the gloom; there's still no sign of Bangkok, but I steel myself for an attack anyway.

As the gates slam shut, a cheer goes up. I can't believe it. I am being welcomed 'home' by my brothers. Not one of them shows any aggression towards me. Many shake their heads, knowing without knowing what has happened outside. They are disappointed but not surprised that I am back. I am a survivor of Black Beach. I've earned their respect. For now, even though I am innocent and have done nothing wrong, I am one of them.

As one of the lost among the damned, united in our suffering and misery, I make my way into the belly of the beast, murderers, rapists, bank robbers and drug dealers at my side. Strangely, I almost feel safer here than I have over the past few months making my way around the streets of Malabo where the police prowl and the political elite rule from behind their lofty palace walls. Fearing what lies ahead, I remind myself that God is in control. I must trust in Him and have faith that this is not yet the end.

PART 4

'I go to the place of no return,
to the land of darkness and the shadow of death;
to the land of deepest night,
where even the light is like darkness.'

– Job 10:21-22

PART 4

42

Why Is This Happening?
Hoekwil, South Africa
July 2014

My life is disintegrating like a sandcastle swept away by the incoming tide. Everything is falling apart, and I am powerless to stop it. The burden of my loss is too much. I've shut the door to my bedroom and vowed never to set foot in there until Daniel comes home.

Now I lie curled up on the couch, struggling to understand, struggling to find meaning. Even the simple act of breathing is almost impossible, the pain just too much for me, the fear overwhelming. I have nothing left to live for...

How can this be happening to us? Daniel loves God so much. We are good people. We have always treated others with dignity and respect. We have loved God and the church. We have honoured God in our daily lives. We've been kind; we live a simple, happy life. That's who we are; that's what we believe in.

I haven't moved from the corner of the couch since Abigail went back to university in Cape Town. I've lost track of time. I just want to be left alone in my grief, in my anguish and despair. I don't want company. I want to lose myself in the mists of my memories, a cocoon where I can choose what happens next. It's a place to mourn, because my Daniel is not coming back this time. I know it and I hate knowing it. He tried to prepare me for it.

Why? Why is this happening? Why are we being punished? Why do we have to suffer? What did we do to deserve this? Thoughts tumble through my mind, but mostly I feel broken, the thoughts in my head incomplete. I feel cheated. I want to embrace the rage threatening to overwhelm me, run wild, escape, break things, rage, vent my frustration. It's not fair! It's not right! Daniel is innocent, but who will believe that now?

I imagine people whispering behind me in the church, discussing our lives like they know everything about us, questioning Daniel's story, murmuring behind their hands in their kitchens over tea, debating his innocence. I imagine men gathered around the braai, beers in hand, judging, speculating, wondering what the real story is. Surely no one goes to jail twice if they are really and truly innocent?

But I know my husband! I know he has done nothing wrong, but who will believe me? God knows the truth, as I do, but I don't want to walk around in our community, go to the shops, go to church, knowing that people are talking about us behind our backs. How do I hold my head up and confront the petty hypocrites who I know are discussing me, Daniel and our lives while pretending to care?

I curl up in a ball and pull the covers tighter around me, burying my head between the cushions in the corner of the couch. Bubbles paws and scratches at the blanket trying to find a way in.

I don't want to go through the rest of my life without Daniel by my side. What is the point of carrying on alone? If Daniel doesn't make it out of Black Beach, I will be alone. Forever. There is no way he can survive that place again; he barely survived the first time.

Someone is knocking at the door. I ignore it, hoping they'll go away, hoping they don't. I am in mourning. My life is pointless without Daniel. I can't bear to think about what they are doing to him. Has he been beaten? Tortured? Is he dead? I feel in my heart that he's never coming back. I am so scared and alone. No one can save me, only Daniel.

I sink into oblivion, returning to the void where, at least for a moment, I can ignore the voices in my head. I embrace this in-between space, taking refuge in the infinite emptiness of a place where I am frozen in time, existing, breathing, but not living.

I don't know how much time passes. I sense a presence in the room, but I am too far down the deep pit of despair to care. I don't look up. I don't want to look into the light; I don't want to see that the sun is still shining and that life carries on. I don't want to have to deal with the kindness of someone who just wants to show me that they care. I feel the weight shift on the couch as they sit down beside me. I feel them reaching across and gently squeezing my shoulder, resting a reassuring hand on my back, murmuring familiar words:

'The Lord is my shepherd; I shall not want. He maketh me to lie down in green pastures: leads me beside the still waters. He restores my soul: he leads me in the paths of righteousness for his name's sake. Yea, though I walk through the valley of the shadow of death, I will fear no evil: for thou art with me; thy rod and thy staff they comfort me. Thou preparest a table before me in the presence of mine enemies: thou anointest my head with oil; my cup runneth over. Surely goodness and mercy shall follow me all the days of my life: and I will dwell in the house of the Lord for ever.'

I lie silent and still, closing my eyes, unable to stop the flood of tears until finally I give in and allow the shroud of grief to envelop me, burying myself alongside Daniel in a secret space between the horror of my reality and the infinity of my dreams.

43

Enter the Dragon

Black Beach Prison, Malabo
July 2014

Everyone here knows that you cannot beat the 'house'. Outside, I was watched and followed. I took risks to stay in contact with my family, and I wasn't going to stop living, but all the while I felt like I was one step away from being abducted and murdered. And now I'm back in Black Beach.

After my unexpected hero's welcome, my old acquaintances gather round, wanting to hear about life outside, some shaking their heads in resignation – if I couldn't make it out, what chance do they have? When you are locked behind these walls for months or years, there is nothing better than hearing talk of the city, but it's late and I need to find somewhere to sleep, hopefully among the murderers where I set up 'camp' during my previous stay.

I need to avoid 'Baghdad', which is what the prisoners call the area where the younger gang members hang out. Among them are the drug-addicted scumbags who have no control over their cravings, not to mention the certifiably insane who are prone to hallucinations and are often volatile and unpredictable. In Baghdad, it's not unusual for a petty squabble to turn into a full-blown hurricane of savagery. The murderers are actually more stable and less inclined to outbursts, too busy battling the demons within.

There is a slight disturbance at the outer edge of the crowd as the Jefe de Castel pushes his way through the throng, clearly heading in my direction. I didn't have much to do with him during my previous stay, but I've since learnt that he's an ex-policeman who was caught colluding with a team of bank robbers and received a hefty sentence. He's been living *la vida loca* in Black Beach for a number of years. He's an unremarkable fellow – short, as are many in the region, and without any specific skills qualifying him for the job as the inside man for the guards other than that he follows orders, no questions asked. Nobody really respects him, but he is tolerated out of fear of those who appointed him.

The warden doesn't show up much, but when he does, he strolls about freely inside with no fear of us 'animals'. The Jefe de Castel is our circus trainer; the inmates fear the whip, not the man. He does what needs to be done, leaving the warden free to turn up around the time that the Red Cross puts in an appearance on their biannual visits to check on the political prisoners. The Jefe knows that he holds the whip, as do the inmates, so in the interests of survival you stay under the radar or suffer the consequences, and for most it's just not worth the trouble.

I greet him politely, knowing that it's best not to make enemies here. He's carrying an old, filthy, hand-me-down mattress which, much to the amusement of my fellow prisoners, falls to pieces as he shoves it towards me and beckons me to follow him as he heads up to the first level without a backward glance. I tag along behind him, dragging the disintegrating mattress, trying to salvage as much of it as I can. I know how important this crumbling piece of foam is on a bare floor overrun with rats and cockroaches.

The Jefe turns down the passage at the top of the stairs and the first thing I notice is a sickly, sulphurous odour that grows stronger as we make our way along the corridor until he stops outside a cell. He leans in and talks to the inmate inside. A loud argument ensues as I catch up, still juggling the pieces of the mattress. It seems that this is where the Jefe has decided I'll be spending the night. I peer over his shoulder. A young Chinese guy by the name of Chan is complaining bitterly, and as I look through the cloud of stale cigarette smoke hanging over the room, I can see why, and I'm not impressed either. This place is a rathole with barely enough space for one person.

I manoeuvre closer and hoist my mattress through the entrance, squeezing in against the wall, and suddenly determine the source of the stench. Another Chinese guy is lying in a stinking swamp of faeces on the lower bunk against the opposite wall. He looks dead, his skin yellowish-green. I gag and quickly point him out to the Jefe who shrugs, telling me: 'It's okay, he just has malaria.'

I consider taking the tatty remains of my mattress and heading back to general population on the ground floor, and my resolve is quickly reinforced as the guy on the bunk groans weakly, his body contorting spasmodically as he leans over the edge of the bed and retches violently. The spray of vomit splatters my feet and I jump away, shuddering with revulsion as the man falls back on the bunk, a string of sickly green slime sliding down his chin. Looking around, I'm fairly certain that this is not suitable accommodation for a roughly six-foot-tall South African *boerseun*, or anyone else for that matter. I don't know where the Jefe expects me to fit in this tiny space as there is barely enough room for its current occupants. I'm not a five-star kinda guy, but I definitely prefer accommodation where, at the very least, my feet are not going to get spattered with someone else's puke.

The Jefe doesn't give a damn, though, and walks away, leaving me with no choice. I turn back to the cell to see Chan fish a fresh cigarette out of his pocket and proceed to light it using the stub of the one he has just finished. He throws the butt on the ground and grinds it out. Sighing, I realise that I've been officially checked in to Hotel China, Black Beach, room on the mezzanine level.

It's late and I'm exhausted, so I drag my pieces of mattress into the narrow space between the beds and the bricked-off corner of the cell, which once housed a toilet and shower but is now just a stinking cesspit, the drain clogged and no running water in the pipes.

While I am trying to find a space to lay my mattress, one of the brothers from the church group turns up with an old sheet. It's been a long and emotional day, so I arrange the bits of mattress on the floor and sit down, trying not to be bothered by Chan's chain-smoking. He's already on his third cigarette since I arrived. The cell has one small window, but it's cloudy with smoke and the air is hot and dank, steeped in the lingering smell of death lurking patiently in the corner, waiting to carry away the wretched soul of the man languishing on the bunk beside me.

I stretch out my legs, but there's too little space, a subtle reminder that I am in the land of the Pygmies. It makes me remember that in Equatorial Guinea, tradition still plays a role in the everyday culture and the beliefs of many of the inmates. Having got to know my fellow prisoners during my first stint behind bars, I know that the crimes some of them committed were to honour the spirits of their ancestors or to appease the gods and involved performing atrocities that are the stuff of nightmares: slaughtering and sacrificing their wives or performing acts of depravity that defy belief in the hopes of absorbing and harnessing the power of their enemies.

Knowing these people not only exist but are imprisoned here with me, and that there is no escape from them, makes sleep a luxury. But at least here in this cell, I have little to fear from Chan and his friend, who is hanging on by a thread, and we can lock the door from the inside, making it a little safer from the dangers lurking in the passageways.

As my first long night back in Black Beach wears on, sheer exhaustion takes over, and I doze fitfully until morning.

44

Evil Spirits

```
Black Beach Prison, Malabo
July 2014
```

Most nights I lie listening to the strange yet familiar sounds of the prison. It's a little safer in the cell, so I've found I can rest easier than I could last time I was here, but night-time is still punctuated with the screams and cries of people haunted by the ghosts of those they've wronged, keeping me awake.

Some prisoners speak about visions of demonic beings, snakes, mighty men, and beasts who come to devour them, feasting on their manhood before carrying them away into the night. Owls roost around the building, hooting ominously, giving rise to much discussion about bad luck and the horrors that await when darkness descends. During my first stay, I became accustomed to watching tortured souls run howling through the prison, heading for the pastor's room, seeking protection or divine intervention from the evil spirits preying on them. Strange things happen behind these walls, things that defy explanation, things that make no sense or should not be possible, feeding superstitious minds and making even me wonder about the power of belief and manifestation.

While Chan smokes, his friend is trapped in a hell of delirium. I've been there and it's not pretty. He retches throughout the night, even though there is nothing left inside him. I know that he's dying. Sometime in the morning, a few inmates come to the cell, lift him up in his sheet and carry him out to the prison entrance. Around midday when I go outside for some fresh air, I see him lying next to the fence, not moving. The ambulance arrives around lunchtime, and a day or two later news filters through the prison that he passed away. No one mourns his passing; it is what it is. That's how life and death go here.

Time only means something when you know there is an end date, and as I have none I have no choice but to face each day as it comes. I have settled into my new home with Chan, a gutless whiner who uses what little Spanish he knows to bellyache interminably or demand something from me. As annoying as he is, I feel sorry for him. He is young and has been badly abused. He's here because he accidentally killed a friend in a fight. Both were drunk and couldn't agree on who would be first with the prostitute they'd hired. They came to blows and fell through a glass table. Chan's friend bled to death, and someone had to pay. I know he suffers great remorse, and being locked up here doesn't mean that justice has been served; he must live with the guilt and is constantly bullied by the other inmates. He does, however, have one friend, Oscar, who works in the kitchen and is able to source or smuggle in anything that you need, provided you have the resources to pay for it.

I'm moving up in the world, having inherited the dead guy's metal bed, but my gratitude is short-lived when Chan announces that I must pay for it. With no money, I'm now in debt before I've even settled in. Sleeping on the pieces of my thin foam mattress against the metal bars of the bedframe is torture, but Oscar brings me a few cartons to use as cushioning. It's marginally better than sleeping on the floor, but I still spend most nights tossing and turning in an effort to find a comfortable position to sleep. There is precious little ventilation, and the small barred window doesn't let in enough air to clear away the constant cloud of cigarette smoke hovering overhead. Mosquitoes are the only thing that make it through, adding to my suffering, each one potentially carrying a single-dose lethal injection.

On the first weekend following my return, I stand at the fence, hoping to spot a familiar face. The courtyard is crawling with visitors, and I am ecstatic when I recognise the embassy staff making their way down the embankment carrying plastic bags of supplies. I can tell they are relieved to see that, despite the appalling conditions, I am unharmed and in relatively good health, and they reassure me that they're doing everything they can. They add that the ambassador encountered the judge at an event where he apologised, saying that he had no control over the 'chiefs'.

I'm told that Teodorin Obiang, as the minister in charge of prisons, authorised my incarceration. This is not news to me. Many of us are here because we've pissed someone off and will rot here until bribes are paid so the charges can be dropped. Sometimes, it doesn't pay to have 'friends' in high places, especially if those friends turn on you. It's not only the government that authorises tickets to Black Beach though; I've learnt that in this country you cannot trust the people you work with or even your friends and family. Some people are here because the wrong girl fell in love with them and someone else with more power wanted her. These issues have nothing to do with the courts or the justice system, as I well know.

We discuss my options, and I tell the embassy staff that I am entitled to make one local call a week but don't think that I can rely on the warden to make good on this and will use the drug dealers and weekend visitors to send messages, adding that I can get money in the form of a 'loan' which can be paid outside to the wife of the moneylender. I come away from the meeting feeling a bit happier, knowing that I will soon have access to funds to buy the things I need. Having been here before, I know that life is easier if you have money.

45

Broda-Broda

Black Beach Prison, Malabo
2014

In Black Beach, the positions of power are constantly changing. There are many brothers who manufacture stories to gain favour with the guards or to bring trouble to an enemy. When any one person or group becomes too powerful, the warden is quick to see that they are destroyed.

Many of the guys here have ended up on the wrong side of an official or someone in government by being greedy and taking too much out of the till in a government contract. Certainly, this type of activity is a punishable offence out in the real world, but this is not a normal society with the usual rules. Nepotism – called *broda-broda* in Pidgin – is the standard operating procedure. The presidential family effectively controls all big business – oil and gas, telecoms, shipping, construction, logging – and there is really no other way but to include them in any deal. You're all right unless you move outside the lines or take more than your share, in which case you'll find yourself in handcuffs on a one-way trip to Black Beach in the back of the meat wagon. There is more than enough in the trough, but the greed is endless, and sometimes even their own family members are sent down the hill. I once saw a bumper sticker that read 'Don't steal! The government hates competition.'

The fact that Chan and Oscar have set up shop in our cell selling their contraband just adds to my misery in this place. Their stock consists mainly of alcohol and cigarettes, which are popular items and guarantee a steady stream of customers at all hours of the day and night. Many wealthy prisoners, or those who have honed their entrepreneurial skills, involve the guards in their illicit dealings. Because the guards can move about freely in town, they will often strike a deal to purchase stock, drinks and even prostitutes to take care of a prisoner's needs.

Although the cell offers a little privacy and a small degree of protection, helping me to get a little more sleep than if I was with the general population, there are times when I feel that being in my own tent on the 'boulevard' below would be more appealing than this tiny smoke-filled hovel. I decide that when I have money, I will buy myself a bed and move to where I stayed last time, among the murderers and other long-term residents.

During the day, I spend a lot of time in the yard between the two main buildings of the prison. The side known as Baghdad is supposed to house younger prisoners, but this is not enforced by the guards. Everyone ends up mingling in the yard, so you learn quickly who to avoid.

On the opposite side of the yard is the multi-purpose hall where we line up to collect our food or go for 'court' appearances for internal problems and punishment. On Sundays, the Christian group uses it to conduct a church service that can go on for hours. The bloodstains on the tiles where we sit praising the Lord and singing are still there, evidence of the previous night's floggings.

Stealing, fighting or getting up to any serious mischief inside does not go unpunished, and transgressions are dealt with swiftly and with enthusiasm. The guards will collect the culprit and, in a public display, take them outside and stretch them out on a frame. Water is poured over them and then they are beaten with a cable until the blood flows, the screaming stops or the guard gets hot and goes inside, leaving the victim to bake in the blazing sun. Often, the inflicted wounds swell up and become infected as there is no way to keep them clean living in the filth of Black Beach. The medical staff are not motivated to help ease the suffering, taking the attitude of 'you get what you deserve'.

Most people working here are looking for ways to line their pockets, and sometimes they intercede on behalf of an innocent person who's been 'dropped off' here by whispering a word in the right ear. But usually the inmates are delivered from the courts by the meat wagon with the proviso that they will be collected the next day to have their case heard; in reality, the 'next day' never arrives. I've met some who have lost track of how long they've spent trapped behind these walls. They have no connections and no money, are forgotten by their families and loved ones, and exist without hope.

Every day is a struggle. A struggle to get food. A struggle to find enough water to drink. A struggle to stay healthy. A struggle to avoid the mosquitoes and vermin that outnumber the inmates. A struggle to wash and attend to matters of hygiene. A struggle to stay hopeful. A struggle to survive. A good day here is when you don't get robbed, threatened or harassed. The language of Black Beach is to the point; there are no innuendos or euphemisms, no ambiguity:

'I will *KILL* you.'
'I will *STAB* you.'
'You are a *THIEF*.'
'You are a *RAPER*.'
'You want to *KILL* the *PRESIDENT*.'
'You come to our country to take our *MONEY*.'
'*Waka Waka*. DO IT!'

46

Tales from the Dark Side

```
Black Beach Prison, Malabo
           2014
```

I've accumulated sufficient funds to buy a bed and am now living in 'gen pop', creating a home for myself alongside some of the worst criminals on earth. Avoiding negative people is tricky as most are always complaining, but as time passes I slip into a routine that sees me rise each morning and thank God for getting me through the night. I greet my neighbours and head outside, grateful for the 'fresh' air, grateful for the warmth of the sun on my skin or the rain to wash away the filth. I do my exercises in the courtyard, grateful for the open space outside the furnace in which we are locked up each night. Out here I can breathe better.

Living a life of gratitude, despite the circumstances, changes the way my mind works, filling me with positive energy. Some days it takes an effort to silence the despondent voices whispering in my mind, so I have started to teach English to the younger children and my reward and motivation are seeing their faces light up from the attention that I am giving them knowing that I expect nothing in return.

It seems almost unreal that I could learn such a transformational lesson in this wretched, miserable place, but it's the catalyst for change in me and applying my faith. Building my strength through exercise feeds my spirit so that I can hang on to the hope of getting out of here someday. I have also tried to organise a routine of cleaning the space so that the children feel like they have a small element of control over their environment.

Cleanliness is next to godliness, but the walls and floors are layered with decades of grime and abuse. I know it will take a monumental effort to make a difference, but as they say, idle hands are the devil's workshop, so I feel it's important to keep these young minds occupied and their hands busy. They are always so willing and grateful for the attention.

Sometimes it's hard to make sense of God's plan, but I never waver in my faith, sticking to my ritual as I settle in and pray for protection to get me through the night. I don't ever really sleep, as I'm always on edge, wary of anything out of the ordinary in a place where everything is out of the ordinary.

The nights are the worst. Sometimes there's action outside involving the guards. Whenever they can, they drink to pass the boredom of guard duty, and it always ends up in some or other altercation. Inside, the sounds echoing through the building often chill me to the bone: sudden blood-curdling screams or angry outbursts as someone catches a thief and delivers swift justice. Then there are the walkers who pace endlessly, driven by demons. Others have headphones and listen to music to drown out the sounds of the night, and still more can be found deep in conversation with imaginary people.

Pedro, my neighbour, is already asleep, but I can hear that he is being troubled by the spirits that haunt him. He speaks to them in a language that no human can understand; I think he is pleading with them. Now he's getting up. I've long since given up trying to figure out what he's doing and have come to the conclusion that he is somehow interacting with the ghosts that torment him without end.

In the background are the low rumblings from the night owls playing board games like checkers with pieces made from bottle tops. They're whiling away the time as they wait for sunrise, which is when they retire to sleep away the day. For those with money to burn, there is a gambling room in one of the upstairs cells where they bet thousands of dollars; one of the prostitutes who consistently makes good profits sends out her earnings every Saturday. Gambling is hugely popular. It's mainly limited to card games in here, and some take it very seriously. There are frequent arguments and violent fights, which is great entertainment for the people watching from the shadows. The stakes are high, and I've seen gamblers place everything on the line and come up short, losing their whole cell with everything inside it.

Sometimes I retire to my 'tent' and wake up to find a rich drug runner, who until the night before was the proud owner of some serious real estate in the form of a fully equipped and furnished cell, lying beside me on a filthy old mattress, where he remains until visiting day when he can get his hands on some cash and relocate. Until the next time, that is.

Every night is filled with dread, and going to the bathroom is too dangerous to contemplate – it's far better to keep a bottle with you for that purpose. I lie back, thankful for the hot, stale air from my small fan blowing over my sweating body, helping to keep the mosquitoes at bay. Pity that it does nothing to ward off the cockroaches. Until I lived here, I never knew that cockroaches could bite, but they do! There are millions of them, like a biblical plague, but it's the rats and mice that I worry about. I live in fear of being bitten by them and becoming ill. They always manage to find any food that I've managed to squirrel away; it seems that they too are starving.

I try to block out the sounds of the prison and ignore the insects, and after what seems like an eternity I doze off. Sleep is measured in minutes, not hours, and I wake with a start. There is a mosquito buzzing near my ear and my sheet is drenched in sweat that flows off me like a river, pooling in my crotch and under my arms. I'm itching all over. The power is off again, so my fan has stopped working. But it isn't the fan stopping that woke me. Someone is going through my pockets!

'*Ladron*! THIEF!'

Smack! Smack, smack! I swat him like a fly, and it feels great to channel my frustration, but he disappears in a heartbeat, a silent shadow against the darkness of the night. I lie back against the sticky sheets, my adrenaline pumping, and sleep eludes me for the rest of the night.

The following afternoon it's unusually quiet. People are irritable and restless, but no one seems to have the energy or inclination to fight. I watch two guards walking alongside the fence, sharing a beer. That would go down so well right now, I think, just as they start arguing, tussling over the bottle. Neither of them wants the other to have the last sip. I lose interest and focus my attention on tuning my radio. Moments later, gunshots ring out across the courtyard.

There's no time to take cover or run and the firing stops almost as soon as it started. Some of the prisoners race over to the fence where two bodies are slumped on the ground. I head over to take a look. Both guards lie dead in a pool of blood, the empty beer bottle beside them.

They say a man's true character comes out when he's drunk. These guards are violent, aggressive tormenters who treat us like animals, so it's not surprising that they've died in such a horrific manner. Apart from the entertainment value the incident has provided, we feel little compassion for them; their deaths are not worthy of any sympathy from the people they have bullied, tortured and victimised.

The heat brings out the worst in people, and a few days later the prisoners are angry for some reason or another. The atmosphere is tense and I get the feeling that the situation is going to escalate and things will go off the rails. Having lived here for some time, I've learnt to recognise the signs. I've witnessed the Christmas riots and multiple other insurrections and have been lucky to make it through them alive. I have a sneaky suspicion that this powder keg is about to blow.

No one ever really knows the why of the situation, but on this day some of the prisoners vent their frustration by throwing stones at the guards. It all happens so quickly, and before I know it there is an all-out riot as everyone goes on the rampage, driven by rage, hunger and the heat, and fuelled by drugs and alcohol – a lethal combination that guarantees things will not end well.

Within moments it's a free-for-all. The best thing to do in this situation is to fight your way to the safety of a cell where you can lock yourself in and wait for the rioters to be brought under control. But the turmoil is short-lived. Retaliation from the guards is swift and deadly; they cock their rifles and fire at random into the crowd of frenzied prisoners, injuring six. Game over!

Later, the number of injured prisoners rises substantially as the instigators are dragged away and flogged. More than half the inmates are beaten, and things die down for a while as they retreat to lick their wounds. Considering the aftermath of this minor riot and the one I survived at Christmas, I'm glad I missed 'the big one', when special forces abseiled into the prison from helicopters. Nobody knows exactly how many died that day, but the prisoners tell me it was like shooting fish in a barrel.

It seems that, for most, their memory is selective when it comes to the carnage of a riot, but I know that none of us who have come through it relatively unscathed want to go through this again. Sadly, we all know that it is just a matter of time before it happens again. There is no justice here; there are no rights. Nobody cares.

47

My Adopted Son
Black Beach Prison, Malabo
2014

I've acquired a little shadow of late. It's John, the young lad who looked after me when I had malaria and typhoid during my first time here. He speaks a little English and is always trying to get close to me. I'm not sure where he came from or what his real story is; out of a survival instinct he tells me only what he thinks I want to hear. What I am certain of is that he has spent most of his life surviving on the streets.

His story goes that when he was around sixteen years old, he worked for someone who didn't pay him for three months – a common problem in Malabo. Starving, John told his employer that to cover his wages he was going to sell the old laptop the man had given him. Obviously, the law here favours the guy in a suit over a starving urchin, and when the employer called the police to report the 'theft', John was arrested, beaten and locked up in Guantanamo, where he was promptly forgotten.

After a few weeks in the holding cells, the police put him in the meat wagon and dropped him off at Black Beach, where he's been living ever since. It will be his eighteenth birthday soon. Two years in this wretched place and no charges have ever been brought against him. Even if he is eventually released, his options are limited as he is destined for a hand-to-mouth life on the streets. I know I can't change the injustice, but a little kindness can go a long way.

John is resilient and always has a ready smile. Having grown up on the dirty backstreets of Malabo, his survival instincts are finely honed, and he knows that life is simpler and more bearable if he has someone looking out for him. He sought out the wealthier, more stable residents of Black Beach, offering his services carrying water, washing clothes or cooking for them in return for shelter and sometimes food.

This is how most of the youngsters survive here. If they make themselves useful and are willing to work, there is a good chance they will survive this place until somebody eventually remembers that they are here or decides they should be released. These kids have no access to funds to bribe their way out, so for as long as they are here, they'll work for inmates they trust (as much as that is possible) in exchange for food and protection.

John has been working for 'the General', one of the so-called political prisoners, for quite some time, but I think he realises that having more than one master is safer, especially as you never know who is getting out and when.

Political prisoners are never allowed to leave their cells, so everything is done through the bars. Most are wealthy, former members of the elite who managed to piss off someone in government, and they pay someone outside the prison to cook and prepare meals for them. John delivers these meals and bottled water to the General, and on visiting days he carries messages back and forth, and delivers supplies from the General's family. During the week, he washes the General's clothes and bedding. Now, John has started collecting my clothing – just one spare shirt and a pair of ragged shorts – and uses the General's washing powder to wash my things too.

I know that doing these little chores for us makes him feel good about himself. He actually enjoys helping others, which is probably why he has had such a hard time here. He is a sensitive child and reminds me of my kids back home. It feels good to nurture this young boy and offer him a little happiness, a glimpse of a different side of humanity, letting him know that not everyone wants to take advantage of him.

I spend a lot of time with him just letting him talk, sharing meals, saying prayers and treating him like a son. I know he believes that if the others are aware that he is my friend they'll leave him alone. Sadly, this is not always the case. As a street kid, old habits die hard, and the lure of the night is something he struggles to resist. He often walks around after dark, when everyone with good intentions is trying to sleep and only those looking for mischief are still on the prowl. Just like the streets of Malabo, a lot goes on after lights out. But if you get too close, it can suck you in and spit you out.

As I've learnt with my children, you have to let them be, let them make their own decisions and be prepared to face the consequences. They must make mistakes to learn and grow, so, as much as I want to protect John, there's not much I can do when he wanders around in the dark where the hyenas lie in wait.

Learning to trust must be very difficult if not impossible for a kid like him, and I'm not sure if he wants to or is capable of changing this part of who he is after surviving on the streets for all this time. 'Normal' life is something that is probably as alien to him as walking on the moon.

John is a warm and positive influence in my life. Having someone to nurture, protect and guide, someone who makes me smile, someone to hug or share a meal with, helps divert my attention from the things I know I can't have. I look forward to his visits, enjoying the look of gratitude that shines like a beacon in his eyes, making me realise that these simple gifts are moments that he has never experienced or shared with any other. I am glad that I am able to offer this to him with no expectation of anything in return.

In my letters to Melanie, I tell her about our 'adopted' son. I don't get many letters back, but when I do she always includes a little note especially for him. In October, with his birthday coming up, I try to arrange a cake through my infrequent visitors, but unfortunately I am unable to pull this off and we settle for some lime-flavoured instant pudding made by Ugo at the impromptu birthday party in my makeshift tent.

Taking John under my wing has given my stay here a sense of purpose, and I have grown to love him as a father loves his son. I am probably the only father figure he has ever had, or will have.

FRIDAY 17 OCTOBER

DEAR FAMILY,

IT HAS BEEN A HARD WEEK HERE, BUT BY THE GRACE OF GOD WE ARE STILL FULL OF HOPE THAT THIS WILL END VERY SOON! ON THE LOCAL NEWS, I HAVE BEEN TOLD THAT THE SA MINISTER OF MINES AND ENERGY (SHE USED TO BE MIN OF AGRICULTURE) IS HERE IN MALABO WITH A DELEGATION! SURE HOPE AND PRAY THAT I AM ON THE AGENDA? PRAYING!

JUST AS I THINK NOTHING WILL SHOCK ME, SOMETHING NEW COMES UP! THEY HAVE INCREASED THE NUMBER OF PEOPLE HERE BUT NOT THE FOOD, AND A HUNGRY MAN - IS A ANGRY MAN!

BUT ON THE POSITIVE SIDE, THEY DO REMEMBER TO OPEN THE DOOR AND FREE SOME GUYS, BUT SOMEHOW THEY ALWAYS SEND IN MORE THAN GO OUT, NOT SURE THEY REALIZE OR CARE!

LIKE YOU KNOW ME, I AM BLESSED AND HAVE ORGANISED MYSELF PRETTY WELL IN MY REFUGEE ROOM. WORKING ON THE SECURITY PROBLEM! (STOLE MY SHORTS THIS WEEK!) WAS THINKING THAT I GET BUBI HERE TO HELP? BUT, SMALL PROBLEM, THEY EAT DOGS HERE AND HE IS (SSHH) FAT! HAHA! AND HE WILL GET SO DIRTY, THAT EVEN I WILL HAVE A PROBLEM GIVING LOVE TOO! SURE MISS HIM... OH DON'T WORRY I MISS YOU ALL ALSO (HEHE). APPARENTLY, SO THEY TELL ME HERE, THEY PREFER EATING CATS!! ALWAYS WONDERED WHY I NEVER SEE CATS!! OOPS MY PEN JUST RAN OUT OF INK, I USE ONE PER WEEK, SORT OF A PROBLEM, BECAUSE WE ARE NOT ALOUD TO BRING IN PENS (OR SEND LETTERS.... SHHH) THIS PLACE IS CRAZY, YOU ARE NOT ALOUD NAIL CLIPPERS, BUT THEY SELL RAZOR BLADES INSIDE? LOTS OF OTHER CRAZY STUFF, BUT THAT WILL HAVE TO WAIT.

PTO

48

Ebola

```
Black Beach Prison, Malabo
            2014
```

It's been another tense and rough week, dangerous times for those of us who just want to live to see another day on our endless journey to a freedom that remains elusive. And now there are rumours of an Ebola flare-up on the mainland. It's not the kind of news you want to hear in this place, where everyone is confined to a small area and you know that there is no way for the incompetent thugs in charge to implement an effective containment protocol.

The news spreads like a virus throughout the prison, and the inmates are terrified, restless and on edge. I wouldn't be surprised if there's an outbreak of another kind. All that's needed is a spark.

On one of the news broadcasts that I manage to pick up, I hear that the virus is out of control and primed to explode. Usually, Ebola, which has been present in West Africa for decades, is limited to remote rural areas and easy to contain within a timeframe of three weeks to three months, but in this report it seems that a few scattered cases in Guinea, Liberia and Sierra Leone have been incubating for a few weeks and the virus is now being detected in cities outside of the initial containment zone.

I feel uneasy. I grew up watching films like *Outbreak*, and I realise that if Ebola makes it to Black Beach, we are probably all going to die. There is no way to contain such a contagious disease in an overcrowded prison with no sanitation or proper medical facilities. But Ebola is not the only threat I have to contend with here. The tension is mounting. As I did the previous time when we were expecting riots, I write another will and send it to the embassy.

For about a week or so, visitors are not allowed. We are cut off without updates on the local Ebola situation, apart from what we hear on the radio. As far as implementing a virus protocol, the most we've heard is that there were some cursory checks of those coming in and out of Malabo. We are the forgotten ones, certainly not worth worrying about or trying to save. In any case, Ebola is soon forgotten in the wake of an attempted breakout at the prison. The risks to life here far outweigh the threat of a virus in a country more than a thousand kilometres away. Here, if something goes wrong, we all suffer the consequences, we are all punished, and life just gets harder.

When you sleep in gen pop, it's best not to keep anything of value with you, as that is when you are at your most vulnerable, as I've discovered. This is a lesson I learnt quickly the first time I had some money. Earlier that day, I'd bought some Maggi spice to mix with the rice to make the food a little more bearable. Stupidly, I'd put the change, about five US dollars, in the pocket of my shorts. That night, no matter how hard I tried to stay alert, my body eventually shut down and I fell asleep, switching off from sheer exhaustion. That's when the skulking hyenas crept closer, emerging from the shadows where they'd been lurking, watching and waiting for an opportunity to pounce.

The following morning when I woke up, I knew instantly that something was wrong and soon realised I'd been robbed. I hadn't felt anyone going through my pockets, and even though this was by no means a large sum of money, the loss felt disproportionate, as I was also forced to face my vulnerability and helplessness. Knowing I had no way of protecting myself hit me like a punch in the gut, and I was plagued by thoughts of how long they'd been watching me. What else had they seen that they wanted? Were they coming back? Had they followed me from a distance, waiting for an opportunity to strike? I felt violated, and the worst was that I had absolutely no idea who'd invaded my space as I slept. My skin crawled as I looked around, wondering who'd managed to get close enough to put a hand into my pants pocket without me stirring. They had probably been watching me all day.

After that, I asked the others for suggestions to make sure it didn't happen again. Some ideas are really good, like putting your money in the sole of your shoe or inside the elastic loop of your shorts behind the drawstring. In the end, I decided to set up a line of credit with a Muslim inmate and arranged for a friend on the outside to give his brother the money to pay my debt. Now, if I want to buy something, I loan the exact amount so I won't need to worry about where to store the change. It helps to know the ropes.

Some prisoners are robbed of large amounts by other inmates because theft is a sickness with them – it's all they know, and it's how they survive. It's so bad that, despite the risks, they will even steal from their own pack. They can't stop themselves, even though they are wary of being caught and local justice is often far worse than what the prison authorities dish out.

But these incidents pale in comparison to the crimes some of the prisoners committed before being sent here. One of my neighbours is here because he chopped up his wife and fed her to their children. And he is just one of many. How do you make sense of such outrageous crimes? In my life before Black Beach, the likelihood of encountering men such as these was close to zero, and yet now some are my closest neighbours, with not even walls or a garden fence to separate us. Nevertheless, it's not up to me to judge them, or their actions, abhorrent as they are, and despite My neighbour's horrific crimes, I don't believe he will harm me. I know that he suffers for his actions and his greatest punishment is living with the guilt for what he has done. I can see that it's slowly driving him crazy.

Many believe that their brutal acts were carried out unconsciously. Perhaps it's a way to assuage their guilt, saying they were driven by irrepressible urges. Some claim that they are possessed by evil spirits or carried out gruesome acts to appease their deceased relatives or to gain favour with the spirits. On an island where ancient African folklore still thrives, these cases are more common than one would imagine. I've heard of incidents where entire villages have been wiped out by neighbouring villagers on a murderous rampage. It's hard to comprehend that such barbaric acts are still taking place in the mountains and rainforests of this region, but the things I've witnessed and the stories I've been told in Black Beach make me believe that it's true.

The nights drag on, hot and stuffy, the darkness punctuated with anguished cries, the faint whimpering of those too fearful to draw attention to their suffering, the babble of prisoners speaking in tongues, general bickering and arguing, and the screams of women being raped. Night after night, month after month. I lie in my tent, just a thin sheet separating me from the others crowded in around me, vulnerable to the pickpockets, murderers, drug addicts, and lunatics driven by demons and malevolent forces, who will stop at nothing to get their hands on whatever others have.

49

What's Your Name, Where You From?
```
Black Beach Prison, Malabo
2014
```

This afternoon, we gather at the gate to see who has purchased today's one-way ticket to hell. As I squeeze between the crowds of onlookers, I remember what it felt like when I arrived so many months ago, the terror, the anger, the fear, the anguish. Now, here I am on the other side of the fence. I have survived and, in the process, learnt how savage and cruel humanity can be.

It's as if years have passed since the horror I felt taking my first steps into Black Beach. I'll never get used to existing in this place, but I know how things work now and take each day as it comes. My life plays out against a backdrop that never changes: hot, dirty and volatile.

The guards emerge from the hut and amble towards the van. The inmates are chanting and shaking the fence in anticipation. The bush telegraph is very effective, and we often know in advance who is coming to join us as information is passed between the officers at Guantanamo to the guards here. There was a murderer who arrived at the prison a few months back, and there was a lot of hype about him before he arrived. He was said to be a vicious killer who had hacked his friend to pieces over sharing the spoils from a robbery they'd committed. When the van arrived, everyone rushed to the fence to see this crazy, musclebound savage, but he turned out to be a scrawny, diminutive chap, hardly the stuff of legend. He stepped out of the van in ankle chains, his hands bound and chained at his hips, the guards reluctant to approach him. He was processed and placed in solitary confinement, where he remained for three months. One day I happened to notice him wandering about in gen pop, indifferent to his surroundings and seemingly disconnected from reality. We all gave him a wide berth, and not long after that he disappeared.

Black Beach is like an airport terminal. People come and go. How many times have I stood at the fence waiting to see who is inbound, as if standing at the airport waiting for a flight to come in? How depraved are we that welcoming someone new to this place has become a form of entertainment? But it can't be denied, anything that gives us a taste of something new is welcomed, and every now and then I get a thrill to see a high-ranking official or politician climbing out of the vehicle in shackles.

On a few occasions, usually when political prisoners are brought in, we are taken around the back because the guards don't want us to know who's arriving. I've learnt that there is seldom a paper trail; everyone knows not to sign your name to a document – if there are no signed papers, there is no one to blame. The ones who end up here probably signed something they shouldn't have. Sometimes, an infamous criminal is finally caught or someone who was released but forgot the lessons learnt comes back for another reminder. And then there are the escapees who are recaptured.

Keeping track of people in here is impossible, and there is no point to it, but some days you realise that you haven't seen so-and-so for a while. There's no point speculating where he went or if it was by choice. All escape attempts are successful up to a point – getting out of Black Beach is not too difficult, especially as the guards are drunk and negligent, and sometimes they're even in on an escape. The problems arise once the escapees are over the fence and outside the prison. Of course, as I am still the only white man in Black Beach, it would be pretty difficult for me to leave without my departure being noticed.

One of the things I observed early on is that prisoners are united by common heritage – Equatorial Guinean, Nigerian, Malian, Cameroonian – or by religion. If you're lucky enough to find someone from the same region as you, you're infinitely safer than going it alone. The locals are contemptuous of foreigners, treating them like second-class citizens. Even in Black Beach there is xenophobic discrimination and a hierarchy, which is why Ugo, a Nigerian, will never have the honour of leading the Christian group, even though everyone knows that he is the power behind the throne. Luckily for me, even though I don't have any fellow South Africans to hunker down with, being the only 'European' African provides a novelty factor, and of course whenever I have visitors, everyone is suddenly my friend.

As we stand at the gates today, waiting for our new brothers to make their appearance, I'm surprised to hear a loud cheer erupting as two badly battered and bleeding young men emerge. They look like any of the other Malabo youngsters here, so I'm curious to know who they are and why everyone is so excited to see them.

They're handcuffed and in a sorry state, clearly in a lot of pain as they limp down the hill. The minute they're through the gates they are surrounded by solicitous admirers, full of concern for their well-being. My brothers explain that the newest additions to our flock are the famous Miami-based rapper and rising star Ismael Sankara and his boxing hero brother Emilio. It appears that not even celebrities can escape prosecution in Equatorial Guinea.

For me, it's rare to find someone here who speaks English fluently and has experienced a completely different life. Although the brothers say 'fuck' a lot, they're always polite and respectful to me. Ish, as we come to know him, and his brothers were raised in Miami by their mother after moving there from Burkina Faso, and in 2008 Ish took a trip to Africa to connect with his roots. The experience had a profound effect on the way he made music, and he is considered one of the leading acts representing African beats on the international stage. I have to wonder what they are doing in this place.

It turns out that they came to the island to visit family, and Ish hired a car which he then lent to a friend and the vehicle was spotted fleeing from the scene of an armed robbery. Ish and his brother said they had no knowledge of the crime, but they were arrested, accused of participating in the heist and beaten. They swear they were not involved, and, listening to their story, I believe them. Two young men with such big dreams and promising careers ahead of them – it doesn't make sense for them to have done that.

I am horrified when the brothers describe the brutality they suffered under interrogation at Guantanamo, where they were suspended on a pole attached to the roof, their hands cuffed together at the wrists and their feet bound at the ankles while being repeatedly beaten. Even though the wounds have healed, both complain about the constant pain and numbness in their hands and wrists. Emilio is concerned that he won't be able to box again, but for Ish things are a little different. Perhaps his time in Black Beach will bring him street cred; it certainly seems to be a badge of honour in the rap fraternity to spend time behind bars. I'm pretty sure Tupac and his crowd would not have been impressed with the conditions here, but Ish takes it in his stride and revels in his star status, with all the young thugs from Malabo basking in his reflected glory.

After about six months of living in gen pop and suffering along with the rest of us, their names are called. And just like that, they're gone. Released with no charges ever having been brought against them. *Liberdade!* Freedom!

And yet I remain here, no end in sight, battling my sense of isolation and abandonment every day. I have to trust that God is in control and remain grateful for the brief distraction the brothers brought. Now that they've left, I must stay busy and hopeful; it's the only way I'll survive until the day my name is called and I get to walk out of here, irreparably damaged but alive.

50

Nothing to Declare
Black Beach Prison, Malabo
2014

While I turn to my Bible for solace, many take a different route when they need to escape the harsh reality of life in this dark underworld. Since the days of the slave trade, Equatorial Guinea has served as something of a gateway to Africa, and in modern times drug smuggling and human trafficking top the list in the exploitation of Bioko's strategic location. During the years I have spent working here, I've seen a steady increase in the cocaine trade, but it's all very hush-hush, with the authorities keeping a tight lid on it, especially as this mostly affects the privileged kids of the elite.

Most children from wealthy Equatorial Guinean families are given huge allowances and sent off to the US and Spain for school or university where they mix with the wrong crowd, use cocaine and pick up other bad habits from their new First World friends. Everyone knows about the cocaine trade in Malabo, but no one talks about it; it's best not to ask too many questions, as high-ranking officials with diplomatic immunity and easy access to funds operate within these circles with impunity. Cocaine is the drug of choice for the social elite, who take full advantage of flexible border controls and diplomatic passports.

Around Christmastime, a young dealer, the son of a senior politician, finds his way to Black Beach. He's a smooth-talking hustler and a popular figure in the drug community, which guarantees him a comfortable spot among the dealers and upper echelon of the prison. His nickname is Scissors, and he's the preferred supplier to the rich kids of Malabo.

Scissors' father has sent him here in the hopes of teaching him a lesson, as all other attempts to set him straight have failed. He is a real charmer and I have my doubts about his rehabilitation – he's soon the go-to guy in prison for those who have money. He tells me that he buys his drugs in Brazil, flying them back aboard an official aircraft and using his diplomatic passport to bypass border control.

At Christmas, he offers to get me a bottle of Jack Daniel's and a whore.

Much to his disgust, I tell him a pair of nail clippers will do, which he duly arranges, and I add them to my small collection of prized possessions. For some or other reason you can buy a razor blade in here but not nail clippers.

Only wealthy prisoners have the resources to buy hard drugs, but drugs in general form part of the fabric of society in the prison. People are divided along the invisible lines of those who do drugs and those who don't; those who can afford drugs and those who can't. Drugs fuel much of the crime committed by the inmates, although as I've witnessed first-hand, alcohol, which is the more acceptable and accessible drug of choice, is by far the most damaging.

Today is just another Sunday afternoon, very hot and humid. There are visitors for the lucky ones, which means everyone is happier than on other days in this hole. The youngsters controlling the flow of drugs into the prison are often caught and pay a hefty price in lashes, so they're always coming up with ingenious strategies to smuggle in the drugs under the noses of the guards. For the most part, though, they are reluctant to cut a deal with a guard to look the other way in exchange for a share of the profits.

We know something is up today and watch with interest as one of the gangs carries in a five-litre tub of butter. It's fairly obvious that their sudden interest in a large quantity of butter has very little to do with culinary pursuits and a lot to do with what is probably a stash of drugs concealed inside; the leader of the gang looks particularly smug as he carries it like a trophy into the prison. A rival gang smells profit and immediately ambushes him, and it soon turns into a free-for-all with everyone trying to make off with the prize. When I pass by the scene a few minutes later, there is butter everywhere and no drugs to be seen. Both gangs are called to the gate and beaten – it seems that cutting the guards in on the deal would have been cheaper and less painful in the long run.

Recently, there was another incident when a group of young inmates, all members of the same gang, were summoned to appear before a judge to have their case heard. As usual, they were paired two together and cuffed before being delivered to the courthouse in the meat wagon. This particular gang of delinquents are roughly between seventeen and twenty years old and had been living the thug life on the streets of Malabo until they ganged up and kicked some poor guy to death after he'd tried to save his girlfriend from being raped by them.

Most of these young guys have girlfriends, and whenever there is a court appearance the waiting area is swarming with them, as well as lawyers, parents, babies, relatives and friends. Despite their crime, these boys were deemed 'not dangerous' and therefore required minimal supervision from just one lethargic guard who made the most of the situation by extorting 'gifts' from the visitors.

When the guard went off to answer the call of nature, one of the guys noticed that the door to the evidence room had been left open. The temptation proved too much, and he managed to convince the guy handcuffed to him to tag along to take a look at what was inside. Apparently, in plain sight on the table lay a pile of packets, all containing white powder. Quick as a flash, the boy managed to grab one of the packages and shoved it into his underpants, where it remained undetected throughout the rest of the day.

It was quite late when they finally returned to Black Beach. It's standard procedure that everyone is searched when entering or leaving the jail, but on this day, because it was late and there were nine boys to be processed, the search was not thorough, and so against the odds, a two-kilogram packet of cocaine made its way into the prison hidden inside the underpants of a young hooligan.

This unexpected windfall definitely landed in the wrong hands. The boys are from a low-level street gang who've never used cocaine; I doubt they'd ever even seen it, except maybe on television, especially in such a large quantity. But this didn't deter them in the slightest. It was a free-for-all. Some snorted it, others ate it, and some even mixed it with water. I don't know if anyone experienced a high from drinking it, but it was all very entertaining for the onlookers who watched these kids go wild, shaking their heads at their ignorance, especially the dealers who have a pretty good idea of how much money they could have made by selling it. This went on for a while as everyone climbed in, trying to get their hands on some of the 'magic' white powder.

I am amazed that none of them overdosed; clearly, none of them experienced any kind of euphoric high as they ended up puking or passing out. Later, to add insult to injury, they were taken away by the guards and flogged, never knowing that they'd just blown their one chance to make some serious cash.

Easy come, easy go …

BLACK BEACH

51

Fair Game

```
Black Beach Prison, Malabo
2015
```

Every now and then, the warden and his helpers chase us out of the building and do a headcount. We stand in the blazing heat of the courtyard crammed to way beyond maximum capacity as we're ticked off a list and searched. Today, we're on edge, waiting as the guards search everywhere, confiscating contraband, drugs, weapons, or anything that they want for themselves. If they find something, we all know that the punishment will be swift and brutal.

Afterwards, I return to my spot and find everything turned upside down. The small, precious items that make life here just a little more bearable are gone, including my nail clippers and 'gym' equipment. I feel violated, but that's how things are; you can't complain.

It's easy to fall foul of the 'law' in this place. Committing a crime in Black Beach is often as simple as doing something the guards deem suspicious, such as exercise. I've joined the 'Virgin Active' again, along with a few others, but when the guards see us working out in the yard they call out and aim their rifles to intimidate us.

Out on the Esplanada is where I get to know the other inmates, listening to stories about their lives and how they ended up here. There's always a lot of discussion about their cases, even though three people sitting together is considered a crime by the guards, who assume that we must be plotting something. Another serious offence is to be caught writing with a pen and paper – a rule still in force since the warden declared it during my last stay. If during a search these items are found, they're confiscated and destroyed. At one time even owning a Bible was not permitted.

There is a strong Catholic heritage on the island dating back to the days of colonisation, and it's still the predominant faith of the region. Followers of the Claretian missionary movement are encouraged to share the word of God around the world, living frugally and rejoicing in all the torments and sorrows they suffer to honour their faith. Ana Maria, a devotee of the faith, used to visit Black Beach with her church group, despite all the difficulties that they faced to get here. This was before my time, and she is now banned from coming here, but Ugo tells me about how she spoke of passing trucks filled with soldiers who fired at her and her group at will, and yet despite the intimidation she made regular visits to the prison, bringing Bibles for the prisoners and holding Bible study classes. Many inmates attended these classes as they were an escape from the horrors of their daily existence. For them, God represented freedom, and Ana Maria brought hope to many abandoned behind these walls, forgotten by their families, most presumed dead.

Ana Maria also supplied pens and paper to the inmates so that they could take notes during Bible study, but when the prison administrator heard about it, he took the information to his superior, who had a fierce reputation for relying on violence and intimidation as an effective means of coercion, and when he heard about the Bibles, he immediately demanded that the books, papers and pens be seized. Somehow, they ended up at the office of a senior official in the presidency who looked through them and ordered that they be returned to the prison with instructions that they should not be taken again and that Bible study should be encouraged as a step towards rehabilitation and to bring about positive change in the prisoners' lives. God does indeed move in mysterious ways.

My most prized possession in this place is the small, well-worn Gideon Bible dating from 1956. Although pages are missing, it still gives me solace and comfort on the worst days and guidance on others. After hearing the story about Ana Maria, I look at it a little differently, wondering about the other hands that have held this book. What has become of them? What crimes did they commit, or were they innocent like me? What suffering were they subjected to?

Not long after the guards complete their search, heading off with their prizes, we go back to life as usual, spending the afternoon sheltering from the sun at Old Man Luis's shack on the Esplanada. In Black Beach, soccer forms a huge part of our daily routine as the guards realise that the younger guys need to burn off their excess energy, although 'soccer' is a very loose description of the game that's played behind these walls. It's a combination of various physical sports, with very few rules. Usually, it's a free-for-all with lots of action, and a great source of entertainment for the spectators sitting against the side of the building watching in anticipation for the next fight to break out. Most fights are not excessively violent and don't last long, but there have been times when a small ruckus starts a battle that can go on for days.

As usual, the fun starts in the afternoon. We've gathered along the sidelines, ready to watch the action. *Gentlemen, place your bets!* From the outset, it's a boisterous match with a few slaps and tussles, but the game continues – no red or yellow cards here. At first, there is nothing to indicate that it's any different from any other day, but it will soon turn out to be one of the worst incidents I've witnessed in this place.

The sudden escalation in violence is impossible to explain to someone who hasn't lived here, where respect for others is non-existent. Sometimes, there is no reasonable justification for what unfolds in an instant, especially when many exist on the edge of madness and you never know whether they're going to catapult beyond the point of no return.

As the game progresses, I notice two youngsters, brothers, who are playing on the same team. They've already had a few scuffles in today's match, kicking and lashing out at one another. Now they're fighting again. Someone wrenches them apart, but they're soon back at it. The game goes on, with the crowd enjoying the action, until suddenly and without warning the two of them pile into each other in a sudden fit of rage.

The crowd watches, dumbstruck, as one of the boys wrestles his brother to the ground, grinding his face into the searing hot concrete and, in a split-second impulse, with no discernible motive, grabs an empty Coke tin from the gutter, crushes it into the dirt and, as viciously as a hunter ripping open the belly of its prey, tears at it with his teeth. The thin aluminium peels away, providing him with a weapon, sharp as a raptor's beak. Without a thought, the boy slashes at his brother's face, slicing through his cheek to the bone.

It's carnage as blood spurts over them and the terrified shrieks from the injured boy rise above the cries of horror from the onlookers. His wound pours a red river down his face, covering them both in blood and puddling on the ground beneath them. He collapses, his head lolling to one side, the skin of his cheek flapping loosely, exposing his entire jaw and teeth through the gaping hole.

The soccer match is quickly abandoned and a few of the players lift the boy and carry him to the gate, still unconscious. Most of us are certain that he will not survive, that he will bleed out right here at the entrance to Black Beach.

After the dust has settled, we make the most of our last moments of freedom before being locked in for the night, and later I hear through the bush telegraph that the boy is going to be okay, although it was a close call. When he arrived at the hospital, there were no bandages or surgical sutures available, so his family had to go and buy them in the marketplace and take them to the hospital so that he could be stitched up. He will no doubt bear the scars for the rest of his life. The sudden and swift descent into madness is hard to process; it seems almost surreal when I think about what happened. One moment we were laughing, and the next we were watching a real-life bloody horror show right in front of us.

All in a day's entertainment when you live in Black Beach.

52

Crimes Against Humanity
Black Beach Prison, Malabo
2015

I've been here for more than eight months, and I'd be kidding myself if I said it was getting any easier. Yes, I have adapted, because if you don't, you die. Each day is still a struggle against the heat, to find enough water and food, to stay healthy, and to avoid pickpockets and thugs, not to mention battling mosquitoes and the constant threat of malaria.

The morning fog comes in from the sea and burns off as the day wears on, only to be replaced by the smoke from the kerosene stoves and cooking fires. In the background is the sound of gunshots and blasts from the neighbouring naval facility. We're always grateful when it rains; it's possible to collect water for drinking, cleaning and washing, and the stench is much less overpowering as it flushes out the sewerage pipes.

I spend most of my time on the Esplanada. It preserves my sanity and is infinitely better than being stuck inside, fighting off the others, pushing, shoving, and avoiding the shadows where danger lurks. The men who worked with me before sneak in over weekends, bringing me food and taking letters to the embassy. They've been turned away by the prison officials many times, which possibly explains why I haven't seen the embassy staff for months. Life is hard enough here without reminders of what lies outside my reach, but at least there is always something going on to distract me. The constant altercations between prisoners alleviate the monotony of the day, as the onlookers offer commentary and place bets on who will emerge victorious.

The prison-issue brown uniform is reserved for court appearances, so most of us wear civilian clothing with open sandals ('slippers' as they are called here). For some reason, it's really hard to hang on to your footwear, and in this place you don't want to be walking around barefoot. I don't know if it's for sport or malice, but often inmates will steal just one shoe and put it in the dustbin or throw it over the fence. Others throw their shoes at the lights or steal a pair and hide them until visiting day when they give them to their families to keep for when they get out.

We all have a way of marking our possessions, using sharpened plastic spoons to carve a small symbol into the item so that we can identify it. I've realised that having anything of value makes me a target, so my clothes are old and tattered, and not even the pettiest of thieves is interested in stealing them. Even my slops are hand-me-downs, thrown away by someone who felt they were no longer worth keeping, but I've repaired them and they're a good fit and fairly comfortable. They serve their purpose.

The Esplanada is crowded, with some people exercising, always under the watchful eye of the guards. Most of those who exercise are policemen or military men who serve their time, even getting paid while incarcerated, and as soon as they get out, they simply return to their old jobs. They tend to stick together, helping one another, given a wide berth by the general prison population. I remember the night a policeman who had been caught stealing from the wrong man – someone in politics – arrived. He was tossed inside the gates, hands still cuffed behind his back, after being beaten to a pulp by the guards. When no one was watching, some inmates helped him under cover of darkness, and after a few days he started to recover. I recognised him then; I'd seen him around in Malabo, and so I sat with him sharing a drink of water. He told me that the worst was yet to come, that the authorities were waiting for him to recover enough to be taken away again. He was right. A few days later they came for him, and he did not return.

Once, an argument broke out between a civilian and a soldier who I'd spoken to a few times, providing the catalyst for a massive riot so violent that the warden's 2IC, Paul, arranged for the soldier to be immediately transferred out of Black Beach to a prison on the mainland. He won the lottery that day – there is no place on earth that can possibly be worse than Black Beach.

I am learning more about the shameful history of the prison and the country. Black Beach was reconstructed shortly after independence and came to be known as the 'Auschwitz of Africa'. Francisco Macías Nguema, the son of a Fang witch doctor and the president at the time, was a ruthless dictator; some say he styled himself after Hitler. He'd grown up on the mainland and came to power in 1968, only to be overthrown in 1979 by his nephew, the current president, Teodoro Obiang Nguema.

After the coup, Francisco Macías Nguema escaped into the forest, but was apprehended after hiding out for ten days and brought to Black Beach. Found guilty of genocide, treason, human rights violations and embezzlement of public funds, he was sentenced to death. According to local legend, he vowed that his ghost would return seeking vengeance on those who had condemned him, so the local military refused to carry out the execution. Moroccan soldiers were subsequently appointed and delivered swift justice by firing squad at Black Beach later that day.

Superstitious folklore is not unusual in Equatorial Guinea. People from all walks of life consult shamans, from the destitute wanting to escape poverty and those needing healing tonics to young men looking for potions for matters of sex, rivalry and romance. The elite will often call on a marabout, looking for powerful spells to fast-track their trajectory or to gain protection from a perceived enemy, eliminate competition or ward off evil. Many of my brothers believe in the power of witch doctors, and their families bring them potions. I am recovering from yet another bout of malaria and am offered a concoction and almost drink it, but I smell quinine and, as I am allergic to it, I decline.

Outside on the Esplanada, I'm sitting with my eyes closed against the glare. In my mind, I travel to the heat and dust of the Karoo, the sun baking down on a landscape as endless as time. My memories and dreams blur in a mirage of thoughts and emotions. I'm intensely aware that it's a miracle that I have so far survived without medication. It's at moments like these that I think about God.

How is it possible that I have survived cerebral malaria without any treatment or medication? From what I know, it doesn't happen very often. Time has been stolen from me as I lie in this dark hovel, rats and cockroaches crawling around and over me, with no access to proper health care or clean water. I shouldn't be alive, and yet here I am. Is it divine intervention? Does such a thing exist? And if so, why? I must believe that there are unseen forces at work, and if that is so, then I must honour my faith and use this time to grow in spirit, to stop searching for a way out of here and use the time to find my way back to God and my core beliefs. Perhaps God is not done with me.

I still struggle with questions that haunt me: Why am I here? When, why and how did everything fall apart? I simply don't understand. I've devoted a lot of time to these questions, but right now does it really matter how I ended up on an unofficial death list? I know that I could have handled things differently, simply agreed to Angabi's demands and then looked for another project. It's not as if I didn't know about how things work in this country, so if there is any blame, I need to lay it at my own door and take responsibility. This is *not* God's doing.

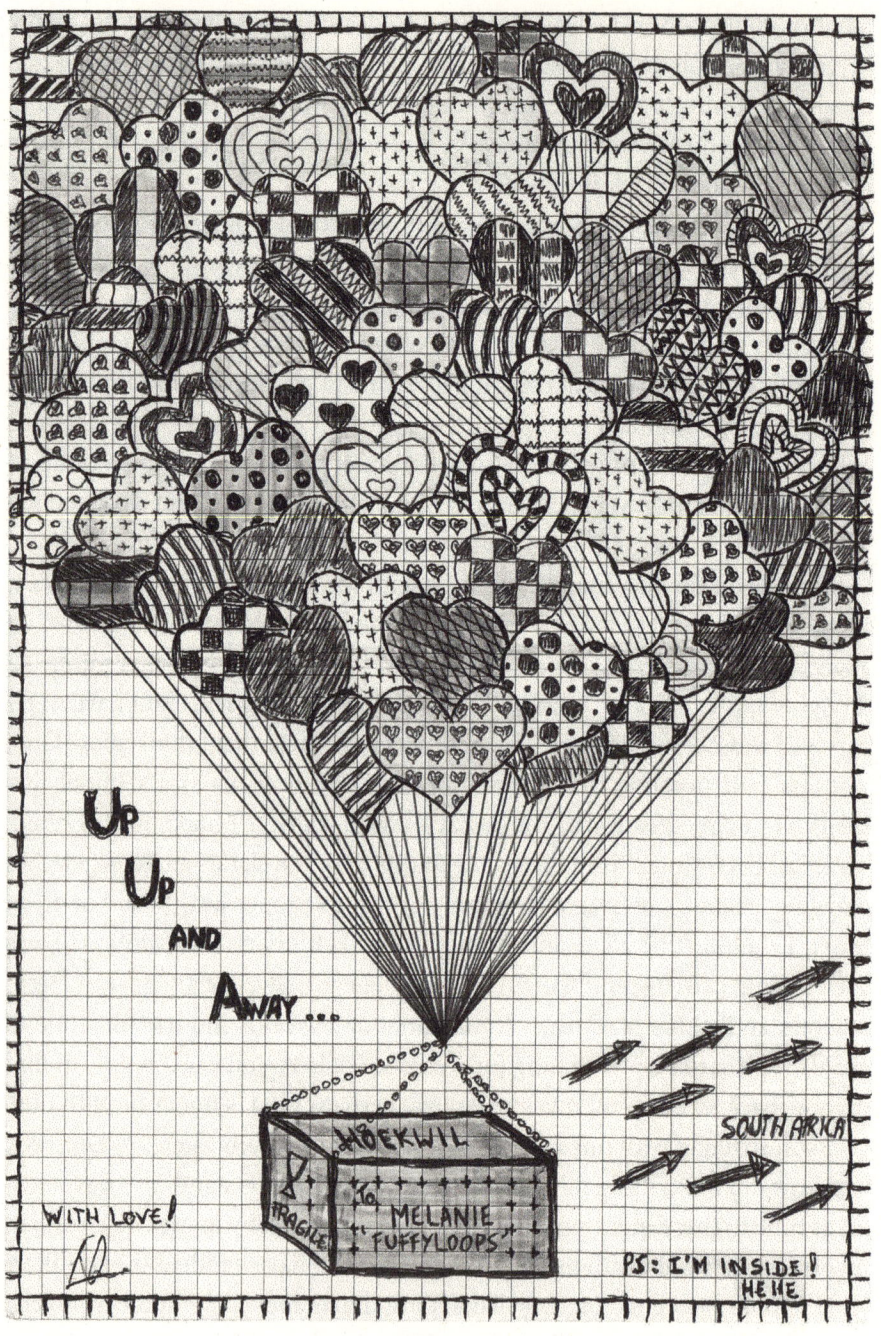

I am in control of my actions, decisions and choices. God is not overseeing the minutiae of my existence, but here in Black Beach, I know that the only way I will get through the ordeal is if I walk with God at my side. Even though I have accepted a scenario in which I don't make it out of here, a part of me feels that by putting my trust in God, I *will* get out. There is still so much to live for, to fight for. Just the chance to see my wife, my family and even Bubbles again keeps me on the path to redemption.

As I sit leaning against the wall, I notice a teenage boy sketching me. He is something of a celebrity artist around here, producing 'selfies' and behind-the-scenes glimpses into daily life at Black Beach. I have built up quite a collection of his work and look forward to seeing his latest portrait. They are prized possessions, little 'snapshots' confirming my existence.

Close by, a young boy is washing some clothing in a trickle of water. When I first saw this kid, I was astonished that such a young child was in this place. I asked the others how old he is. They told me that he is around ten, at a push maybe eleven. It makes no sense. What is he doing here? How long has he been here? It turns out his crime was, in the eyes of some, worthy of this ultimate of punishments: he'd stolen a mango from the main market. Timing is everything, and it just so happened that a member of the presidential family was in the market at the time and she instructed the police to take him to Black Beach to teach him a lesson.

So here he is, in the worst possible place for a child to be, suffering repeated sexual and physical abuse, forced to work as a slave washing clothes, running errands for the very people committing these heinous crimes against him.

I look at him sadly. This is not a life for an innocent child. What hope does he have, a forgotten victim of an uncaring society? He's spent a year in this hell, yet somehow his spirit endures. What must he have come from to find this life tolerable? Is stealing a mango when you're hungry really a crime? Isn't the crime that he, a child, was hungry? It is not my place to judge the actions of others, that is up to our Lord, but surely we need to provide a stable society where children are not forced to steal to survive, where children have a stable home environment where they can learn, grow and thrive? It's difficult not to condemn a society where a child is forced to steal because his stomach is empty and then forced to live in this place because someone felt that he should be taught a lesson.

Sadly, he is not the only child in this place. There are many children in ragged clothing being forced to do unspeakable things, and there are women too, degraded and forced to prostitute themselves to survive. I see it every day and am powerless to stop it. There is no way to intervene when human beings are forced at the whim of wealthy or influential politicians, and sometimes even their friends, lovers and colleagues, to live together in a cage like animals guarded by savage watchdogs.

Black Beach exists so that someone can get rid of someone else. Black Beach exists because someone wants to teach someone else a lesson or has an axe to grind. Black Beach exists because someone got rid of someone else by killing them, chopping them up into pieces, squeezing the pieces into a sack and dropping the sack in the creek. Black Beach exists because someone made a mistake and their lawyer is afraid or can't be bothered to find out both sides of the story or the accused did not understand the language of his interrogators. Black Beach exists to punish a child who took some fruit because he was hungry. How is this just? How is this fair?

Many times, I have wanted to intervene, to fight for this boy and the others like him, but my brothers hold me back. They know that to meddle will not end well, not for me and certainly not for the child, because after I am gone, he will still be here. He is worth more to those abusing him than I am. For these savage men, it's just as easy to kill me as it is to swat a mosquito.

How do I remain faithful to God despite what I see? How is it possible that I still believe that my God is loving? I don't have an easy answer to that, but the truth is I believe that God's role is to guide us, not to make choices for us. There is evil in this world, but there is good too, and if I am here, then there must be a reason for it. It's not up to me to question it. I must do what I can to get through it, one day at a time.

I know many people would question my faith. If God loves us, why do we suffer, why does he allow a child to suffer? These are really questions for all who value good over evil, Christian or not, and they are always asked during times of hardship, suffering, tragedy and injustice. We want to make sense of it; we want to find someone to blame. But ultimately, God is not at fault; we walk our own paths and make our own decisions, and when we suffer we want to know that God cares and that we are not alone.

As the sun beats down, warming my skin and nurturing my soul, I consider these questions again and realise that there is both good and evil trapped within these walls. There are people like Ugo and the other church members who work tirelessly to ensure that there is a place of solace in this wild and untamed hell. And there are people like Bangkok and the men who are merely an abomination, just plain and simply pure evil. There seems to be no grey area. On some days I lose hope, but I know that I will never feel abandoned by God. I am not alone, and as long as I don't give up I will be protected. I will endure. Survive. I will return to the Karoo and the ocean, rivers and mountain paths around my home in South Africa.

There is no doubt that God has saved me numerous times since my ordeal began. I cannot think of any other explanation. For example, when I was held in the torture chambers at Guantanamo, how is it that I walked away unscathed while others were beaten? How did I survive in the cells among the other prisoners who could have raped, abused or killed me? In Black Beach, I have suffered starvation, cerebral malaria, dysentery and typhoid. I have somehow survived the wrath of Angabi, and I am sure that as long as I am here, living in filth, on a knife's edge, I will encounter many more life-threatening moments. But, by the grace of God, until now I have endured.

I have to trust that, as it says in Proverbs, there is a bigger plan, each step ordained by God to bring me closer to my destiny. I must not question the path that led me here. My only goal is to make it through, make a difference, and find my way home. I must have faith; I must *not* give up hope. I must believe that I will hold my wife close again.

53

Fresh Meat

```
Black Beach Prison, Malabo
2015
```

We're sitting outside in the courtyard late one afternoon when the meat wagon comes down the hill and pulls up outside the guard hut. Fresh meat incoming! We amble over to the fence, not expecting anything out of the ordinary, but I'm shocked when a beautiful and obviously refined young woman steps out of the van. She's in her early twenties, immaculately dressed, and looks completely out of place. It's clear that she comes from a wealthy family and she has an aura of sweet innocence. I'm sure that, like my daughter, she is the apple of her father's eye. My heart fills with dread, terrified for her safety. What is she doing in a place like this?

All around me, the frenzied pack is immediately on the scent, their lust tangible, raw, savage and intense. They fill the air with obscene howls that make my skin crawl as they jostle one another, pushing and shoving, arguing over who will take her first. I know that this night will be long and violent, and that my brothers and I are powerless to stop these animals in their mania. Having seen how the women, mostly street-smart prostitutes capable of taking care of themselves, are treated in here, I know that this young lady is about to step into an abyss, a place so depraved that I'm not sure she'll ever find her way back.

She hesitates at the top of the hill, catching a glimpse of her future, and fear seems to take hold of her, hitting me too. Is death a better option than what she is about to encounter? She whimpers, obviously petrified as the guards lead her like a sacrificial lamb to the slaughter.

If only I could protect her. I'm thinking of my daughter, who is around the same age, and as a father and someone who has seen the dark side of this place, I know that this young woman's life is about to be irrevocably damaged just at the moment that she is making her way in the world.

But then, as she enters the prison, she is granted a stay of execution. The 'madam' who takes care of the women here whisks her off to the other side of the prison, an area supposedly just for women, and for now she is safe. My prayers, delivered frantically like a 911 call, have been answered.

Later, I hear that the local bank where the young woman worked was targeted in an armed robbery and the authorities believe she can identify the culprits, but she's not talking. Someone decided that a stay at Black Beach might jog her memory. Who is she covering for, I wonder. Why is she so afraid to reveal their identity? She's playing Russian roulette with her life by taking her chances here. Then again, damned if you do, doomed if you don't.

A day or two goes by and the madam keeps her safe, ensuring that she is never alone, even having her escorted to the bathroom. Four nights later, just as in nature, the young get reckless. It's late and the madam is elsewhere, so the young woman makes the fateful decision to walk to the bathroom alone, not realising that this careless mistake will change her life, if she gets to live at all.

Skulking in the shadows are six boys driven by one desire. They are slaves to their insatiable lust, impatient to mark their territory and stake their claim, growing bolder with each passing moment. They watch her, stalking her silently in the dark, just out of sight. As she passes them on her way back to the women's section, the trap is sprung. They pounce, surrounding her, and she is at their mercy. There is no hope of escape as they grab her, dragging her into a cell, barricading themselves inside, tearing and ripping at her clothes, biting in a fever of unbridled lust, each one violating her while her blood-curdling screams echo throughout the building.

The prison is in an uproar as inmates rush to stop them, but it's too late and we are powerless, unable to break through the bars, screaming at the boys, witnesses to a sickening attack that has no end. The young woman's cries fade to a pitiful whimper that tears at my soul as we are unable to save her.

I am almost ashamed to be a man. I feel impotent and powerless to change what happened and will happen again, not just to this girl but to the other women and children in this desecrated place. I am one man against many, and some battles cannot be won. At last, the guards manage to break into the cell and drag the boys away.

What justice is there in the world that a bright and hopeful young woman is subjected to such depravity? The sad truth is that it happens all over the world, not just in prisons, not just by lustful predators, but by men that girls and women trust, men they call Dad, brother, or uncle. Men they think are friends. So much of this exists beneath the surface of society. These men put on their suits and ties, going about their day, masquerading as princes, when in fact they are no better than the boys here. Witnessing the attack on the young woman, I realise that despite the trappings of modern life and the rise of gender equality and liberalism, just beneath the surface little has changed in the world.

We're outside on the afternoon that the rapists are carried back inside. Although beaten and handcuffed, they show no remorse. One guy shouts that he hopes she has rested as he is coming for her again later. In a gesture of defiance and bravado, he takes a small piece of wire and quickly jimmies the latch on his handcuffs, releasing them and brandishing them skyward before tossing them over the fence. He stops next to one of his friends and brazenly removes his cuffs too, throwing them over the fence and hollering insults at the guards. This, at least, does not go unpunished, and in a matter of minutes the guards have dragged both boys out and are beating them senseless. We don't see them again for a few days. When they do finally return, they are quiet and subdued for a few weeks.

Sadly, there is no happy ending for the young woman; she is permanently damaged by her experience. Learning that in order to survive it's easier to cooperate, she hooks up with one of the young gang leaders. She's safer prostituting herself with him as he protects her, until it becomes clear that she is pregnant and she leaves the horrors of Black Beach behind, carrying the memory of that fateful night in her heart, her soul and her womb.

I try to bury the memory deep, in a dark and hidden space where it can never be found. Much of the evil committed in this place is too terrible to speak about out loud, but this atrocious act plagues me, constantly rising to the surface, refusing to be buried. The abuse she suffered should not be forgotten. I feel it must be spoken about in all its appalling detail, because if we don't speak about these horrors, it's as if they didn't happen and things will never change. Her beauty, her gender and her status in society made her a target, a trophy to be possessed and mounted, then tossed aside.

Not long after this incident, another young girl is repeatedly raped by five guys. Her injuries are so horrific that she doesn't survive, and the guys are caught dumping her body over the fence. These are not men but animals reduced to their base, carnal instincts, the devil unleashed in their hunger to take these innocent young women and violate them in ways that are an affront to God and humanity.

If you believe in good, then you have to believe that evil exists too, and somewhere along the way the two must find balance. Evil is present in its most hideous form in this wretched place. The men that prey upon these young women have no respect for them as human beings and certainly not as women to be cherished and treasured. They are simply seen as playthings to satisfy savage desires and are later discarded when the men tire of them or a new girl arrives.

For many nights after these incidents, I lie in my tent curled up with my eyes shut tight, feeling myself slipping into a dark place. I must get out of here if I want to preserve my sanity, but as that's not an option I decide to create a more comfortable living space. My friends outside are managing to visit more often, so through them I buy John a bed, expanding my tent structure to make space for his bed opposite mine with a small table and a plastic chair between us. There is even a bucket with fresh water for washing. Against the opposite 'wall' of the tent is a small shelf with a light fixture and a fan.

I have a 'library' that includes an old copy of *Landbou Weekblad* which I've read from cover to cover many times. My most prized possession is a small mp3 player that a visitor smuggled in for me. He even visited the embassy to download my playlist from my laptop onto a USB drive, and it's not long before the whole prison is subjected to all my favourite eighties and country classics and Afrikaans gospel music.

My days are filled with Bible study, exercise, giving English classes, soaking up the sun and attending prayer meetings. At one of these meetings, we decide to pray for change in the prison. It feels good to challenge the wickedness and depravity that surrounds us. The warden often relies on the respect that prisoners have for men like Ugo and Pastor Fernando, so he sometimes asks them to help resolve problems in the prison. Despite being banned, alcohol is still a major challenge. A woman is caught smuggling in vodka by filling plastic water bottles with it, deceiving the guards until she gets greedy and they grow suspicious. She pays the price in lashings, but she is not the only culprit.

We know that without alcohol, life will be easier, so we pray, and are surprised at our success as it is suddenly and noticeably less available – disappointing for some but a small victory for us. We decide that considering we have God's attention, we can address the drug problem, and almost unbelievably no drugs come in for a while. Sadly, this does not have the outcome we anticipated as we notice an uptick in violence and restlessness.

As we know, weed has a calming effect on even the worst offenders, so it seems that we must be specific about *which* drugs we want to block, because without weed tensions rise. Perhaps even God understands that we mere mortals need something to help us cope with life behind bars. For some of us, the Bible is enough, but for our brothers a little weed goes a long way in maintaining peace.

One day, shortly after I completed the extension to my tent, Pastor Fernando pops by for a visit. I enjoy welcoming guests to my new, improved space and the pastor always lifts my spirits. I glance up as he announces himself at the 'door', smiling happily.

'Hello, Daniel,' he says. 'Do you eat pussy?'

I stare at him, completely flabbergasted. These are not words you'd expect to hear from a man of the cloth, but as he enters the tent, I see that he is referring to the bowl of food he is carrying. I decline, hiding my distaste. I seldom see cats around the place, and I haven't really wanted to think about why, even though I'm aware that some prisoners eat dog meat. It also explains the out-of-control rodent population.

Pastor Fernando tells me that the warden has asked him for help with a sickness going around. Disease here is often a death sentence because many inmates have AIDS. Over a period of about a week, seven have died, but one of the sick men visited by Ugo and the pastor is showing signs of improvement, so they've decided that the whole prison should do a three-day fast. As I watch the pastor sucking on the cat bones, polishing off his meal and licking his fingers, I decide that perhaps fasting isn't such a bad idea after all.

Committing to a spiritual fast may seem strange in a place like this, but it's only for a short period during which we will abstain from all food and drink, apart from water. I've never voluntarily done a fast, but in here there are times when you are forced to fast anyway because you have nothing to eat. The idea of a spiritual fast intrigues me. When in Rome ...

The pastor tells me to drink plenty of water in preparation and then heads off to tell the warden that everyone, including the guards, *must* participate. I keep my opinions to myself about whether that's likely and seek God in prayer, asking for guidance on matters out of my control. With something to focus on, before I know it a few hours have passed. This is just what I need, something to do with intent and purpose. Deep down, I hope that my own prayers will be answered.

54

Mucho Gusto
Black Beach Prison, Malabo
2015

I have recently acquired a small television for my tent. I must watch whatever the guy with the remote elsewhere in the prison wants to watch, but the novelty of having access to the outside world from inside my tent is worth celebrating. Routine helps to pass the time, and I'm always looking for a new pen, as I write and draw so often that the ink runs out. Sometimes, I have to stop mid-sentence and continue only when I've found a replacement. They're not always the same colour, but I like how it separates the content on the page.

You never know what to expect here. One week may be peaceful and then suddenly there's fighting and blood flows. Many are flogged; even my friend Ugo has not escaped the sharp end of the whip. After the incident with the bank girl, the women's section is quiet, but most of the prostitutes are used to life on the streets, so they get bored and venture into the yard, hooking up with the gangsters. When a new woman arrives, it doesn't take long for the wealthier inmates to court her. Life has not been kind to the women who arrive here, and they're probably not prostitutes by choice. However, in here there is less competition, and some end up better off than on the streets. One of the prisoners, a moneylender known as the Money Man, takes a shine to one of them, telling his minions to see that she has a nice breakfast, courting her in a true gentlemanly fashion, buying her clothes and gifts, and even paying for her hair to be styled. No one touches her, as he is a powerful man and it's not worth the risk. Before long, she succumbs to his charms and is infinitely safer than she would be in the slums of Malabo.

One day, Ugo manages to pay a 'fine', and soon after that his name is called. After eight years in this hellhole, he is finally free to return to Nigeria. I'm happy for him, and I will be forever indebted to the man who protected me from certain death at Bangkok's hands on the day I first arrived here. Although I now have other friends, the prison does seem emptier without his cheerful smile and positive attitude. I miss our chats and hope he has not lost too much while being trapped so far away from home. For many incarcerated here, it's common for their friends, family members and others to steal their things while they are locked up, and sometimes prisoners return home to find that even their wives have been taken.

There is one guy here with a very beautiful wife. They were very much in love, and she visited him every weekend despite constant harassment from the guards, who told her that he would never be released. One was particularly persistent, and now when she visits she spends her time with the guard, her husband watching helplessly from the courtyard as the two flirt shamelessly. Just the other day, she told him that she no longer loves him and it's over. It's not that unusual. Many of the men here are not guilty of any crime but suffer nonetheless and have come to expect betrayal and heartache.

This place offers all the drama, intrigue, twists and turns of a reality show like *Big Brother*, and a big part of the story is, of course, to wait at the gate to see who is coming to join us for this week's episode.

Today is just like any other: a group of young thugs, probably in dire need of an attitude adjustment, climb out of the meat wagon. I lose interest and am about to turn away when I notice one more passenger emerging from the vehicle. I stop and do a double-take. Not only is he much older than the boys, but there is another major difference between him and almost everyone else in the prison.

'*Blanco! Blanco! Blanco!*'

The white population at Black Beach has just doubled.

I am no longer the only white face in here. Intrigued, I wonder what this man has done and who he's offended, but every time I try to engage with him using my basic Spanish – '*Mucho gusto*', pleased to meet you – his response is lukewarm at best. He wants nothing to do with me, avoiding me if he can, and for the first time since the prison gates closed behind me, I truly see myself through a stranger's eyes and realise that living here for so long has taken its toll. It's a harsh environment, and I probably look much worse than I think I do. I'm scrawny and gaunt, a few of my teeth are missing, I'm in scruffy slops and my clothing is old and tattered. I'm wearing the rags out of necessity as these items are less likely to be stolen, but he wouldn't know that, so I'm pretty sure he believes that I am a lowlife scumbag who probably deserves to be here.

His name is Juan, a wealthy, well-connected Spanish citizen with a lot of influence as a professional fraudster forging official documents, visas and passports. He has joined us here not as punishment for his unlawful activities, but because he did not share enough of the profits. We all know that the Equatorial Guinean government officials and politicians grow fat off bribes and kickbacks, although this phenomenon is not restricted to just this part of the world.

Juan likely believes, much as I did when I first arrived, that he'll be out the gates pretty soon, but after being here for two weeks he's starting to understand what it means to be stuck in a forgotten swamp in the arse-end of nowhere and is becoming despondent as the reality of the Black Bitch takes hold. Once she has you in her clutches, she is reluctant to let go ...

Juan is used to the good life, with all the trappings of wealth, having enjoyed power through his connections. I watch as he visibly shrinks, depression taking hold, and he just sits day after day doing nothing. Every morning, I invite him to join me on my walk, but he consistently ignores my attempts to befriend him until one day he follows me outside. We stroll around the courtyard chatting, and I think that telling him my story helps him come to terms with just how bad his own situation is. After that, he joins me every day and I sense a shift in his demeanour. He seems more positive, and he talks about getting out of here. I know that he has access to more resources than I do, and once he begins the process it's not long before the Spanish ambassador turns up to visit him. Juan doesn't fill me in on the details of what he's planning, but almost as suddenly as he arrived, one morning I hear that the warden is calling for him, and just like that he is gone!

Details about how he managed to pull this off are sketchy, but I don't doubt that it involved a large sum of money changing hands. It seems that he's paid for a sick note stating that he requires special emergency medical treatment for a life-threatening disease. He was clearly *dying* to get out of here…

55

Pay the Ransom
Black Beach Prison, Malabo
August 2015

Once again, I feel a sense of abandonment. I've been here for more than a year now – when will it be my turn to leave? But to my astonishment, Juan returns the following Saturday bearing gifts, food and money. I can't believe the change in him; he's clean, healthy and vibrant and tells me he is grateful that I was there for him during his time here and appreciates my efforts to make his life a little easier. Most importantly, he says he wants to help me get out too!

As desperate as I am, I'm not sure I can trust him. So many people have said they can help and I end up getting my hopes up for nothing, so I tell him I appreciate his offer but decline. He persists, but eventually gives up when I refuse to be swayed. He leaves, shaking his head.

On Tuesday I am called to the gate for a visitor, which is extremely unusual. No one, apart from new arrivals or very rarely a visiting official, is allowed to come here during the week, so I hurry to the gate. It must be someone important, maybe from the embassy, but when I get to the guard room, it's Juan! I'm immediately struck by how his eyes seem disproportionately large behind his thick glasses – something must be seriously wrong.

My first thought is that something has happened at home, because when he left on Saturday he said he would call my family. My knees go weak and I lean heavily against the desk. Seeing my reaction, he quickly assures me that they're all fine, but there is a much more serious problem. I can't imagine anything more serious, but he explains that his lawyer looked into my case and has found nothing. All the documents have disappeared. Once again, it is as if I don't exist; there is no record that I'm being held at Black Beach.

No entiendo. I don't understand. How can the official records relating to my case and my situation with Angabi have disappeared? Still struggling to make sense of it, I tell him that maybe my file is on someone's desk or mislaid – the officials do after all use an antiquated manual filing system. He shakes his head, insisting that there is no trace of me or the case against me. As far as any officials are concerned, there is no record that I am currently being detained.

Ultimately, if I died here no one would be able to confirm my death officially, especially if my body disappeared. Juan believes that they intend to have me killed or let me die from the hardships of life in Black Beach and then simply deny any reports or rumours of my demise by saying that as there are no official documents, it can't be possible. I suspect that a cover-up of this magnitude would have had to come from a higher authority than Angabi.

I have been rotting here for months on end, distracting myself by trying to survive each day, trying to work with the others to make life more bearable, erecting a structure to live in, getting to know the people that make up the fabric of this place, experiencing hardship and suffering, facing starvation, being forced to exist on rotten meat and at the mercy of the guards and other prisoners, not to mention the filth, trying to avoid mosquitoes, battling malaria, typhoid and dysentery, but apparently all of this is just a bad dream as I am supposedly 'not here'.

Juan says we must move quickly as Angabi is out of the country for medical treatment and a new judge has been appointed. According to Juan's lawyer, the new judge is willing to free me as there is no case against me. My heart soars, and then immediately sinks. This is probably going to cost a whole lot more money than I can raise, but Juan again assures me that the only fees necessary are the legal fees for the lawyer to draw up the documentation – around US$20 000.

On a roller-coaster of emotions, I almost don't believe this is happening. Hope and joy sing through my veins. For the first time, I truly believe that this can work. I am elated and give Juan the go-ahead, and he rushes off to call my family, saying we can't waste a minute if we're going to pull it off; we need to make sure it happens before Angabi gets wind of our plan.

I always hoped that an opportunity like this would come along, but had wondered how I'd ever pay the fee. Can Juan be trusted? He's wealthy, so 20K doesn't seem exorbitant to him. I just hope that my family will be able to raise that amount: in rands it would be over R200 000. They've been through months of suffering and anguish, and not just emotional pain but the financial burden too – I was the breadwinner and always took care of our finances. As I sit here, contemplating freedom, hoping they can raise the money we need, all I can do is believe that God will find a way.

On Wednesday, Juan is back and very angry. He tells me that my family is not interested in helping me and that my mother put the phone down on him. I immediately realise that they would never trust anyone asking for money unless they heard from me first, and the last time we had any communication was months ago. I explain this to Juan and he organises a thirty-minute phone call for me. Even that seems incredible – how is it possible that whatever this man demands, he gets?

Having been denied contact with my family for so long, my hands shake as I dial Melanie's number. I almost can't believe that I am going to speak to my wife for the first time in so many agonising months. I know we won't be able to talk for very long, so as she answers the call I tell her not to cry or get emotional, that there will be time for that later, and explain that I can get out of Black Beach, but we need to pay the lawyer and she needs to make a plan fast! She tells me that when I was first imprisoned she sat at a table in our small village with a sign, humbling herself and begging for money, and has raised R75 000. I tell her that I love her and that she must organise with my mother to get the money to Juan. I end the call, the guards and Juan watching me intently.

I then call my mother, my dear, sweet mother, who has been tireless, working relentlessly, hounding the embassy with daily requests for updates, plans and suggestions to try to secure my release. I quickly explain the situation and she says to give her fifteen minutes and she'll call back.

Hurry! Hurry! Hurry! Fifteen minutes later, she calls me back to confirm that my brother-in-law and cousin will make up the difference and then she pauses and asks: 'Welman' – she always calls me by my middle name – '*kan ons hom vertrou?*'

Can we trust him? I look at Juan standing impatiently beside me and think: *hell no*! I answer her in Afrikaans, saying that there is no way that I would *ever* trust this man, but we trust in God and must believe that when all else has failed to get me out, He would use Juan to help secure my release.

And that's that! Juan leaves and I head inside, daring to hope my prayers have been answered. Later, looking around the little structure that I share with John and so recently renovated, I wonder if God has decided that I'm getting a little too comfortable here in Black Beach and maybe it's time for me to go home…

PART 5

'Each friend represents a world in us,
a world not born until they arrive,
and it is only by this meeting
that a new world is born.'
– Anaïs Nin

56

Western Union

Garden Route Mall, South Africa
August 2015

After so many long, lonely and heartbreaking months without answers, I can't believe that my Daniel could finally be coming home. Just hearing his voice, knowing that he's alive, is a miracle, but I'm terrified that something will go wrong. We've been disappointed so many times. It's hard to have faith that this time it's real and he will be set free.

But before that can happen, I need to pay the money. It's all up to me now, and I must make sure that I do everything right. If I make a mistake, they won't let him out. I've hardly slept, worrying about all the things that could go wrong, and I've been up since dawn so I can be at the mall when the bank opens. I need to make the payments early in case things don't go according to plan.

My head is spinning and my thoughts are all over the place as I drive towards George. I have to concentrate and get this right, otherwise it will be my fault if Daniel doesn't come home. I sigh heavily, reminding myself to stop saying that and focus on the instructions and everything will be okay.

I can do this! I can do this! I can do this!

I don't notice the beauty of the drive as I head down the hill, the vast Indian Ocean ahead of me, the early morning mist evaporating over the lake. My thoughts jump to the man who called us ... Juan? The Spanish guy. What if he's not trustworthy? I don't know anything about him except that he's a criminal! There are too many unanswered questions, and I'm terrified that after I transfer the money Juan will disappear, Daniel will still be stuck in Black Beach and all the money will be gone.

Before I know it, I have left Wilderness and Kaaimans Pass behind and am pulling up outside the mall in George, parking near the Pick n Pay entrance. The shops only open at 9 a.m. I'm too early and will have to wait for the Western Union office to open.

I don't know why Juan insists that we use Western Union; I've never used them, so I hope it's not too difficult. Daniel normally takes care of these kinds of things. He'll be so surprised by everything I've learnt to do while he's been gone, but bank stuff like this is totally out of my league and it's all a bit intimidating. It's a lot of money. Luckily, my sister's husband, Piet, has been helping me to take care of the financial side of things. I am so glad Nicky married him; he is the best brother-in-law I could have wished for, he knows about things like this and I am so grateful to have them to rely on for guidance. They have supported me through thick and thin. It's true what they say about finding out who you can count on when the chips are down.

I glance at my watch; the shops are opening soon. Time to go!

My legs are wobbly as I climb out of the car and hurry into the mall. It's filling up with early-morning shoppers, and shop assistants are bustling about opening the doors and beginning their day. I doubt that any of the people have something as urgent or life-changing on their minds as they amble along while I rush past towards Western Union.

The staff are busy, but someone spots me and waves. They'll be opening soon. My body feels electric with fear and anxiety as I wait impatiently to get this over with.

Someone's coming to open the door. Thank God. I'm the first customer, but when they hear what I need to do, there's already a problem. They tell me that regulations only allow for the transfer of R30 000 per person and I am only able to process two payments a month. I don't have months; I need to transfer R220 000 now!

I start to cry, feeling like I am going to melt into a puddle on the floor, and pull out a tissue to wipe away my tears, trying to take control of myself as they look at me helplessly, shrugging their shoulders, saying these are the rules and none of them has the authority to change them. I feel so defeated. What am I going to do? Daniel would know what to do, but he's not here! I'm so frustrated I want to scream and rage at the world, at these people going about their day like nothing is wrong. But standing here looking at them isn't going to solve the problem. I need to get out of here and think.

I leave in a daze, walking towards the entrance of the mall, trying to breathe while I figure out a plan. I've transferred the first R30 000, I just need to make sure that the rest is sent before the end of the day. Juan said that it has to be today or it won't happen …

My mind is racing. Who can I call? Who can make this better? There must be someone who can help me figure this out. Just at that moment, I see a man walking towards me. He seems to know who I am, even though I don't recognise him, and waves a greeting as he gets closer. I frown, wondering who he is.

'You must be Melanie,' he says, introducing himself as a manager at the Pick n Pay supermarket where I shop and telling me that he's followed Daniel's story, which my friend Fran Kirsten has written about and worked hard at keeping in the public eye. It's been in all the major newspapers, on television and radio. I nod, but I don't really feel like socialising, as I'm struggling to hold back the tears, but he sees I'm upset and asks if everything is okay. His kindness and concern overwhelm me. My legs feel weak; I am on the verge of collapsing. I dissolve into tears, blubbering while trying to explain what's happened. It's all so overwhelming, and I'm scared that if I don't figure this out then Daniel will never come home.

He puts a hand on my shoulder and tells me not to worry, he has an idea. I follow him to the manager's station at Pick n Pay where he switches on the announcement system and asks all employees who have their ID books with them today to please come to the office immediately. Within minutes, a crowd of Pick n Pay workers surrounds us. I only need seven people!

The manager tells them what I need, and gives me a little wink and a thumbs up. I am overjoyed looking at the crowd of smiling faces, overwhelmed by the readiness of these strangers to help me. I rush back to the Western Union with seven new friends hurrying along beside me and once again the tears flow as I hand each one a sizeable wad of cash and watch as the teller processes the transactions. It doesn't take long at all, and then it's done! The spirit of ubuntu is alive in the mall today, and it gives me shivers to know just how simple it is to get help from my fellow South Africans, who are unfailing in their willingness to help someone in need.

I am so grateful and relieved and can't thank them enough as they surround me, hugging me and shaking my hand, but I need to rush off. I still have to get home, scan all the receipts and email them to Juan before he can go to the Western Union in Malabo and withdraw the funds. The trip home is a blur. Once there, I manage to send the scans without a hitch. Now I just have to wait to see if Juan holds up his side of the bargain.

The nightmare is not over yet. I have no idea if Juan has collected the funds and the wait seems endless as I hear nothing from him. Has he made off with the money? Is he still in Equatorial Guinea? What if he's returned to Spain with our money lining his pockets?

Days pass and I grow more and more desperate. Almost a week goes by, and then finally the phone rings. It seems that Juan could be trusted after all. Thank you, God, for this miracle. I've never wanted to give up, but it's been more and more difficult facing each new day with no news.

A week ago, five thousand kilometres away in Malabo, Juan downloaded the receipts, but when he arrived at the local Western Union, there was a power failure, so nothing could be processed and he left empty-handed. He returned later and thankfully the power was back on and he was able to collect the money, taking it to the lawyer later that evening. Finally, it found its way to the courts and the release papers have been signed.

Daniel is free!

57

Liberdade

Black Beach Prison, Malabo
August 2015

It's been a long wait since Juan's visit, but I don't want to get my hopes up, and worrying about whether it will happen this time won't change anything. It's in God's hands now. I'm in my tent when there's a sudden commotion, shouts echoing through the prison. I listen curiously.

'*Blanco, Blanco!*'

'*Liberdade!*'

Freedom!

How long have I waited to hear these words? I feel like Mel Gibson in *Braveheart*, wanting to shout out to the heavens, to roar.

Within minutes the vultures appear, looking for gifts to inherit, anything to ease the suffering and make life more bearable. It's chaos, and my friends quickly surround me as prisoners storm into the space that's been my haven during my seemingly endless struggle. Everything has value.

I rush to Old Man Luis's cell, hugging him, telling him the news and thanking him for his kindness and friendship. He hands me the clothes I stored with him so many months ago, and I quickly discard my rags and pull on my shirt and jeans. It feels strange wearing long pants again after all this time, and man oh man, those Levi's 501s hang loosely on my skinny ass!

News spreads through the prison and I make my way through the crowd, wanting to sing, dance and punch the sky. I am surrounded by friends, hugging me and shaking my hand, celebrating freedom with me, in stark contrast to the horrific memories of my first arrival at Black Beach. Only a few hang back, jealous that it is not their time.

I am so overwhelmed; it's all happening so quickly. The van arrives, and now I'm heading out the gates and leaving Black Beach behind, a free man! In my hands are my Bible and a notebook, in my heart a feeling of joy that knows no bounds, in my mind a sense of relief. I can breathe again.

Even the guards seem more human and the driver friendlier as he asks me where I want to go. I'm not taking any chances.

'Take me to the South African embassy ... and don't spare the horses!'

Minutes later, we pull up outside the embassy. The guard opens the gate, looking confused to see the prison van here, until he sees me climbing out and his eyes widen in recognition. He rushes towards me, embracing and almost kissing me in his joy, tears running down his cheeks. We walk inside together saying 'God is great!' He tells me that he thought he would never see me again.

By now the staff have heard all the commotion outside and come rushing towards me, enveloping me in warm, heartfelt hugs and kisses. Everyone is talking at once; they can't believe that I'm finally free. The ambassador comes downstairs, hugs me, and then leads me to his office so we can call my family. He chuckles as he picks up the phone to dial my mother's number. I think he knows it by heart as she's been so persistent.

It's very emotional talking to her, so we keep it short. Then I call my beloved Melanie, but we are both so choked up that I end the call quickly, promising to phone her again later.

I'm whisked back downstairs, where work has been abandoned. Champagne corks pop and the air fizzes with excitement as we celebrate the end of my ordeal. While we're raising our glasses, Ambassador Rambau asks if I've been issued any documentation confirming my release.

'No,' I say, 'nothing.'

Seeing the expression on his face, I know that this is not what he wants to hear. Perhaps we've been a little premature in opening the champagne. Houston, we have a problem ... I'd never 'officially' been imprisoned at Black Beach, so I can't officially be released. Once again, I'm reminded that if there's no paper trail, there is no one to blame.

We begin the process by sending a letter from the embassy advising the Equatorial Guinean government that I've been exonerated by the courts but don't have a passport or identity documents. We then meet with the 'judge general' – the chief justice who appoints the president and judges in the judiciary. He's considered the most powerful man in the country after the president, and in a place mired in corruption, he is one of the few people with integrity. He's new to the job and apologises that he's not been fully informed of my case, promising to investigate immediately.

After an agonising two-week wait, we meet again, and he tells us that there are no official records, so he can't understand why I'd been sent to Black Beach at all. He apologises, saying that this is what must change in Equatorial Guinea, and we leave with an official letter. Meanwhile, the embassy has received the necessary documents from the minister of security stating that I am permitted to leave the country.

This must be the worst case the embassy team has had to deal with. They knew I was innocent and tried everything from a diplomatic perspective to resolve the situation, going above and beyond what's required in the job description. Gift, who helped me when I was first released, inherited my problem when he took over as consul from Thandi, and I think he is as grateful as my family that I am free and on my way home. I'm sure he's looking forward to closing my file, while I am forever grateful for his kindness, patience and wisdom as we walked the tightrope through the minefield of diplomatic relations in my quest for truth, justice and freedom.

58

Final Boarding Call
```
Malabo International Airport
      September 2015
```

I can't believe this day has finally arrived. I'm walking on air, excited to fly across Africa on the first leg of my journey home. I'm booked on an Ethiopian Airlines flight departing this morning with a night stop in Addis Ababa, then on to Johannesburg tomorrow, where I'll catch a connecting flight to George.

It's been an endless road getting to this point, and the whole experience is something none of us will ever fully understand. At times bewildering and terrifying, it took every ounce of my faith to keep believing that truth would win in the end. My bags are packed and I know in my heart that today I am finally going home. I've even been reunited with my Malabo stray, who will be accompanying me. I only hope Bubbles isn't too jealous and welcomes the new addition to the family.

My paperwork is still not in order, as the Malabo police have my passport and are refusing to return it, even though I've been cleared by the High Court. A new team has been deployed at the South African embassy, as Gift and Ambassador Rambau are back in South Africa on holiday, and my case has been placed in the very capable hands of Madame John, the chargé d'affaires, who is a force to be reckoned with. I'm very glad to have her in my corner. The entire embassy team are coming along to see me off and we're hoping to collect a second passport that is apparently at the airport, and failing that we have a temporary travel authorisation which will be my only other option, but whatever it takes, I am leaving today.

We head out early. Check-in is at 9.30 a.m., but I want to make sure that we have enough time to resolve any issues. We're all anxious – I've been down this road before and, as I know, in Malabo they make their own rules. We leave for the airport and head straight to the counter where we confront our first obstacle when the staff refuse to release my passport, saying that if I have a problem with the government, I cannot leave.

Déjà vu.

I'm taken to the airport commissioner and, despite facing the might of the

South African diplomatic authority, he refuses to listen to reason. We show him the letters from the chief justice, which he tosses aside. I point out to him that the chief justice is the man who appoints the president, so surely on his authority they must allow me to leave the country, but he refuses to budge. We leave his office having accomplished nothing.

We head back to the check-in counter where it seems that, despite the commissioner's reluctance to assist, I've been cleared on the 'system' and my boarding pass is issued. Feeling relieved, we go to the restaurant to wait, and while we're sipping coffee, I see the aircraft refuelling outside. I can almost taste freedom. I can't believe that I'm finally getting out of here! This nightmare is almost over.

Back home, it's a long weekend as South Africa is celebrating Heritage Day. In the Malabo airport, the embassy staff, my local friends and I are happy and excited, taking photos together and sending WhatsApp messages. I'm thanking everyone, saying goodbye and enjoying the camaraderie and spirit of friendship. These are good people, and I feel blessed to know that even though we had no history prior to this horrible experience, they've put everything on the line and tried their best to help me.

The airport is crowded, the airport staff briskly attending to passengers while the ever-present airport security patrols the area. I notice a man standing by the window looking out at the runway. He's well dressed, wearing civilian clothing, but he looks 'official' in the way 'they' always do in movies. He's not carrying any luggage, doesn't seem to be seeing anyone off, and remains standing there. I get the feeling that he is watching us.

I tell myself not to be paranoid and look away, immediately spotting two others a little further away in a corner. They're watching me while talking on their phones and a shiver runs down my spine when I recognise one of them.

Something is not right.

Please, God, I can't go through this again. Am I paranoid or are they really watching me?

Just then, one of the embassy officials tells me he's heading off to deal with some last-minute paperwork. Now there are just three of us left: me, my good friend Carlos, and an embassy official who is new and only recently arrived in Malabo.

I notice that two more men have arrived. Something is up, and as one of them reaches into his jacket, I see a concealed weapon tucked into his waistband. I turn to Carlos and ask him if he thinks they're watching us, and he confirms that he's noticed the men too.

My heart sinks. Not again.

We need to come up with a plan, so I ask my friend to find the rest of the embassy staff and inform them of this new development while I head for the departures lounge to be closer to the plane. I am ready to make a run for it if I have to …

He immediately gets up and sets off, while the chap from the embassy and I walk in the opposite direction, trying to look casual. I glance behind me and notice that the men all leave their positions and begin to follow us. There is no doubt that they are undercover officers from the elite secret police, and as they get closer they converge around us, matching our pace. My suspicions are confirmed when they 'suggest' that we accompany them to the office. I nod. Sure, no problem. But my heart is racing as I keep walking casually despite the frantic alarm signals blaring in my head. Please, God, not again.

Two of them are on the phone, obviously taking orders about what to do with me. The men appear calm, assuming that we are coming along willingly. As we near the main airport entrance, I almost can't believe my luck as I spot the official South African embassy vehicle parked right outside the door, the driver seated behind the wheel. I turn to my companion, who is looking increasingly uncomfortable, and in Afrikaans I tell him, 'I'm going to make a run for the car, are you coming with me?'

He replies, '*Dis reg*' (that's right), and I don't hesitate. I won't get another chance. I shove the guy nearest me aside, counting on the fact that we're in a busy, public place, so I doubt they'll pull their weapons on us. I bolt through the doors of the building and jump into the back seat of the embassy vehicle, my companion diving in after me.

'Go! Go! Go!'

Without asking questions, the driver speeds out of the parking lot. I tell him to make for the embassy and hurry, hurry, hurry, as I look out through the back window where the men are standing on the pavement outside the terminal building watching us. Taken by surprise, they look at one another, unsure of what to do. One of them is making a phone call.

I turn back, watching the road ahead in case they are communicating with someone elsewhere in the town. I glance over at the embassy official in the car with me; as he's new to the job, he doesn't know much about my story.

His eyes are big as saucers and he looks horrified by what's just happened. He's probably wondering what he's signed up for ...

As we race along the highway towards the embassy, I see an unmarked police vehicle giving chase. Luckily we have a good head start, and I think we'll make it to the embassy before they catch up. I have little doubt about who is behind this – the list of people who can override the chief justice can't be very long. I still don't understand how I got to this point, but it definitely doesn't pay to have enemies in high places, and I wonder if I'll ever be able to stop running.

How is it possible that I am still stuck here on this island after spending almost five hundred days behind bars? Right now, there is no way out. I'm going to miss my flight and will have to figure out a way to survive while all around me people are trying to stop me from leaving. If they get their hands on me this time, I'm as good as dead. The only barrier between us is the South African embassy. I know that the staff are ill-equipped to deal with a siege, but I'm out of options and have no choice but to trust that the rules governing international diplomacy will not be broken.

Within minutes, we pull up outside the embassy. The guard is having a smoke break and the driver leans on the horn, gesticulating wildly for him to open up. He drops the cigarette and rushes through the pedestrian entrance, opening the main gate so we can pass through. We pull in and jump out of the car, yelling at him to shut the gate as we hear the roar of an engine and the unmarked police vehicle screeches to a stop, blocking the street outside. The five men from the airport bail out and start pounding on the gate.

We race inside, but it's ominously quiet and I remember that it's a South African holiday. The staff on duty are still at the airport and haven't a clue about what's just happened, so it's just me, the new guy and an unarmed gate guard! The new guy grabs the phone, frantically dialling the Department of International Relations and Cooperation in Pretoria, telling them that we're under attack. The exchange is brief; on the other end of the line is another junior staff member as the South African office is closed for the public holiday too. Neither are qualified to deal with a situation like this.

Outside, there are now two cars blocking the street; it's a one-way and the vehicles are facing both directions, ensuring that they're ready to give chase if I try to leave the embassy. The gate guard is terrified, staring goggle-eyed in horror as the men hammer at the gate, yelling and demanding that he open up. My phone rings. It's my friend Mike and his words chill me to the bone.

'Whatever you do, don't leave the embassy,' he shouts down the line. 'They're going to kill you!' He rings off abruptly.

My heart is racing and I'm not sure that I can count on the relative safety of being on 'South African soil', but there's nowhere else to go! This is my only refuge, the only place where I have any kind of protection. Just then, another vehicle pulls up and I feel like I'm on a movie set, the drama unfolding at breakneck speed, action all the way, as I rush back to the window and peer out.

An embassy vehicle has pulled up outside and I can hear raised voices. It's Madame John and she's furious. She threatens the men, telling them that if they touch the embassy gate again, it will be considered an act of hostility. She adds that there is a South African naval vessel 100 kilometres off the coast and she will see to it that it is deployed, as this is tantamount to a declaration of war against South Africa.

I can't believe that, at the eleventh hour, they're still trying to block my departure, that this is happening in broad daylight. Is there no end to this madness? I collapse onto the couch in reception and sigh deeply, putting my head in my hands, knowing that I will need to make the one call that I don't want to make: to my family.

Back in South Africa, they have no idea what is going on. The last they heard was that I was at the airport about to board the plane. Less than half an hour ago, everyone was in high spirits, excited to know that I was on my way home and that we'll soon be able to start rebuilding our lives. They have no idea what's just happened, and the thought of calling them to say I'm not leaving today fills me with dread.

I left home in October 2013 on a five-day trip. Now, almost two years later, I still can't leave this island. Once again I've been plunged into a dark chasm, and I don't know how I'll make it out of here or if I'll be killed. It's like I'm a character in a video game, thwarted at every turn, chasing an impossible outcome until I run out of lives and it's game over.

Thankfully, the thumping at the gate has stopped and Madame John hurries inside. She comes over to me, gives me a big hug and sits down beside me; she is outraged and promises me that this will end today. She will not allow them to intimidate me and will personally make sure that I am on the next flight out of here. She is a force of nature and, listening to her, I feel like God has sent me yet another guardian angel. If anyone can get me out of here, it will be this little firecracker with a big heart, yet another selfless champion at my side throughout this long and terrifying ordeal.

On this special day, when I should already be winging my way home, I am once again reminded of just how incredible my fellow South Africans are and reluctantly reach for my phone to call my family. I keep it brief, telling them it will just be a few hours and I'll be on my way. They're devastated and I end the call quickly, their howls of despair echoing in my soul.

I sink back onto the couch, feeling numb. Madame John tells me that, for now, we should keep the story out of the press so that we can try diplomatic intervention to get the issue resolved. Things quieten down, but it's too late for me to catch the other flight to Addis Ababa.

Everyone at the embassy has left. I'm alone with the guard to face the long night ahead. I try not to think about the fact that he's not authorised to carry a weapon so there is no real protection other than the flimsy concept of diplomacy. There is nowhere to sleep, but I can't sleep anyway, so I make myself as comfortable as I can on the couch and close my eyes, focusing on switching off the myriad thoughts tumbling in my head. My phone rings. It's my friend Mike calling to check up on me. He asks if I've had anything to eat and I tell him, no, I'm not hungry.

'Good!' he says. 'Don't eat anything that's brought in from outside – they will try to poison you.'

He tells me that if I'm hungry I must only eat something out of a can or sealed packaging. I don't have much of an appetite anyway, but this doesn't make me feel very confident about making it out of here alive. The long weekend will mean more delays, and the ambassador, who is on holiday in South Africa and only expected to return on Wednesday, so it looks like I may be holed up here for at least a few more days.

Once again, I have to believe that the situation is in God's hands and there is nothing I can do to change it. I must have faith that everything will work out in the end, but apparently for me, it's not yet the end.

59

Stop the Press

South African Embassy, Malabo
September 2015

I spend a sleepless night on the small couch in the embassy reception, where every sound makes me sit up in alarm, acutely aware that if the men outside get their hands on me, there is no way they'll let me live. If they somehow manage to break in, I know that I'll be taken to be killed and my body fed to the sharks.

There is no shower here, so I use a bucket in the little bathroom to try to freshen up, and memories of Black Beach come flooding back. Once again, I am trapped. I go to the small kitchen, switch on the kettle and make a cup of strong coffee, grab a handful of cookies for breakfast and get ready to face the day. God willing, my last on this wretched island.

I call my family. Melanie is incoherent as she sobs uncontrollably. It tears me apart to know how much she is suffering, and I'm grateful that our children are home from university to comfort her. Talking to my mother makes me feel better; she's been a rock throughout this nightmare, determined to set me free by sheer force of will, and my heart is heavy when I think about how much she and my father have suffered too. There is nothing worse than feeling helpless to put an end to their suffering.

The day passes in a blur of phone calls, messages, and trips to the small kitchen for a refill of coffee and cookies. I get a call from Fran Kirsten, who has been acting as the official spokesperson for the family, another in the long list of people who have gone beyond the bounds of friendship to help me and my family, expecting nothing in return. When I explain the situation to her, she says that the time for diplomacy is over; we need to use the might of the pen and get the story into the headlines.

My friend Carlos has turned up again to give me moral support, and he takes a photo of me sitting on the embassy couch, the poster of a couple enjoying a meal at Cape Town's V&A Waterfront behind me. We send it to Fran. Within hours, the press has pounced on the story and there are headlines in media around the world. The photograph of me and the story of my struggle for freedom are everywhere.

'SA man fears for his life after two-year nightmare in Equatorial Guinea hell.'
'"Kidnapped" SA man in Black Beach jail.'
'SA man tells of Guinea prison hell.'

I'm in constant contact with my family over Skype, trying to keep Melanie calm by talking to her as much as possible when all I want to do is reach out and hold her tight and never let go. A little while later, Madame John returns victorious from her meeting with the chief of security where she's been battling it out with him on my behalf. Fortunately, she is well versed in matters of international cooperation and not the least bit intimidated by these men who believe that they are above the law. She says that she has advised them that their actions are in direct violation of international protocol, that the chief justice has approved my request to leave the country, and if they do not accept this then they are contravening international regulations and will be held accountable at an international tribunal.

Hallelujah!

We're ecstatic to hear the news, but unfortunately it's too late to catch the last flight out of the country and I am forced to spend another interminable night on the small couch in reception. In the morning, I get up, rinse, repeat, using the bucket of water. Although my body is taut with nervous energy, I'm feeling hopeful, somehow believing that today is where my ordeal will finally end.

Madame John and the staff arrive early and we're all feeling optimistic. Carlos turns up and we discuss the final plan for my departure. Carlos insists that he's coming along too, as he won't be satisfied until he sees my flight take off. My ticket has been rebooked, and just as I'm gathering my things together, Mike calls to tell me that this time he's sure it's going to work out, but not to take any chances and only travel in the embassy vehicle to the airport with no stops along the way. Once we're there, he says, the embassy staff must accompany me every step of the way. He wishes me well and promises to visit next time he is in South Africa. I tell him not to worry, Madame John has vowed not to leave my side, promising Melanie that she will personally see me aboard the aircraft, buckled in and ready for take-off.

Shortly after I end the call, we head to the airport, and everything goes like clockwork. Once again, I have my boarding pass in my hand, and my Malabo stray who will be accompanying me on the flight, my baggage and my backpack with my laptop in it don't leave my side. I have some snacks and juice for padkos on the journey home.

We go to the VIP lounge and have a last coffee together, the mood festive, and although I will not rest until the plane takes off with me on board, I am starting to feel like we just might pull it off!

It seems like minutes later that I hear the overhead announcement that check-in has opened for my flight. I decide to go for a quick pitstop at the bathroom and get up. Madame John immediately looks at me and asks where I'm going. I laugh and tell her it's okay, I'm just going to spend a penny, but she's having none of it and escorts me to the bathroom where I have to work really hard at convincing her that she doesn't have to accompany me all the way in. Finally, she relents, but stands just outside the door and doesn't budge until I'm done and we can leave.

I gather my things and hug everyone goodbye, once again believing that everything is going to work out and not sure how I'll cope if it doesn't – there is only so much that a man can take! Madame John marshals the troops and I march to the boarding gates surrounded by my flotilla of supporters. No one bothers me and I don't see anyone watching me suspiciously.

Madame John unleashes her secret powers on the check-in staff and is permitted to accompany me onto the aircraft, waiting by my side while I find my seat and buckle in. Only then is she satisfied and leaves to call my mother to tell her that I am aboard the flight and will soon be on my way.

There is a tense hour-long wait sitting on the runway and I'm convinced that they're coming for me, that once again my plans have been thwarted, but it turns out to be a technical issue and finally the engines start up and we're speeding down the runway. I am finally on my way home, with no souvenirs apart from my Malabo stray and the scars in my mind, on my body, in my heart and in my soul.

As the plane lifts off, a wave of relief washes over me. I cannot believe that my interminable struggle has finally come to an end. Initially, I find it difficult to relax as we rise towards the heavens and encounter a few bumps, but once we enter the smooth air of the jet stream, I feel a sense of release. Suddenly we're soaring above the clouds, the sky an endless blue vista, the vast expanse of the African continent spread out beneath us.

What an incredible feeling! I feel free and light, and it's as if I can finally breathe again. I just hope I don't wake up to discover that I'm still on the couch at the embassy and it's all been a dream.

The four-and-a-half-hour flight feels like a few short minutes as we begin our descent into Addis Ababa where I'll spend the night before boarding an aircraft bound for Johannesburg.

As I gather my things and prepare to disembark, I think fleetingly about the fact that I am travelling with temporary documentation and I hope there will be no issues getting through border control here. Madame John is not here to unleash her fiery might on the officials who may question the validity of my papers, so I approach immigration control with some trepidation, my temporary travel documents to hand. There's a slight delay as they check thoroughly, making sure everything is above board, and I have palpitations as I look on in silence, hoping that everything will go smoothly. I'm filled with relief when, finally, everything is stamped and handed back to me and I head off to the shuttle to join the other passengers going to the hotel for our stopover.

As I leave immigration, two gentlemen in civilian clothing approach me, asking me to accompany them. My heart almost stops. I feel paralysed, my feet glued to the ground. I'm aware that Ethiopia and Equatorial Guinea have a long history of collaboration; does this mean that Angabi's reach extends this far and he has 'friends' here who will see to it that I never make it home?

The stress is almost too much, especially when the men identify themselves as officials and say that I must come with them. My body is shaking but I manage to keep my composure as I follow them down a passage, saying a quick prayer to give me the courage to keep moving forward.

To make matters worse, the area seems to be going through some sort of renovation and is dimly lit and ominously quiet, with not another soul in sight. The officials show me into an office, shut the door and tell me to put my things down, announcing that they're drug enforcement officers. They show me their identification cards and then politely ask permission to search me and check through my luggage. I feel weak at the knees; I'm sweating and remember I haven't had a proper shower in two days! Man, oh man, how much more can a guy take?

The search is brisk and professional; they ask me to extend my arms and search the length of my body but find nothing of interest, then open up my bags. On top of my suitcase are my very large Bible and my Malabo stray. One of the officers looks at me curiously, does a cursory inspection of my bags, shakes his head, and then turns to his partner, shrugs, and they tell me I can close up and leave. Before they can take another breath, I'm out of the room, racing out of the airport building looking for the shuttle to take me to the hotel.

It feels strange to suddenly be in another country so far from Equatorial Guinea and even further away from home, and I can't wait to get into a warm shower, freshen up and head downstairs for dinner. I get some food and then go back to my room to rest. It seems unimaginable that tomorrow I will touch down in South Africa and be reunited with my family. I finally allow myself to believe that I am on my way home and nothing is standing in my way.

In the morning, after a quick breakfast, I board the shuttle and go back to the airport to check in for the flight to Johannesburg. The flight is on time, and before I know it we're airborne and I'm finally winging my way back to my beloved. The trip is uneventful and all I can think about is that in a few hours I will be back home, holding my wife in my arms again, hugging my mother, my father and my children. I wonder if Bubbles will remember me, it's been so long.

It's mid-morning when we touch down at O.R. Tambo in Johannesburg, and I'm overwhelmed with emotion to be back home. As I walk towards the exit, I see another passenger switching on his cellphone and ask if I can borrow it very quickly. He obliges and I dial the number and wait impatiently for it to be answered.

'*Moeder, ek is hier, ek is veilig*' (Mother, I am here, I am safe), I say, fighting back the tears and ending the call as I hear my mother crying with joy. I hand the phone back to the man and he asks if I'd like to use it to call someone else, my wife maybe? I decline with a shake of my head and choke out a reply: 'I'll get too emotional if I speak to my wife ... That call will have to wait for later.'

It's noisy in the airport terminal – hordes of journalists and cameramen are gathered at the entrance. I take a deep breath, mentally preparing myself for the barrage of questions. How do you condense what I've lived through into a few short answers when so much went wrong and so much still needs to be processed?

As I walk through the doors, I spot Ambassador Rambau at the entrance. He sees me and quickly escorts me away from the crowd with an armed officer at my side. We have a quick chat and he gives me some time to compose myself before facing the press. It feels strange to be flung into the spotlight like this; I am just an ordinary man, a husband, a father, a son, a trusting man just trying to earn a living and provide for my family.

It all passes in a blur of lights, cameras and action as I try to answer their questions.

One of the journalists asks if I'd ever go back to Equatorial Guinea and I laugh, saying, 'I would, but I don't think my wife would let me…'

Another wants to know what the first thing is I'd like to do when I get to George.

My answer is simple: 'Kiss my wife. I haven't kissed her in two years.'

The ice is broken and the questions flood in. Eventually, the ambassador rescues me and the media circus is over, for now. He invites me for a quick bite to eat while I wait for my flight to George. We're shown to a booth and the waitress hands us a menu. After spending so much time at Black Beach eating rotten meat of unknown origin, stale bread and rice infested with weevils, it seems strange to hold a menu with so many choices.

I flip through the pages, looking at pictures of beautifully styled, bright, colourful food, delicious pastries, generous burgers, vibrant salads and then a whole section just for beverages! It's this page that stops me in my tracks and I look over at the ambassador and tell him that there is something on the menu that is very special to me as it reminds me of home.

'I'll have a pink milkshake, please.'

60

Until Death Do Us Part
O.R. Tambo International Airport, Johannesburg
Sunday, 27 September 2015

For the third time in twenty-four hours, I board a plane and speed down the runway and into the air, finally on the home strait. In just over an hour I'll be back home where I can hold my wife tight and never let her go...

These moments alone and anonymous on an aircraft give me a chance to gather my thoughts. Here, no one knows the hell I've been through; I am just another passenger looking out of the window, watching the distant earth below as we soar through the skies. I thank God for getting me through this and for the gift of a loving family to come home to. I know that the path to healing will be long and difficult for all of us; so much time has passed, so much suffering and anguish, but now I only want to focus on the joy of loving them, being close to them and being able to wrap my arms around them and feel their love surrounding me, protecting me, and giving me the strength to walk the long road to healing.

In a heartbeat, we cross the vast Karoo. Somewhere below is the little town of Loxton where I celebrated with friends just before the nightmare began. The flight is smooth and the weather is clear; it's late afternoon so it's not too bumpy as we descend over the Outeniqua Mountains and I catch my first glimpse of home: the green hills and farmlands of Hoekwil, the beautiful lakes and rivers of Wilderness, and the wide expanse of the Indian Ocean rolling endlessly against the shore.

We come in over the ocean, circling past Mossel Bay and approaching from the west. The windsock next to the runway waves gently in the breeze as we touch down.

I almost can't believe that this is real. I want to sing to the heavens and take this moment and preserve it for eternity. The other passengers are restless as we taxi to the apron, gathering their things together, leaning out of their seats to look down the aisle and waiting for the doors to open. As we come to a stop, I grab my Malabo stray and shuffle towards the exit along with the others, impatient to head down the stairs into the waiting arms of my beloved family.

My heart is exploding at the thought of being reunited with them, every step bringing me closer. I look up, hearing their voices squealing from inside the building, and the woman walking beside me looks at me and asks if that's for me. I look at her with tears in my eyes and nod. My smile says it all.

I have hardly made it through the doors when Melanie and my daughter grab me, screaming with joy and holding on so tight that I can hardly breathe. Behind them, I catch sight of my son and my parents. The tears flow as I gather my girls into my arms, smelling their sweet scent and feeling their hearts beat against my chest as they hold on like they will never let me go.

After an emotional few moments greeting everyone, we walk out the doors and I spot Fran standing next to our pastor, Dawie le Roux, and it seems as if they are surrounded by the entire congregation of our small church in Hoekwil. Everyone is smiling and hugging me, welcoming me home. The pastor gathers us in a circle, leading us in prayer, thanking God for my safe return and for blessing us with a fairy-tale ending that sees me reunited with my family.

Afterwards, we follow Fran to a room where she has arranged for me to meet the press. Once again I am bombarded with questions and it all passes in a blur. I am mentally exhausted and physically drained after the past few days of emotional turmoil and the chaos of my final exit from Malabo.

We head out to the car and begin the journey back home along the highway past George where everything looks the same, but doesn't. Has the town changed so much in my absence, or am I seeing it through new eyes?

We drive through Kaaimans Pass and come around Dolphin Point, and I catch my breath at the beauty of this moment, seeing the ocean and the small village of Wilderness ahead of me. It's warm and summery, the light so clear, the air fresh, and the water sparkling in the afternoon sun. My heart fills with gratitude that I've been given a second chance to experience the beauty of the place I'm lucky enough to call home and to experience the love of my family, and I feel a thrill of pleasure thinking about climbing on my bicycle and rediscovering the hidden forest trails and mountain paths around our home.

My heart has settled into a rhythm that feels stronger with each passing moment as we drive up the hill towards Hoekwil and wind our way past the retirement village, the corner shop and the school, following the road down into the dip and pulling to a stop outside our home.

As the engine switches off, Bubbles dashes out to greet us, barking excitedly. He gives me a quick sniff and then rushes around the car greeting all the others. Suddenly, he stops in his tracks; it's as if the penny has dropped and he runs back in a frenzy of joyful barking, jumping up against me. I pick him up and squeeze him tight, tears of joy streaming down my face.

Thank you, God.

I am home.

Epilogue

I can't believe that almost seven years have passed since I was set free and came home to my family. Praise God! Sadly, my father is no longer with us; those two years of anguish proved too much for him. He was my role model who walked with deep footprints before me.

As for Bubbles, we do not know how dogs suffer when we're away; we can only measure how we feel. For the five years following my release, he was my shadow, even going to church with me, and in 2020, as I walked my daughter down the aisle, Bubbles, by now an old fellow, walked beside me with a jaunty stride, dressed for the occasion with a bright green ribbon. Bubbles helped me to heal, especially that first year when it was tough even to breathe sometimes; he would often nudge me to remind me that he was there. The walks that he would force me to do around Hoekwil with him were the highlight of my day.

I read somewhere that it takes a village to raise a child, and that goes for my healing too. Knowing that I had the love and support of my Hoekwil community and the people from our church who stood by me went a long way to help me on my healing journey, and I am forever grateful.

My doctor told me that I should write this book to help with the healing. It hasn't worked yet, but at least I am able to share a little of what happened. To find someone who listens to your stories and ramblings, incoherently told, repeated differently at times, and put it all together in a book for you to read, well that was a blessing from above. Tracey did not have an easy task – it took a long time for me to try to remember things and some memories are still lost somewhere inside my head. I think that the words in the book tell you all about her; she expressed how I felt.

While I celebrate seven years of freedom, nothing has changed in Black Beach and Malabo, and there is no end in sight. I thank the men in Black Beach like Ugo, Old Man Luis, Pastor Fernando and my adopted son, John, who helped me navigate a path through my time there, the South African embassy staff who had to deal with the impossible task of trying to negotiate my release, and the judge who finally stood up to the tyranny and took a chance to allow truth and justice to prevail against the odds.

EPILOGUE

There are many others who, through their actions, kind words and selfless gestures, made a difference in our lives as we walked this path as a family. I can't mention them all by name, but we are all forever grateful for the role you played in getting us through the horrors and nightmares, making the burden a little lighter in some small way. God bless you.

DANIEL JANSE VAN RENSBURG
HOEKWIL, JULY 2022

Author's Note

What an honour and a privilege it is to share Daniel's story and shine the spotlight on the horrific abuse taking place in prisons around the world today. I met Daniel many years before his imprisonment when his children and my daughter attended the little farm school in Hoekwil, a small community where our children grew up in an idyllic rural setting. Daniel had begun working in West Africa then and helped me with some research about the small island of São Tomé for a book I'd been wanting to write since 1991.

At the time that Daniel was first imprisoned, I was working in Dubai and the story found its way there. I was horrified and could not imagine the suffering that he and Melanie were going through. After he made it home, I bumped into him in the village and we chatted about his experience. I wanted to know all the gory details, but what struck me was his incredible resilience and the fact that he hadn't allowed this awful experience to taint his spirit. In passing, I said that if he ever wanted to tell his story, I would love to be the one to write it with him.

I didn't think much about it again until August 2019, when he called me up, asking if I was still interested in telling his story. Without hesitation, I said absolutely, yes!

At the time, Daniel was embroiled in protracted litigation over his illegal detention in Black Beach against Equatorial Guinean vice president Teodorin Nguema Obiang. As minister of state security and prisons in Equatorial Guinea during the time of Daniel's ordeal, which spanned 549 days of detention, 491 of which were at Black Beach, Teodorin, who has gained international notoriety for his lavish, playboy lifestyle, was ultimately named and held responsible for Daniel's unlawful arrest, imprisonment and torture by the Western Cape High Court.

Daniel's landmark case, which began in 2016, was concluded in 2021, with acting High Court judge Dumisani James Lekhuleni awarding him R39.8 million in damages and ordering the Equatorial Guinean vice president to pay this amount in restitution, although to date Daniel has yet to receive compensation.

AUTHOR'S NOTE

Against the backdrop of this litigation, we began writing Daniel's story in August 2019, with no idea what lay ahead of us as the world was flung into chaos by the Covid-19 pandemic. However, during this time of uncertainty and lockdowns, we were able to focus on telling his story, using his affidavit from the court case against Teodorin and letters that had been smuggled out of Black Beach during Daniel's incarceration as a starting point.

It was a daunting and lengthy process, made all the more difficult as Daniel has been severely traumatised and neurologically damaged by his experience and found it difficult to revisit those dark days, suffering frequent panic attacks while we burrowed into the details that formed the basis of our narrative.

His experience at Black Beach was a blur of unspeakable suffering, punctuated by incidents of extraordinary violence that have left him with acute and chronic PTSD and enduring neuropsychological deficits associated with cerebral malaria. Yet despite this, Daniel was willing to face his demons and persevered, until finally, over two and a half years later, we held the first completed draft of our manuscript, which included additional information gathered from voice notes sent via WhatsApp by Ugochuku, Daniel's friend and former Black Beach inmate who is now free at home in Nigeria.

The next stage involved the difficult task of trimming our story down to an acceptable word count for publication, and we'd like to thank Alice Inggs and Robert Plummer of Penguin Random House South Africa for their insight and suggestions during the editing phase. In my personal capacity, I would like to thank Daniel, Melanie and his family for giving me an opportunity to tell his story, and to Blaze Abrahams for reading the initial draft of Part 1 and 2 and giving me the encouragement I needed to forge ahead. I look forward to hearing his feedback on the finished book as he never did find out how it ends...

To Chelsey and Terence, thank you for believing in me, and to my husband, Peter, who not only provided encouragement but also built me a special writing desk so that I could sit on the couch during the cold winter nights, under a blanket surrounded by dogs, and tap away at my keyboard bringing Daniel's story to life. I know that you have spent many long nights and weekends wondering when this would finally be done so that our lives can return to normal, and I am forever grateful for your input and advice, and for reading and listening to me talk about the book, Daniel and his experiences.

For me, the spirit of ubuntu is brought to life in Daniel's story, and in the process of telling his story we are united in a universal bond of humanity. Without the commitment and friendship of those who have helped Daniel on his journey back to his beloved Melanie, this story could never have been told.

Having the opportunity to work with him on this book is a precious gift, and I hope that I've told his story with respect, in a way that will not only help him to heal but also help others facing hardship to dig deep and find the courage to keep moving forward. Daniel is a humble man who does not expect any special treatment. He is kind and unassuming, putting his family first, advocating old-fashioned values, and is always cheerful and positive, with an infectious laugh and a twinkle in his eye. I hope that taking this journey helps him heal and recover the missing parts that will make him whole again.

During the more than two years working on this book, making sure we covered everything and leaving no stone unturned, I found it incredibly inspiring to sit with Daniel, reading his letters that had been smuggled out of Black Beach and listening to him relate his experiences against the backdrop of his incredible faith, love and courage.

His love for Melanie, his mother, his children and God sustain him. One of the things I remember most during the process of writing down his story is that I would often have to dig into old wounds to bring the true horror and magnitude of his suffering to the surface. I was always apologising as I know how painful these memories can be for him, making him relive the unimaginable moments that he faced each day behind bars. In response, he would always say: 'Don't worry, keep going, it's okay. I know how it ends.'

As a spiritual rather than a religious person, I was a little concerned that I would not be able to portray Daniel's relationship with God with empathy, and yet the more I understood about him, the more I found myself profoundly moved by Daniel's unwavering faith, knowing that this is a huge part of the reason that he found the courage to face each day in Black Beach. Ultimately, though, this is not a book about religion, it is a book about love and the power of the human spirit to endure against insurmountable odds.

This is the true story of one man's struggle to survive the horrors of a prison that should not exist. It's a haunting story of immense suffering and dark places, but mostly it is about love and courage in the face of adversity. It's also a book about friendship in the strangest of places, human rights, abuse of power, corruption, greed, inequality and poverty.

As we join Daniel in his ultimate fight – a struggle against injustice – we

AUTHOR'S NOTE

must understand that the journey will be hard, the road long and the darkness often impenetrable, but we will find our way to the light, despite the odds, against the odds.

Daniel's story is one that must be told, not just as part of his healing journey, but also on behalf of the countless other innocent victims of an unforgiving system. There are prisoners illegally detained without trial and still incarcerated at Black Beach and other prisons around the world, faceless, nameless, innocent men, women and children who have no power or opportunity to tell their story. May this book be the first step on our journey to setting them free.

TRACEY PHAROAH
JULY 2022

Ecclesiastes 3:1–8
Everything Has Its Time

To everything there is a season,
A time for every purpose under heaven:

A time to be born,
And a time to die;
A time to plant,
And a time to harvest;

A time to kill,
And a time to heal;
A time to break down,
And a time to build up;

A time to weep,
And a time to laugh;
A time to mourn,
And a time to dance;

A time to cast away stones,
And a time to gather stones;
A time to embrace,
And a time to refrain;

A time to gain,
And a time to lose;
A time to keep,
And a time to throw away;

A time to tear,
And a time to sew;
A time to keep silent,
And a time to speak;

A time to love,
And a time to hate;
A time of war,
And a time of peace.

Read more about Daniel's experiences, Black Beach and Equatorial Guinea at www.daniel.africa.

Twitter: https://twitter.com/danielafrica_
Facebook: https://facebook.com/danielblackbeachprison
LinkedIn: https://www.linkedin.com/in/daniel-janse-van-rensburg-africa